SYMBOLICAL MASONRY

An Interpretation of the Three Degrees

By

H. L. HAYWOOD

EDITOR OF *The Builder*

NEW YORK

GEORGE H. DORAN COMPANY

[1923]

WITH LOVE AND AFFECTION TO MY WIFE

EDITH AGNES HAYWOOD

ISBN: 1505686776
ISBN-13: 978-1505686777

THE M. S. A. NATIONAL MASONIC LIBRARY presents, in a series of volumes of uniform binding and competent craftsmanship, the best results of Masonic research by masters of the Craft in America and abroad. The LIBRARY will cover every aspect of Freemasonry, its ritual, its symbolism, its philosophy, its past history and present activities and development. Representing all recognized schools of Masonic thought, it will bring the best literature of the Craft within reach of lodges and members.

Symbolical Masonry
by H. L. HAYWOOD

The Great Teachings of Masonry
by H. L. HAYWOOD

The Beginnings of Freemasonry in America
by MELVIN M. JOHNSON

Speculative Masonry
by A. S. MACBRIDE

The Builders
by JOSEPH FORT NEWTON

The Men's House
by JOSEPH FORT NEWTON

The Philosophy of Masonry
by ROSCOE POUND

Symbolism of the Three Degrees
by OLIVER DAY STREET

WASHINGTON, D. C.: THE MASONIC SERVICE ASSOCIATION OF THE UNITED STATES

PREFACE

Shortly after taking my degrees in Masonry I asked my friend, Brother Newton R. Parvin, Grand Secretary of the Grand Lodge of Iowa, for a book to explain the ritual in which I had just participated, so much of which had escaped or confused me like a foreign language. He told me there was no such book in existence and said it was the most badly needed volume in the whole field of Freemasonry. Later, I chanced to report this remark to a group of friends at Waterloo, Iowa, consisting of Alfred E. Longley, Raymond Folk, Louis Fowler, and P. J. Martin, the last mentioned of whom, now deceased, was one time Grand Master of Masons in that state, whereupon these gentlemen challenged me to write such a book myself, and offered to co-operate in publishing and marketing it after my MS. might be completed. The upshot of it all was that after engaging a young man to assist me in the work I spent the larger part of one year in the Iowa Masonic Library at Cedar Rapids, Iowa, a magnificent collection of Masonic literature founded by Theodore Sutton Parvin and maintained by the Grand Lodge of Iowa. I owe very much to the unfailing kindness of Brother Newton R. Parvin and to his Deputy, Brother C. C. Hunt, and wish at this time, and publicly, to extend to them my most sincere thanks. Also I wish to extend my thanks to Brother John H. Cowles, Sovereign Grand Commander of the Scottish Rite, Southern Jurisdiction, for his permission to read Albert Pike's unpublished manuscript on the ritual of the Three Degrees, which is preserved in the vaults of the House of the Temple, Washington, D. C., and which, according to Pike's own written directions, can never be published.

While prosecuting those necessary researches—an arduous task since I was new in the field and found no previous books to guide me in my particular undertaking—I became Associate Editor of *The Builder*, the journal of the National Masonic Research Society, and later, Editor of its Study Club Department. Because of this connection it fell out that instead of publishing my MS. in book form I published it in *The Builder*, or at least all of it except the first few sections, and in such shape as could be used by Study Clubs as well as by individual students. Owing to the delay thus occasioned the book is just now appearing. It has been so widely used by Study Clubs, and is still so much in demand by them, that I have placed in an appendix a list of questions for discussion, and I have also included such bibliographies as experience has shown to be useful for their purpose.

I may say that since its appearance as a serial in *The Builder* I have entirely revised and in many cases rewritten the whole. The Introduction, except for two or three paragraphs, is entirely new, and so are the first four or five chapters. One chapter has been omitted.

The work undertaken originally as an apprentice task proved so attractive to me that I was at last drawn to surrender all my other duties in order to devote myself entirely to Masonic research and the cause of Masonic education, and have found my own particular and quite congenial niche with the National Masonic Research Society, of which I now have the honour to be Editor-in-Chief.

There is no need to tell the veteran Masonic scholar who may chance to peruse these pages that the book was not designed for his uses, but rather for the host of beginners in the field, whose first intellectual interest in the Craft is usually aroused by their curiosity as to what the work "is all about." I have tried to tell the beginners what it is all about, as clearly as possible, within the limits of space and of the obligations to secrecy, and as far as the results of modern Masonic scholarship have allowed.

H. L. HAYWOOD.

Cedar Rapids, Iowa.

CONTENTS

SYMBOLICAL MASONRY

"Unto the divine light of the holy altar, from the outer darkness of ignorance, through the shadow of our earth life, winds the beautiful path of initiation."

AN INTRODUCTION TO THE HISTORY OF SYMBOLICAL FREEMASONRY

The question is often asked, How old is Masonry and where did it begin? The answer must depend entirely on one's definition of the word. If by that term one means a Freemason in the modern sense, who is a member of a subordinate lodge operating under the authority of a Grand Lodge and practising the rites of Symbolical Masonry, then Freemasonry came into existence in London in 1717. But this present day Craft is in historical continuity with lodges or guilds of Masons who in earlier days engaged in the tasks of actual building: if the word Freemason is to be extended to those brethren then we may say that Freemasonry came into existence in the twelfth century along with Gothic architecture and that its cradle was very probably the northwestern corner of France. But if the word Freemason is to be applied to any secret society that makes use, or has made use, of some of our symbols or signs, then Freemasonry goes a long way back into history, because there were organisations among the Græco-Roman peoples, two or three thousand years ago, that had much in common with ours: and it is certain that the ancient Egyptians made use of several of the symbols or emblems that we are accustomed to because we find them in "The Book of the Dead," and in other Egyptian memorials. If Freemasonry is given the widest possible sense of being merely a secret fraternity then it has existed in many parts of the world for thousands and thousands of years, because primitive tribes have made use of such organisations through an untold period of time.

All over the world at present, and throughout the world in the past, there have been existing all manner of secret societies which in many of their characteristics are so much like our own that writers at various and sundry times have been led to attribute to almost every one of the more important of them some connection with Freemasonry; and in many cases have sought to derive Freemasonry from them. This makes for a great deal of confusion of thought and leads men into very absurd positions as to what Freemasonry really is and what Freemasonry ought to do. A student can easily avoid this confusion if he begins his studies with the known facts of the now existing Fraternity and works his way back, step by step, and with scholarly care and accuracy, as far as ascertainable facts can carry him. The student who pursues this method will soon find that our Craft in its earlier days borrowed from, or derived many things from, or was otherwise connected in many ways with, other organisations: having an historical connection with Freemasonry these organisations properly come within the scope of Masonic history and research, whereas all other secret societies that have no such historical connection are of merely curious interest.

If we can judge by the practices of primitive tribes that now exist, and by the evidences of archæology, we are safe in assuming that long before the dawn of history men organised themselves into secret societies each of which had its headquarters or lodge building, produced ceremonies of initiation, carried on a religious cult, maintained law and order, made war, and so forth. A great deal of speculation is now rife concerning such primitive societies, and many very strange theories are being erected upon the basis of what little we know concerning this subject: a beginner in this field will be wisely advised if he is very cautious about accepting these speculations, because as a matter of fact we yet have learned very little, comparatively speaking at least, concerning primitive secret societies.

The first great secret organisations in history of which very much is known were the religious cults in the Græco-Roman world,—Egypt, Rome, Greece, etc., etc.,—which were known as the Ancient Mysteries. These powerful fraternities had very many things in common with our own Craft. Except in few instances men only were eligible to membership; they met in tiled lodge-rooms; employed ceremonies of initiation; collected fees and dues; divided their memberships into grades; etc.

One of the most typical of these Ancient Mysteries was Mithraism. It is believed that Mithra was originally an Aryan sun-god who, after passing through many transformations of form and attribute, was at last introduced into the Roman Empire. By that time he had become a saviour-god who had left his home in heaven to become a human being for a time in order to effect the salvation of the world: it was believed that after his death he ascended to his former place in heaven, there to judge the dead and to keep watch over his followers on earth. These followers were supposed to constitute a great army of militant worshippers who, after the fashion of Mohammedan devotees of present-day Islam, were to conquer the world for Mithra, who was heralded as the god of light making everlasting war on the god of darkness. The meeting place of the cult was known as a Mithræum. Men only were admitted to this membership, and they were obliged to undergo a severe ceremonial of initiation, in some respects strikingly like the drama of our Third Degree. The other Ancient Mysteries were in essentials similar to Mithraism and all of them anticipated in many ways, sometimes startlingly, the rites and customs of modern Freemasonry. The analogies are in many instances so close that some careful students believe that our own Fraternity is lineally descended from the Ancient Mysteries. This hypothesis is intelligible and one that commends itself in many ways, but as yet it has been impossible to establish all the links in the long chain of evolution.

At the time the Ancient Mysteries were flourishing in the Græco-Roman world another form of organisation became very common which also anticipated in many very striking ways our own lodges. I refer to the Roman Collegia. From a very early date all the trades and crafts among the Romans were very closely organised in every community; the bakers, the butchers, the carpenters, the shoemakers, painters, etc., etc., had each their own *collegium*, which was organised according to imperial law, and used as a kind of social and benefit club by its members. It is supposed that most of these *collegia* originated as burial societies to enable the usually impoverished workman to have the respectable burial for himself and for the members of his family which every Roman much desired. As time went on these *collegia* passed more and more under the control of the Imperial Government until it came to pass that by the time of the barbarian invasions the Emperors were making use of them as the most perfect means of controlling the hordes and masses of labouring people in their dominion. Each *collegium* met in its own lodge room; had its own constitutions and by-laws; admitted to membership men only and by means of initiatory services; had a common chest, wardens, masters, etc., etc.

The collegiate form of trade organisation was so very common in the ancient world that it is most probable it existed in the Near East when Hiram, King of Tyre, built for Solomon, King of Israel, the world-famous Temple at Jerusalem. In his exceedingly curious and very interesting book called "The Dionysian Artificers," Da Costa has argued that the *collegia* which constructed this Temple were dedicated to Dionysus and were, therefore, called Dionysian Artificers. Some Masonic scholars agree with Da Costa in his hypothesis, while others impatiently scout the whole theory. Be that as it may, it is most probable that Solomon's Temple, which has become both the head and centre of our system of Masonic symbolism, was built by men organised after the fashion of the Roman *collegia*.

What became of all these *collegia* when the barbarians destroyed the Roman Empire? The question is one about which there has been endless debate, and it is probable that it will be a very long time, if ever, before historians have satisfied themselves that they know the truth in the premises. Some believe that the *collegia* were utterly destroyed; others that they survived in Byzantium, there to act as the seeds out of which later developed Byzantine civilisation; others that some of the *collegia* passed over to England and there became the centres out of which developed English mediæval civilisation; others believe that the *collegia* became transformed into various church organisations. Among all these various historical speculations there is one that holds for us students of Masonic history a peculiar interest. I refer to what is known as the Comacine theory.

In the celebrated book called "The Cathedral Builders," a woman, Mrs. Baxter, under the pen name of "Leader Scott," first brought this theory to the serious attention of Masonic scholars; she was followed by Brother W. R. Ravenscroft who has published codicils to her theory at two various times in *The Builder*, the journal of the National Masonic Research Society. According to this Comacine theory certain *collegia* of architects took refuge from the barbarian invasions in the easily defended territory immediately around Lake Como in the northern part of Italy, and there for two or three hundred years, by means of carefully training the youths, preserved alive the old methods and secrets of the builders. As the barbarians themselves became settled in communities and began to feel the need of walls, bridges, highways and buildings, these Comacine masters, as they came to be called, sent out their skilled workmen here and there to superintend the new activities and to organise schools in which boys could be taught the rudiments of the trade. In this wise the Comacine masters served as a bridge over which something of the old Roman civilisation passed into the mediaeval world. From their own communities, which acted as the centre, the art of architecture, along with its auxiliary arts, passed into other parts of Europe, to Germany, to the Netherlands, to France, to Spain, and also to England. The Comacine masters were organised into lodges, each with its own officials and its own meeting place, with rites, ceremonies, pass-words, signs and trade secrets.

All this according to Leader Scott. The hypothesis is plausible and there is much by way of evidence to prove its validity, but as yet the majority of careful students have refused to accept it, and that because some of its most fundamental positions have not been substantiated. R. F. Gould, the greatest of Masonic historians, described the whole Comacine theory as a vision hanging in the air. Whether it be that he is right in his position or that they who hold to the Comacine theory have the truth on their side, the fact remains, that every careful student of Masonic history must familiarise himself with, and somehow come to terms with, this theory.

It is the consensus of opinion among the best equipped modern Masonic historians that the history of the Craft, properly so-called, began with the advent of Gothic architecture. This style of building was such a revolutionary change as compared with the Romanesque which preceded it that new conditions were created and profound changes were wrought in the habits and customs of the workingmen that had Gothic buildings in charge. Under the new conditions of their labour those guilds began such practices and forms of organisations as led, after a number of centuries of evolution, to the development of modern Freemasonry.

A Romanesque building was very simple in principle. It consisted of a flat roof laid across four walls: if this roof was pitched or arched the walls were thickened in order to take up the side thrust. If the buildings were made large and the roofs high, then it was necessary to make the walls of such great thickness that the buildings had the appearance of military fortresses; and since these walls served to buttress the roof it was impossible to cut very large windows in them lest they be too much weakened and the buildings collapse. As a result of this condition the general character of Romanesque buildings was one of squatness, heaviness and of gloomy interiors. In the twelfth century, and either in England or in northwestern France, the builders discovered a new principle that enabled them completely to transform their structures. Instead of the round arch of the older style, they took up the use of pointed arches, which enabled them to raise their roofs to any desired height, and they learned how to take care of the thrust of these arches by means of flying buttresses. In the course of time this system became so well articulated and so consistent that the skeleton of the building became a thing in itself and capable of standing alone, like the framework of a machine, so that walls were no longer necessary to serve for buttress purposes. Therefore, the builders began to leave out the walls as much as possible and to substitute for them stained glass windows. The thrusts from the pointed arches that were not taken up by the flying buttresses were cared for on the interior of the building by slender pillars and piers. This made these great structures capable of housing thousands of persons at once, and yet gave to them airiness, grace and ease, and such harmony of line and colour as later on led Goethe to describe Gothic architecture as "frozen music."

The principles and methods of Gothic were applied to bridges, walls, domestic structures, to art, ornamentation, dress, and even to household utensils, but of all the manifestations of it the most magnificent and enduring were the cathedrals; and, owing to the devastation of war, in which the cathedrals were ever held more or less inviolable, they are all that is left to us of an art that at one time spread over the whole of Europe and of England. These cathedrals were complicated structures that required for their erection rare skill, knowledge difficult to acquire, and a compact organisation of men. It is believed that in the course of time the guilds of workmen who had the cathedrals in charge were given, in recognition of the unique character of their labours, certain privileges and immunities. Not many cathedrals were built, and such as were undertaken were very naturally placed in the larger centres of population. Since comparatively few men were skilled enough to work at such structures it was necessary to move the guilds about from place to place to such points as they were needed. This set the cathedral building guilds sharply apart from the other guilds of that time, each one of the latter of which was stationary and forbidden by law to practise its trade outside of the incorporated limits of its own community. Some writers believe that the builders, or Masons (the two words mean the same), who belonged to the cathedral building guilds came at last to be known as "Freemasons" in virtue of the fact that their guilds were permitted to move about from place to place and free from most of the local restrictions under which other guilds were compelled to operate. If this theory is true, we may say that Freemasonry strictly so-called began with these cathedral builders and not with the ordinary guild mason, or local builder. There is much debate now going on about this whole subject, and it is very necessary that one move with caution and that one make these statements not as utterances of known fact but as tentative hypotheses, more or less substantiated by evidence but not yet clearly proved.

Whatever may be correct of the guilds of Freemasons we may feel quite certain that their practices were in many important respects very much like the guilds existing everywhere about them. Upon undertaking a new work they would begin by erecting a temporary building to serve as their lodge-room, work-room, store-room, etc. In this temporary building they would hold their lodge meetings. They were governed by a master, and wardens, and they probably had secretaries, treasurers, constitutions and by-laws. When a youth was taken into the Craft, he was vouched for by some Master Mason and received, upon entering the lodge, the obligation of an apprentice. He was then indentured to a Master Mason, who was to serve as a sponsor; his name was entered in the book of the lodge, and he was then for a period of seven years set to work to learn the various secrets of his trade. His time of apprenticeship over, he was brought again into the lodge and given his obligation as a Fellow of the Craft, or Master Mason (the two terms signifying the same thing at that time), and he henceforth did a master's work, received a master's wages, was free to travel in search of employment, and was taught how to prove himself a Master Mason wherever he might go. It is supposed that through the teaching of apprentices their traditions and their various other usages, these Freemasons gradually came to use their tools and building secrets as emblems and symbols whereby to instruct their members in thinking and in moral conduct. Also it is known that these guilds possessed traditional histories of the Craft, and it is supposed that such histories were either read or recited to a candidate at the time of his initiation. In the course of time these traditional histories or legends, along with charges and regulations, were written down in manuscript form and thereby preserved. Many of these ancient documents are now in existence and are known as "Ancient Charges" or "Ancient Constitutions." The oldest existing copy has been dated at 1390.

Gothic architecture began in the twelfth century, reached its apogee in the thirteenth century, and began its period of decline in the fifteenth century. There were many reasons for this decline, the most important of which were civil war and the advent of Puritanism: this applied particularly to England, to which country the present historical sketch must confine itself for a time. When cathedrals were no longer erected a great many of the old cathedral building guilds passed out of existence, but a few of them continued their activities by taking up domestic architecture, especially for the landed gentry, the aristocracy of England at that time. To what extent the now transformed guilds maintained their old customs it is difficult to say because records are lacking; but we know that such as continued to exist remained very jealous of their traditions and very loyal to their landmarks.

There was one exception to this, however, and it is a matter very essential to this story. After the lodges had come to be comparatively weak in number and membership, and after they had been working for many years in close contact with the rich and learned class, they began to admit to their membership men who had no thought of becoming actual builders at all but who developed an interest in this ancient Craft because of its old traditions and its rich symbolisms.

This acceptance of non-operative, or speculative, Masons began in the latter part of the sixteenth century but became much more common in the following century. A certain Boswell was initiated as a speculative Mason in Scotland in 1598, the first event of such a character in the records of Masonry. But either a great many men had been so admitted and left no record, or the custom of admitting speculative members grew with great rapidity, for there was a speculative lodge in full working order in London in 1631. When Elias Ashmole was initiated at Warrington in 1646 his lodge was almost wholly speculative. During the seventeenth century the Fraternity in England was made up of a membership in which operatives and non-operatives mixed together: a few lodges were wholly non-operative; some of them were wholly operative; and many of them were divided between the two. Each of these lodges was wholly self-governed and owed no allegiance to any body higher than itself; but each and all had in common the old traditions and usages so that a man could pass from one to another and easily make himself known wherever he went. This is not to say that there were no important differences among these lodges, because there were: it means that during the period of transition the Masonic bodies continued in the practice of their ancient customs to such an extent as to maintain their identity through the years.

It is believed that during this period of transition a number of influences were admitted into the Craft which were not at all of operative origin and had never been felt by the Craft at the time when it was engaged in actual building. There are few documents in existence to guide us in untangling the clues of history during that period, so we must be very cautious in consequence: but the internal evidence seems to show very clearly that these influences were powerful and in the sequel had a revolutionary effect on the Craft.

Among these non-operative influences the Kabbala must be mentioned as one of the most important. The word itself means "that which has been accepted as authority," and was the name given by Jewish mystics to a body of occult Jewish literature that appears to have come into existence among Spanish Jews in the thirteenth and fourteenth centuries. These books are among the most difficult to read in the world, and they are full of ideas and terms that now seem very bizarre, but in their own period they appealed powerfully to the imagination of mediæval thinkers, most of whom were devoted to theological and metaphysical speculation. When Reuchlin, the great German who shared with Martin Luther the leadership of the Protestant revolution, made his impassioned plea in behalf of the Jews, he brought this strange old literature to the attention of the intellectual world of Europe and gave it such currency that for a time the kabbalistic writings were on the study tables of almost every theologian. The framework of the Kabbala was a kind of theosophy expressed by means of a system of symbolism which centred about King Solomon's Temple. Inasmuch as there are things in the Masonic rituals which appear to be identical with many of the old kabbalistic symbols, and since the Kabbala was very influential in the sixteenth and seventeenth centuries, it is a reasonable supposition that it had a certain influence on Freemasonry during the years in which that society was undergoing a transformation.

There were many other streams of occultism flowing in the same period and there is little doubt but that influences from many of them found their way into the speculations of the Masons of that time. Space does not here make it possible to go into these matters in detail. I have mentioned them as suggestions for lines of Masonic study upon the part of the student who may undertake to follow the chapters in this book: they will serve to remind him that many and various influences were at work among the scattered and independent lodges in England during the seventeenth century, and that at the beginning of the eighteenth century Masonic lodges were scattered here and there through England, Ireland and Scotland; it is impossible to guess how many were in existence at the time, but it is probable that there were not very many; and it is still more probable that there was a considerable diversity of custom and usage among them. In Scotland it came to pass in some localities that a man could make a Mason of another merely by giving him the so-called "Mason's Word." Irish lodges differed radically from those that existed in England.

But the time for the great awakening had come and the first gleams of a new day brightened the horizon in the year 1716 when certain members of a few lodges in or about London "thought fit to cement under a Grand Master as the centre of Union and Harmony." How many of these "Old Lodges" were concerned we do not know, but Dr. James Anderson, a Presbyterian minister, whose story of the period is "the only official account we possess of the foundations of the Grand Lodge of England, and of the first six years of its history," gives us the names of four, those that met in the following places:

1. The Goose and Gridiron Ale-House.

2. The Crown Ale-House.

3. The Apple-Tree Tavern.

4. Rummer and Grapes Tavern.

To quote Anderson, whose "The New Book of Constitutions" was issued in 1738:

"They and some other old Brothers met at the said Apple-Tree, and having put into the chair the oldest Master Mason (now the Master of a Lodge) they constituted themselves a Grand Lodge Pro Tempore in due form, and forthwith revived the Quarterly Communication of the Officers of Lodges (called the GRAND LODGE) resolv'd to hold the Annual Assembly and Feast and then to chuse a Grand Master from among themselves, till they should have the Honour of a Noble Brother at their Head.

"Accordingly, on St. John Baptist's Day in the 3d year of King George I, A.D. 1717, the ASSEMBLY and Feast of the Free and Accepted Masons was held at the aforesaid Goose and Gridiron Ale-House.

"Before Dinner, the oldest Master Mason (now the Master of a Lodge) in the chair, proposed a List of proper Candidates; and the Brethren by a Majority of Hands elected Mr. Anthony Sayer, Gentleman, Grand Master of Masons (Mr. Jacob Lamball, Carpenter, Capt. Joseph Elliott, Grand Wardens) who being forthwith invested with the badges of Office and Power by the said oldest Master, and install'd was duly congratulated by the Assembly who paid him the Homage.

"Sayer, Grand Master, commanded the Masters and Wardens of Lodges to meet the Grand Officers every Quarter in Communication, at the Place that he should appoint in the Summons sent by the Tyler."

George Payne became Grand Master in 1718 and "caused several old copies of the Gothic [i.e., manuscripts] Constitutions" to be "produced and collated," a fact which shows that they earnestly desired to adhere to the old traditions. Rev. J. T. Dasaguliers was elected Grand Master in 1719, and George Payne received a second term in 1720. During the year several manuscripts—copies of the old Constitutions, probably—were burned "by some scrupulous Brothers, that these papers might not fall into strange Hands." In 1721 Grand Lodge elected to the Grand Mastership, John, Duke of Montagu, "the first of a long and unbroken line of noble Grand Masters—and the society rose at a single bound into notice and esteem." So popular did the Order become that the learned Dr. Stukely, writing January 6, 1721, complained that "immediately upon that it took a run and ran itself out of breath through the folly of the members."

At first the Grand Lodge, the formation of which is above described, claimed no jurisdiction except over London and its immediate environs; but it was possessed of such vitality that there was nothing to stay its growth everywhither. In 1721 twelve lodges were represented at the Quarterly Communications; by 1723 the number had increased to thirty. Gradually lodges outside London came into the jurisdiction and the Grand Lodge itself chartered new organisations here and there, one of which was the lodge in Madrid in 1728, the first on foreign soil.

But the growing authority of the Grand Lodge at London was not unchallenged. In 1725 the old Lodge at York began to call itself a Grand Lodge. In 1729 Irish Masons instituted a Grand Lodge of their own; and the Scottish followed in 1736. Moreover, rivals sprang up in England itself, so that at one time there were no fewer than four bodies operating as Grand Lodges and claiming full sovereignty as such.

Upon the very rapid growth of Freemasonry in and about London a number of imitative societies sprang into existence in order to capitalise the increasing prestige of the Freemasonry or else to appeal to the eighteenth century love of fun by caricaturing it. The majority of those societies have passed out of existence—the Gormogons, the Bucks, etc.—but one of them, the Order of Odd Fellows, survives until this day. Also a great many individuals who wished to take advantage of the social life of the Fraternity soon began to secure the pass-words and grips by dishonest methods: and at the same time, and in order to pander to such individuals, a number of exposés were published. In consequence of all this the Grand Lodge found itself very much embarrassed by cowans and eavesdroppers and in order to rid itself of this nuisance and to enable regular Masons to detect the cheats and frauds, the Grand Lodge authorised certain changes in the work. When this occurred a number of the older brethren set up an outcry and alleged that this new Grand Lodge was violating the ancient landmarks and making itself guilty of innovations in the body of Masonry. It is supposed that as a result of this resentment against change certain of the independent lodges that had never affiliated with the Grand Lodge gradually grew together and at last undertook to form a Grand Lodge of their own. It may be that this is not the authentic account of how this new Grand Lodge came into existence, but a majority of latter-day Masonic scholars are of the opinion that this account is the most probable. At any rate a new Grand Lodge came into existence in 1751. Henry Sadler has shown that it and its subordinate lodges were in close communication with Irish lodges and the Irish Grand Lodge, where no innovations had been permitted or found necessary.

This new Grand Lodge came into existence in 1751, thirty-four years after the organisation of the first, or Mother Grand Lodge. Owing to the fact that the 1751 organisation undertook to adhere more closely to what its members believed to be the ancient usages than their rival they began to call themselves the "Ancient" Grand Lodge, and they dubbed the older body the "Modern" Grand Lodge. The Ancient Grand Lodge was fortunate in securing a most able man, Laurence Dermott, to serve as secretary for thirty years and who, during that time, proved himself a man possessed of extraordinary abilities as a leader. Dermott adopted the expedient of army lodges whereby a man in military services could be inducted into the Fraternity and this in itself added power to the Ancients, or Atholl Masons as they also came to be called, owing to the fact that the Duke of Atholl became Grand Master. It is supposed also that Dermott made use of that work which afterwards became embodied in the Royal Arch as a means of inducing prospective candidates to unite with the bodies under his Grand Lodge.

For a long time there was constant strife between the two camps but by the first decade of the nineteenth century overtures began to be made by one Grand Lodge to another, joint committees were formed, and the spirit of Masonic unity began to win its way. In 1813 a great Lodge of Reconciliation was held at which 640 lodges of the Moderns were represented and 359 of the Ancients. The two old Grand Lodges passed out of existence and in their place came the United Grand Lodge of England. From that famous assembly Freemasonry emerged, cleansed from all its feuds, united and triumphant.

Meanwhile, Freemasonry had been established on this continent and soon took root here and developed with surprising vigour. Boston, New York, Philadelphia and Charleston, were among the earliest centres of Masonic activity: there has been a great deal of rivalry among the champions of these communities to determine priority in date, but the subject is too complicated to permit me to enter into it at this place. Comparatively little is known of the activity of the Craft prior to the Revolutionary War, but it would appear that the lodges were social in character. It has been proved by our historians that much of the passion for independence was generated among Masonic lodges, as in the lodges that met in the Green Dragon Tavern at Boston where the Boston tea-party was planned, and from which, it is supposed, it was executed. Dr. Joseph Warren was a member of a lodge which met in that Tavern. The most important event in the Freemasonry of those days was the initiation of George Washington, who was made a Mason in Fredericksburg Lodge No. 4, in Fredericksburg, Va., on the fourth of November, 1752. Later in life he became the first Master of what is now known as Washington-Alexandria Lodge, Alexandria, Va. Hundreds of other patriots and military leaders became members of the Craft, and they with their lodges carried on so much patriotic activity during the war that it is almost not an exaggeration to say that the Revolution would not have been won by the patriots had it not been for Freemasonry. The spirit and principles of Freemasonry had been written into the Declaration of Independence, and they were also embodied in the Constitution, which became the organic law of the new Republic.

As a result of the prestige it gained for itself in Revolutionary times the Craft flourished exceedingly. Some of our historians believe that it flourished more than was good for itself, because its influence became a temptation to politicians to enter its ranks, some of them, in order to further their own aims. Owing to this fact, and owing also to the general revival of a type of religion that condemned secret societies, there grew up a sentiment opposed to the Fraternity. This finally culminated in the Anti-Masonic craze. Anti-Masonry, as a definite movement, sprang into existence in 1826 with the mysterious disappearance of William Morgan, a printer of Batavia, New York, who undertook to print an exposé of the Masonic work. What became of Morgan has never been ascertained, but enemies of the Craft immediately fastened responsibility for the man's murder or abduction upon the local Masonic lodge: in a short time scheming politicians, among whom Thurlow Weed was a leader, fanned the flames in their own interest, and soon an Anti-Masonic political party came into existence. A number of religious denominations joined hands with the politicians in a determined effort to destroy

Freemasonry. For a few years it looked as if they might succeed. Hundreds of lodges went out of existence, several Grand Lodges suspended activities or surrendered their charters. There came a time when men had to be Masons in secret or else in many communities were obliged to suffer obloquy because of bearing that name.

A typical example of the disastrous ravages of the Anti-Masonic furore is furnished by the experience of the Grand Lodge of New York. The proceedings of that Grand Lodge for 1860 contain a paragraph that presents in the most vivid manner the extent of the havoc:

"At the commencement of the present century there were 91 lodges, with a membership of about 5,000, in a population of 588,603. This was the era of Livingston, Morton, Hoffman, Astor, Jay and Van Wyck. In 1810 the lodges had increased to 172, with a membership of 8,600, in a population of 961,888. In 1820 there were 295 lodges (numbered to 128) and a membership of 15,000, in a population of 1,312,812. This decade witnessed the tornado [Anti-Masonry] which swept over the states, so that in 1830 the number of lodges, which in 1825 had run up to 480, with a membership of over 20,000 was but 82, and a reliable membership scarcely exceeding 3,000, in a population of 1,918,131. In 1840 the institution began to exhibit symptoms of resuscitation, and brethren awakened from the blight and persecution of the ten preceding years as from a terrible dream. The number of lodges then was 79–22 in New York, and 27 in fourteen counties west of the Hudson River, with but about 5,000 members, in a population of 2,428,921. The increase was slow, but steady, to the year 1850, when there were 172 lodges in the three Grand Lodges then existing, with about 12,000 members, and the population of the State then was 3,097,304. At the present time (1860) there are 432 working lodges (numbered to 477) and a membership of 30,000, and the population is computed at about 4,000,000. It will thus be seen that the ratio was in 1800, 1 to every 117 inhabitants; in 1810, 1 to 111; in 1820, 1 to 91; 1825, 1 to 80; 1830, 1 to 637; 1840, 1 to 485; 1850, 1 to 258, and in 1860, 1 to 133; and it should be borne in mind that there are computed to be in the state 5,000 unaffiliated Masons, who are recognised as such, making the ratio now to be 1 to every 114 inhabitants—a state of prosperity fully equalling that of the best days of the Fraternity."

No sooner was the Anti-Masonic movement abated than the Civil War came on and cut the Fraternity in two in the same way that it divided the nation. Grand Lodges were among the most vigorous agencies on both sides of the Mason and Dixon's line to stem the tide of blood and after the conflict had come brethren in both camps displayed many remarkable examples of fraternalism; but even so the internecine strife was almost as disastrous in its own way as the Anti-Masonic movement had been. Bitterness and jealousy were engendered and all manner of sectional feelings aroused.

After the Civil War the Fraternity entered a new phase, altogether different in many respects from what it had ever been before. It became more secret than ever, almost secretive, in fact, so that Masons jealously guarded from public knowledge even their most perfunctory activities. To a large extent lodges fell under the control of the older men: Masonry became interpreted as a moral and religious institution so that Grand Lodge proceedings of that period read like the minutes of church conventions; in many quarters the ritual became accepted as literal history and many of the most influential Masons began to believe that that history, incredible and unknown to historians, was Freemasonry's secret.

We are now (1923) entering a new era in which it is very evident that Freemasonry is undergoing another profound inward transformation. One of the evidences of this is found in the fact that the average age of members has become less and less so that Freemasonry may be said to be almost a young man's institution. Accompanying this has been a growth so phenomenal that many of the older heads have looked with some alarm upon it. In 1920 there were in the United States 2,042,706 Master Masons; 551,689 Royal Arch Masons; 173,381 Mark Masons, and 275,989 Knights Templars. No such membership as this has ever been known in the Fraternity before, and it appears that the end is not yet, because everywhere new lodges are coming into existence and new temples are being erected, some of them, such as the great structure in Detroit, of such magnificent proportions as to attract the attention of the world. Along with this growth there has come a new spirit of enterprise and activity: like the churches, Masonic lodges have become possessed of a social conscience, and Masons feel that the magnificent power generated in such a Fraternity should be harnessed up to the work of the world. This new life has already made itself felt inside Masonic circles by the organisation of a great number of new auxiliary bodies, some of which have already become national forces. Nor has the mind of Masonry been asleep during this time. There was a time when Masonic scholarship belonged to a school of thought long outgrown in other circles, so that the carelessness and gullibility of Masonic writers had become almost proverbial. But in the beginning of the last quarter of the nineteenth century a new movement began to make itself felt. In this country its leaders were Albert Pike, Dr. Albert Mackey, Henry Josiah Drummund, Theodore Sutton Parvin, and their colleagues. This intellectual renaissance appeared with greater power in England, which may still justly claim to be the motherland of Masonic scholarship. In r886 the Lodge Quatuor Coronati was established in order to become an academy of Masonic scholars, every member of which had to qualify himself in general scholarship as well as in Masonic studies. The Quatuor Coronati Lodge has flourished beyond the most sanguine expectations of its founders and in the last thirty-six years has made a record that will probably set the standards of Masonic research for generations to come. Its transactions, called *Ars Quatuor Coronatorum*, have grown to be a great encyclopædia of all matters pertaining to the Craft and absolutely indispensable to every serious Masonic student. The end of all this growth is not yet, and no man can see what it is going to be. Perhaps it will never have an end: perhaps the Fraternity will grow from power to power until it has become a great public institution standing in the midst of the world to teach the human race how good and blessed a thing it is for brethren to dwell together in unity.

Freemasonry is in its very nature profoundly religious, but it is not a church, for, though it is friendly to all churches that preach the Fatherhood of God, the Brotherhood of Man, and the Immortality of the Soul, it teaches no theological dogmas of its own. It is not a political organisation, whatever its enemies may allege, though it is vitally interested in the public life of the land and never sleeps in its efforts to keep American governmental life as pure as possible. It preaches no programme or reform, but nevertheless lends itself to every effort made to lift the burdens of life from the common people, and it evermore holds before its membership the high ideals of service and of mutual helpfulness. It is a great body of picked men who are bound together by sacred and serious obligations to assist each other, by means of fraternity, and through the teaching instrumentalities of ritual, to build in each man and in society at large a communal life which is not inadequately described as a Holy Temple of Human Souls.

Such, in brief, is the story of Freemasonry. What a story it is! It began in a far foretime in a few tiny rivulets of brotherly effort; these united into a current that swept with healing waters across the pagan centuries; many tributaries augmented its stream during the Middle Ages; and in modern times it has become a mighty river which sweeps on irresistibly. And now, if I may venture to change the figure, its halls are homes of light and life; therein men may learn how to live the life that is life indeed. Well may one unclasp his shoes and uncover his head as he enters a Masonic lodge; a symbolism white with an unutterable age is there, and voices eloquent with an old, old music, and a wisdom drawn from the thought and travail of a thousand generations!

PART ONE: THE FIRST STEP

CHAPTER I

AN INTRODUCTION TO THE FIRST STEP

In the days before 1717, when the first Grand Lodge of modern Speculative Freemasonry was organised, the First Degree—it was called the "Apprentice's Part" then—must have been a less elaborate ceremony than it is now. In Scotland one Mason could, and often did, make another merely by communicating the "Mason's word." (What it was we do not know now.) In England the ceremony was richer than this, but even so was doubtless very bald as compared with the work as we of the twentieth century have come to know it. There are many scholars who believe that the old Freemasonry of Ireland was more complete than that of England (by this fact they help to explain the famous so-called "schism," and which was "healed over" in 1813), but even if it was it could not have compared with the ritual of to-day which has grown to such proportions as would require a man years of study in order to master its history and meaning.

It appears that the great revival of Freemasonry which occurred in 1717, and out of which grew the first Grand Lodge mentioned above, was in reality a very complete reorganisation of Freemasonry, though it may well be that no such radical changes were made as some of our more extreme scholars have believed. The Fraternity prior to that date had become very much demoralised and divided; lodges had lost touch with each other; and many Masons had no understanding at all of the meaning of the ceremonies they performed. After the Fraternity began to make a new start a centre was established about which Masons could rally and to which they could all furnish their own traditions and records. In consequence of this it seems that the ritual grew with such rapidity that after a few years it became necessary to fabricate more degrees. What had been the First was divided into the new First and the new Second; what had been the Third was continued as such, though much amplified. This division was completed by 1738, since which time and by the addition of Preston's lectures, etc., the machinery of the degrees has reached its present perfection.

II

It is impossible to know exactly how the candidate was given the "Apprentice's Part" in the old days when Freemasons were still operatives engaged in the construction of actual buildings, but many hints have been left us embedded in the Old Charges, as the ancient Manuscript constitutions and traditions are usually called. E. L. Hawkins, who edited a well-known Encyclopædia of Freemasonry, collated all these references and out of them composed a mosaic picture of the old-time ceremony:

"The meeting was opened with prayer—the legendary history of the Craft was then read—then the candidate was led forward and instructed to place his hand on the Volume of the Sacred Law, which was held by one of the 'Seniors,' while the articles binding on all Masons alike were read, at the conclusion of which a brief obligation was imposed upon the candidate, all present joining in it; then followed the special charges for an apprentice, concluding with a longer obligation by which the candidate specially bound himself to secrecy with regard to what was about to be communicated to him; then the secrets, whatever they were (modes of recognition), were entrusted to him, and the proceedings terminated."

Before receiving the First Degree the youth was obliged to prove himself well qualified, of lawful age, free-born, sound in mind and limb, of clean habits, and in good repute. At the same time he was compelled to bind (or "indenture") himself to a Master Mason for a term of years, usually seven: this master set him his tasks, taught him the methods of the trade, and saw to it that he faithfully observed the rules and regulations of the Order and kept inviolate the secrets of the Craft and of his fellow workmen. At first the Apprentice was little more than a servant, performing menial tasks; but as his skill increased he was given more important duties. Meanwhile, "he must be obedient to the Master without argument or murmuring, respectful to all Freemasons, courteous, avoiding obscene or uncivil speech, free from slander, dissension, or dispute. He must not haunt or frequent any tavern or ale-house, or so much as go into them except it be upon an errand of the Master or with his consent, using neither cards, dice, or any unlawful game, 'Christmastime excepted.' He must not steal anything even to the value of a penny, or suffer it to be done, or shield any one guilty of theft, but report the fact to the Master with all speed. After seven long years the Apprentice brought his masterpiece to the lodge—or, in earlier times, to the Annual Assembly ('bodies not unlike the Grand Lodges of to-day')—and on strict trial and due examination was declared a Master. Thereupon he ceased to be a pupil and a servant, passed into the ranks of Fellowcrafts, and became a free man, capable, for the first time in his life, of earning his living and choosing his own employer." (See *The Builders*, by Dr. J. F. Newton, page 129.)

The Apprentice was a learner in those old days; he is a learner still. The word itself is found in many languages: "apprenti" in French; "apprendenti" in Italian; "Lehrling" in German; etc.: but whatever its form it means, at bottom, a "learner." Being a learner he is said to be in the Porch, and his Apprentice Lodge is said symbolically to be in the Porch of King Solomon's Temple. Time was when all business was transacted in a lodge on the First Degree, but now the Apprentice is not considered a full member of a lodge, and is not entitled to vote, to hold office, to walk in a funeral procession, or to receive Masonic burial, though it is true that Grand Jurisdictions differ somewhat among themselves in these last-mentioned details.

In a symbolical sense the Apprentice may be likened to a human embryo about to be born into a new world; he does not have power over himself, and he does not know anything about the new life upon which he is entering, and therefore it is necessary that he follow his guides with implicit and unquestioning obedience, for not otherwise can he advance a step.

From one end to another, accordingly, the great note struck in the First Degree is Obedience, and this virtue—it is a virtue in all strict senses of the word, though many young men of to-day have grown to dislike that fact—is impressed upon his heart by every device of symbolism, by every art of ceremony.

In learning any art Obedience must come first, Obedience to the teachers and Obedience to the rules. The boy who learns to ride a bicycle must obey the laws of equilibrium with slavish carefulness; a girl must abjectly follow the laws of music if she would become the mistress of her piano; and so is it in every trade and in every accomplishment, for he who would master an art must begin as a servant of its regulations, whether it be moulding iron, planting corn, or writing poems. This is not the slavery that leads to slavery; it is the slavery that leads to freedom, for after one has mastered the technique of his art his mind is set loose to work with power. If the vice of our day is slipshod work and slovenly art it is because our young people are lacking in the patience and in the perseverance to win mastership. But the young man who passes through the First Degree learns differently; the Craft causes the great importance and necessity of obedience to bite deeply into his heart, and he is made to know that no man can ever become a master who scamps his work.

III

If obedience must come first in order to master an art or a craft so it is the first of virtues in that which is the most difficult of all the greater arts—LIFE itself. This is the truth which the First Degree emphasises above all else. If the candidate is to be a builder in the speculative (that is, in the moral, intellectual, and spiritual) sense, building and built upon, he must learn to serve the laws of that difficult architecture. If he thinks of himself as a student learning a Royal Art he must obey the rules of that Art. If he considers himself a babe passing into birth and into a new world, he must place himself under the laws according to which that life can alone fulfill itself. If he pictures himself as a type of "the natural man" (if one may thus use the old theological expression) in his ignorance, his raw untutored condition, seeking to live the life of the spirit which rises above ignorance as a temple rises above the crown of a hill, above all he must learn to know and to obey the awful but benignant statutes of the soul.

Of all the various interpretations—they vary as much in value as in theory—of the First Degree, one of the noblest that I have ever discovered is that given by Dr. J. D. Buck in an essay published in *The New Age* (Volume VII, page 161): "Reflect a moment on the condition of the candidate on first entering the lodge room. He is not only in darkness, going he knows not where, to meet, he knows not what, and guided solely by the J.D., but he bears the mark of abject slavery. He is spared the shame of nakedness and the pride of apparel, and his feet are neither shod nor bare. He is poor and penniless, no external thing to help or recommend him. The old life with all its accessories has dropped from him as completely as though he were dead. He is to enter on a new life in a new world. His intrinsic character alone is to determine his progress and his future status. If he is worthy and well qualified, and duly and truly prepared for this, and, if he understands and appreciates what follows in symbols, ceremonies, and instruction, the old life in him will be dead for ever."

These eloquent sentences make abundantly clear the importance of the First Degree, which is the Drama of Beginnings; for, though the Apprentice himself is but a babe, a beginner, a learner, not for that reason is the ceremony to be made easy or careless, but quite the opposite, for it carries within itself all the dignity and the mystery of birth. Therefore should a lodge see to it that the "Apprentice's Part" is conducted with solemnity and with beauty; its impressions are the candidate's first experience of Masonry, and they will consequently remain with him the longest and influence him the most.

CHAPTER II

THE PETITION FOR MEMBERSHIP

I

The first step toward seeking admission into the membership of a Masonic lodge is to file with the Worshipful Master of the lodge nearest one's residence a petition, which is a printed form fundamentally the same in all jurisdictions; this form sets forth the petitioner's answers to the usual constitutional questions and solemnly asserts that he has not been "improperly solicited," but that he has sought the portals of the Fraternity of his own free will and accord. Before this petition can be presented to the lodge, which is usually done at the next regular monthly communication, or business meeting, it must bear the signatures of at least two Masons by way of recommendation; and then, after an interval, usually of one month, is put to the ballot. If the prayer for membership is then granted the petitioner is instructed to present himself for initiation: if the prayer is denied the fee, which has accompanied the petition, is returned, and the petitioner is notified of his rejection. In a majority of American jurisdictions (by "jurisdiction" is meant the territory over which a Grand Lodge holds sway: in the United States it is almost always coincident with the political boundaries of a state) the man is permitted to enter another petition after a certain fixed interval, after which second application the procedure is substantially the same as outlined above.

II

have changed somewhat from country to country and from century to century but for the most part the custom has remained the same in fundamentals. The points to be noted in the petition are (1) that the candidate makes application of his own initiative, and not after having been solicited; (2) that he holds himself to be in accord with the Order's own teachings concerning the "constitutional questions"; (3) that he voluntarily and at the beginning places himself entirely under the authority and laws of the Fraternity, pledging himself the while to a full obedience to the officers as well as to the laws; (4) and that he seeks admittance, not for any gain to himself, but out of having heard the good repute of the Order these many years.

In older times it was often permitted a man to shape the wording of his own petition within certain limits: one of the most beautiful petitions of this type of which there is any record is that presented by the first great American naval hero, John Paul Jones, to the Lodge of St. Bernard, Kirkcudbright, Scotland, under date of November 27, 1770 (see The *Builder, August*, 1920, page 221):

"To the Worshipful, the Master, the Wardens and Permanent Brethren of Free and Accepted Masons of the Lodge of St. Bernard held at Kirkcudbright. The petition of John Paul, Commander of the 'John' of Kirkendal, humbly sheweth—that your petitioner, for a considerable time past, hath entertained a strong and sincere regard for your most noble, honourable, and ancient Society of Free and Accepted Masons, but hitherto not meeting with reasonable opportunity, do now most humbly crave the benefit of receiving and admitting me into your Fraternity as an Entered Apprentice, promising, assuring and engaging to you that I shall in all rules and orders of your Lodge be most obsequient and observant. The complyance of you, Right Worshipful Wardens and rest of the Brethren, will singularly oblige and very much honour, Right Worshipful, your most humble petitioner and most humble servant.

John Paul."

It is worthy of note in passing, and merely as an item of information, that Brother John Paul, afterwards known as John Paul Jones, was entered and passed in the St. Bernard Lodge No. 122, Kilwinning, Scotland, November 27th, 1770, and that his petition was endorsed by one Brother James Smith as follows: "I do attest the petitioner to be a good man and a person whom I have no doubt will in due time become a worthy brother."

III

In the days of John Paul Jones towns and cities were very small as compared with the great urban centres of our day, and men did little moving about from community to community, so that it was usually the case that nearly all the members of a lodge would be personally acquainted with a petitioner; under such conditions it was quite easy to determine his fitness or unfitness. With us it is different. Our country villages have grown to be towns of five to ten thousand population. Our cities are deemed small if they contain not at least one hundred thousand persons. Families live next door to each other without ever becoming acquainted, and men work in the same shop, factory, or offices without coming to know each other. Accordingly it is the rule rather than the exception that a petitioner is not personally known to the members of the lodge to which he submits his petition, and to meet this situation it has become the custom for the Worshipful Master to appoint a committee to investigate into the character and record of the man.

If it be true—as it undoubtedly is—that Freemasonry's future usefulness and present welfare depends upon the quality of membership admitted, then it is instantly apparent that in the whole structure of the Order there is not another office of more urgent importance than that of the investigating committee. The Worshipful Master should make it one of the first of his duties to use great caution in naming such a committee, and he should follow up his appointment by seeing that the committee carefully perform their functions as are necessary. In the old days of Operative Masonry the Master of the Works stood by with a watchful eye to see that no rotten stone was incorporated into the walls of the edifice over which he was superintendent: so should it be to-day with the Worshipful Master, the Master of the Works in a Speculative Lodge. In the long run his Mastership is judged, not by the number of initiations he has given, or by the elaborateness of his ceremonials, or the amount of money received during his administration, but by the quality of the members he has permitted to enter Freemasonry during the days of his authority. For if ever the walls of Freemasonry go down—which God prevent—it will be due to no failure in the Order itself, but to the defective and illy qualified men who are received within its portals.

Many of the larger lodges, and in some instances Grand Lodges themselves, are requiring a petitioner to fill out a questionnaire in which he makes records of all the salient facts about himself, his life, and his connections. This document duly signed and attested is, after it has served its immediate purpose with the investigating committee, filed in the archives of the lodge for future reference.

In some quarters opposition has developed to the questionnaire system, why it is difficult to discover, because the same conditions that have made an investigating committee necessary operate also to make it good sense to use a questionnaire; the information therein entered is merely a substitute for the personal knowledge men had of each other in earlier times when communities were small and men were known to each other. Moreover, modern society has grown very complicated, like the vision Ezekiel had of wheels within wheels, and the Masonic institution has had to readapt itself to changing conditions, so that now a lodge performs functions it did not dream of in older days. Consider how relief work has been organised and systematised; how employment bureaus have been instituted; social clubs formed; and all of that: it is immediately apparent that it is necessary to have "a line" on the men who must be adjusted to and controlled by all this complicated machinery. The information contained in a questionnaire has become necessary, and how that information is to be obtained and preserved is a mere matter of detail, but it is difficult to think of any other method more effectual than the printed questionnaire.

IV

In the petition which a man presents to a lodge no statement is more important than that he has not been solicited. This question of solicitation, why it is an evil, and why it must be strictly forbidden is a subject which, if there were space to go into it with the thoroughness it deserves, would let us into some of the inmost truths about Freemasonry, because it would help us to see, as by a kind of internal illumination, something of the very soul of Freemasonry. As things are in this book it is only possible to touch upon one of the most superficial of the many matters that hinge upon it.

Solicitation is an evil, whenever practised, and utterly condemned by the public opinion as well as by the laws of the Fraternity. Why is this so? Because solicitation is an injustice to the petitioner and a danger to the Craft, and that for many reasons, one or two of which may be suggested.

Solicitation is wrong to a petitioner because at the door of the lodge, when he for the first time presents himself there, he must solemnly swear that he has not been solicited; but if he *has* been solicited, how is he truthfully to make such a solemn declaration? See in what an embarrassment the man's own friends have placed him!

Furthermore, those that solicit—supposing there are such for the sake of the discussion—would usually be the men least qualified to present the nature and claims of Freemasonry to a man with accuracy, and without misleading misinterpretations: and the chances are that they would hold out some kind of an appeal in order to win the man over, and tell him that he will gain such and such a thing for himself if he will submit his petition. But Freemasonry offers no rewards for membership except itself; it does not offer emoluments, prestige, fame, position, commercial advantages or any other such thing, and they who so interpret it do it a wrong, and mislead the man that is persuaded by such means to seek its doors.

Solicitation is quite as great a wrong to the Order itself, for it needs not great numbers but sincere and devoted members, and your solicited member—as every one knows who belongs to a society that encourages solicitation—usually assumes the attitude that something is owing to him, that the promises that were made of the advantages that would accrue must be now fulfilled and consequently he is not useful at all, and becomes not a Mason but a mere member, which is only so much dead timber weighing down the Craft. Unless a man is willing to work, to endure hardships, and to make sacrifices, he should stay outside the Order; his name and his dues are valueless if they are not accompanied by his willingness ever to serve as a loyal son of Freemasonry. It is of his own "free will" that he comes, and that means "willingness" if it means anything, and not otherwise will a man progress far in the attainment of the Royal Art.

V

"But suppose," a Mason may here interject, "that I have a friend who would, I am certain, make a genuine Mason; but he knows so little about Freemasonry that he may never become enough interested in it voluntarily to apply: this would be a loss to the lodge as well as to himself, would it not? Therefore would it not be proper for me to seek to persuade him to become a Mason?" This is a fair and honest question and it has been answered often and often by the wise heads of the Order, which answer may be put into my own words as follows: "Explain to him as best you are able the principles of Freemasonry; acquaint him (as much as your obligations will permit) with its spirit and its aims; give him Masonic literature to read; but do not once, directly or indirectly, ask him to submit a petition for membership, else you will violate your own obligation and make it necessary for him to lie, if ever he stands at a lodge door." Just as one may explain astronomy to a man without urging him to become an astronomer so is it lawful to explain Masonry to men, as is done times without number in publicly circulated books; but solicitation is another matter, for its aim is not to instruct a man but to persuade him to take a step which he must take, if he takes it at all, on his own initiative.

A few of our authorities—Albert Pike for example—have discouraged Masons from going even this far, and they have argued that Masonry's teachings are Masonry's secret and belong only to the initiated: but this, surely, is carrying the matter too far, for Masonry has obligations to the world as well as to its own membership. One might refute Pike's contention out of his own mouth, for no other Mason has ever written more eloquently, or to more effect, of the social mission of the Craft, as when he says: "Masonry cannot in our age forsake the broad ways of life. She must walk in the open street, appear in the crowded square, and teach by her deeds, her LIFE, more eloquent than any lips."

CHAPTER III

THE BALLOT

I

Freemasonry is a social and moral institution that undertakes to build a symbolic Temple of which its members are the living stones; inasmuch as the stability of the structure depends upon the materials of which it is composed it is obvious that the Craft must exercise every precaution lest unfit men weaken its walls. To guard against this it makes use of the secret ballot as an instrument of selection. Because of this most important use the ballot-box may well be described, as one writer has phrased it, "a bulwark of the Order. It is no exaggeration to say that ninety per cent of the trouble and lack of harmony in our lodges arises from the improper use of the ballot." I believe that this statement is an exaggeration, for I have observed that many troubles have their origin elsewhere, but for all that there is much sense in it. The ballot is to the Order what the sentinel is to an army, what the tyler is to a lodge.

Performing as it does a function of such major importance it is natural that the ballot should be the storm-centre of no end of controversies and arguments. One brother has been led to exclaim that "the ballot question is the most irritating of all subjects relating to lodge government and discipline." He had in mind the abuses that creep in through the employment of the secret unanimous ballot. Such abuses are evil enough, but it is a question whether they would not be as bad or worse under any other system, because it would be manifestly impossible to devise any method for the election of members that would not at some point or other or in some hands or other lend itself to misuse.

II

In the great majority of American jurisdictions a petition is put to the ballot one month after first reading, though a few shorten the interval to two weeks. In less than half the jurisdictions no separate ballot is required for the Second and Third Degrees; and in almost all jurisdictions a re-ballot is permitted if only one blackball has been cast: it is almost an invariable rule (and a just one) that a ballot cannot be reconsidered after the result has been declared. In about half the states a rejected petitioner may submit another application in six months: the other states require a year. In no case is a member exempted from voting save in a few jurisdictions where he may be excused by the Worshipful Master or by vote of the lodge.

It is almost a landmark in American Freemasonry that no petitioner can be accepted for membership save by a unanimous ballot. It is at this particular point that many brethren—some of whom have been among the leaders of the Craft—have directed their faultfinding, because it appears to them that such a usage places altogether too much power into the hands of an individual, so that if a member feel some personal slight against a petitioner, or has had a private quarrel with him, such things in no wise militating against the petitioner's real fitness for membership, it would be unjust that a good man be prevented from Freemasonry because of such trivial circumstances. English lodges have long practised the custom of requiring three blackballs, and there is much to be said in favour of that custom. Others there are who go to the opposite extreme and demand that a petitioner be elected by a majority merely; while others go so far as to ask the return of the ancient custom of a viva voce vote.

My own opinion is that the three blackballs rule is a good one, for it would appear to steer a middle course between extremes, but for all that I am quite contented with the system as it now operates in our land. One may agree with Brother J. G. Gibson (see his "Masonic Problems," page 26) when he says that "the lodge certainly owes more Masonic consideration to a member than to a petitioner, no matter how prosperous, popular and prominent the latter may be." If a member believes that a certain petitioner would be unwelcome to sit with him in lodge, or would prove disagreeable in Masonic society, the member has the first rights in the premises, not the petitioner.

The whole question as to how many blackballs should reject is one that must be decided by experience or expediency. There are no landmarks to go by, no ancient usages to bind the Order. On the contrary very different rules apply in different countries, and in the same country different rules have applied at different times, as is the case with England where the three blackball rule is now in force, though there was a time when a unanimous ballot was required. French lodges generally require one-fifth of the votes cast in order to reject. In other countries still the grand governing body sets up a minimum requirement—as, for example, that one-fifth of the ballots are required to reject—and then leaves it to each subordinate lodge to vary its practices at will inside that sine qua non.

III

There may be room for argument as to how many blackballs should be required for rejection but on one matter there would appear to be little ground for dispute: I refer to secrecy. Secrecy of ballot is in keeping with the genius of the Order as a whole, and Dr. Albert Mackey was well advised in putting secrecy among his famous twenty-five landmarks. It is true "that the use of the secret ballot had not even yet begun in 1720," but it must be remembered that the rapid growth of, and the many changes in, the Society since those early years has made secrecy a necessity. If voting were done openly from the floor it would often happen that a member, having just but private reasons for believing a petitioner unworthy, would be driven by the tyranny of numbers to vote with the crowd. Besides, a negative oral vote might be reported to a rejected petitioner and bitter and unnecessary feelings be thereby engendered. Taking it up one side and down the other the present system is as good a method of balloting as can be devised: it is kind to the petitioner himself, it is kind to the voter, and it is fair to the lodge.

At the time of writing (1923) the Fraternity is inundated by petitions. Never before in the entire history of the institution has it been so snowed under by applications as now; one is reminded of the old complaint of Dr. Stukely "that the Order ran itself out of breath through the folly of the members." We are now running ourselves out of breath. Lodges that once were put to it to reach three hundred members are now mounting to one thousand or two thousand and in a few cases more still. In such great bodies it is becoming necessary to devise new methods for balloting in order to expedite business, and in many cases the problem has come before Grand Lodges with the result that new ballot legislation, hitherto undreamed of, has been adopted. It is impossible to go into detail regarding these new usages, or to deal with them critically, because there are too many experiments now being tried, and space does not avail. It would be richly worth while for an individual student, or for a Study Club, to go into this matter thoroughly; it would prove a rewarding field of research in present-day jurisprudence, and many other subjects of cognate interest and importance would be meanwhile encountered, for the whole ballot system is one that insinuates itself into the very core of Freemasonry.

IV

One more word needs to be said. "Be careful how you vote." If you are a member of a board of directors of a business corporation and you are balloting on a new member or on the selection of a new cashier or president your ballot means nothing necessarily more than that you believe that the candidate is not technically qualified; your blackball would under no circumstances be considered an insult. If you vote against a political candidate it may mean, and usually is so considered, that you disagree with his policies, not that you deem him morally unfit for office. But when you vote against a petitioner for membership in our Fraternity it is a different matter, in almost every case, and far more serious, so far as the man's reputation is concerned, because almost all the requirements of membership in the Order are of the moral type; you pass upon the man's CHARACTER. It is unfair to him to blackball him on mere hearsay; or because you chance to entertain a merely private grudge against him, or for any reason less substantial than that he is unfit fundamentally for membership. The thing to be decided is not whether the petitioner is prosperous, or popular, but whether he will make a true Mason, a helpful brother, a desirable associate in the lodge room. If you have valid reasons for believing that a petitioner would not thus qualify it is your duty to vote against him; but you should not vote against him, if he be recommended by the committee on investigation, for any lesser reasons.

CHAPTER IV

"WORTHY AND WELL-QUALIFIED"

I

To many outsiders it may seem that Freemasonry demands too much of a petitioner by way of qualifications, as if it were actuated by some exclusive or aristocratic motive. Masons themselves, occasionally, ask that the bars be let down a little. But those who know the Fraternity FROM THE INSIDE, and who understand well its purposes, are of the opposite opinion, many of them, and believe that the bars should be put up higher still. The Fraternity is not a social club, an insurance society, or a charitable institution, but a body of picked men consecrated to a certain set purpose; therefrom it follows that only those who possess the qualifications for such a fellowship and the abilities for such a work should be permitted membership. The receiving of unfit candidates foredooms the temple now building to future collapse, as was the fate of so many buildings erected by the old Norman architects in England which went down because "they used poor stone, and scamped with the trowel." A wise business manager will not employ inefficient help. A sensible church will not accept unworthy members. For like reasons Freemasonry must guard well its own portals else it fail of its high mission, which God forfend! In his "War and Peace"—a great work that every Mason should read—Tolstoy makes the old Mason say:

"The first and foremost aim and chief foundation of our order, upon which it rests, and which no human power can destroy, is the preservation of a certain mystery and its transmission to posterity, a Mystery which has reached us from the most remote times, even from the first man, and on which, perhaps, the fate of the human race depends. But since this Mystery is of such character that nobody can know it or make use of it who has not been prepared by a prolonged and thorough purification of himself, not everybody may hope to come into its possession."

II

The earliest of the Old Charges, or Manuscript Constitutions, is the Regius, sometimes called, after its discoverer, the Halliwell, believed to have been written late in the fourteenth century, and to have been based on yet older materials: it specifies that the "apprentice be of lawful blood [I modernise the spelling] and have his limbs whole"; and, that the lodge "shall no thief accept, lest it would turn the Craft to shame." It would be of interest to us in this connection, did space permit, to make a careful analysis of the qualifications required by this and other ancient constitutions; fortunately they were embodied, in substance at least, and for the most part, in the Constitution published by James Anderson in 1723. This Andersonian document, one of the most famous of all Masonic productions of any kind whatsoever, has been employed as a model by nearly all our Grand Lodges in writing their own Constitutions. It is important to study carefully the list of qualifications laid down in it. They are as follows:

"The Persons admitted members of a Lodge must be good and true men, free-born, and of mature and discreet age, no Bondmen, no Women, no immoral or scandalous men, but of good Report."

III

Note first in this catalogue the DISQUALIFICATIONS.

1.—"*No Bondmen.*"

In the earlier days of Operative Masonry, slavery, or some form of serfdom, was common in all countries where Masonry flourished. Inasmuch as these slaves or serfs were uneducated and had no legal status and were not permitted to move away from their place of bondage, they were unfit for membership in such a society. As the old Greeks were wont to say, "A slave has slave manners"; such manners could not be tolerated in a Masonic lodge.

2.—"*No Women.*"

Women were freely admitted to a majority of the old craft guilds, of which, says Robert Freke Gould, "not one out of a hundred but recruited their ranks from both sexes"; but to this the Freemason's Guild was an exception, many tales to the contrary notwithstanding. There is one case on record in which the widow of an operative Mason was permitted to carry on her husband's trade, but she was given none of the secrets of the Craft. "Some writers have expressed the opinion," writes Brother A. S. MacBride, in his "Speculative Masonry"—a most noble work—"that women were admitted into the old operative lodges, but so far they have not advanced a single proof of their theory."

3.—"*No immoral or scandalous men.*" On this there is no need to make comment; a child can see that an immoral man cannot qualify for adeptship in a moral art.

IV

Note in the next place what QUALIFICATIONS are demanded.

1.—"*Good and true men.*" How simple yet how profound are these time-worn adjectives! they are not qualities that glitter but they are, in their completeness, as rare as many that do! If it be asked why Masonry does not accept bad men in order to make them good, it replies that such is not its function, for it has a unique purpose of its own to carry out, and its demands are made with that in view. One organisation cannot attempt everything. The reformation of men is left to other agencies.

2.—"*True men.*" Many a Mason has been troubled by the question, If I am fit to be a Mason why not also my wife? Freemasonry had its origin in guilds of men engaged in erecting buildings, a work for which women were not fitted. The customs, laws, traditions, regulations, and ritual evolved by these men continue to form the core of Freemasonry. Modern constitutions are modelled on the ancient constitutions; the ritual of to-day is in outline the ritual of many centuries ago; our laws are of long standing; and so are the usages and customs inside the tyled lodge. To admit women, the entire organisation, from the spire to the basement, would need to be torn down and built anew and in a manner wholly different. Freemasons do not object to women as such: they object to the revolutionising changes that would have to be made in the Craft in order to admit them.

The exclusion of women has offered opportunities for the Masonic humourist times without number and often, one is happy to remark, tempted our heaviest writers to a lighter vein. (Why do so many writers make Freemasonry so funereal and so solemn!) An old French author facetiously remarked that the presence of "the sex" would distract men from the work of the lodge: whilst the old London "Pocket Companion and History of Freemasons" (1764) furnished reasons which may sometimes be in a Mason's mind but which (except behind the Tiler) he wouldn't dare express!

"The Ladies claim right
To come to our Light,
Since the apron they say is their bearing;
Can they subject their will,
Can they keep their tongues still,
And let talking be changed into hearing?

"This difficult task
Is the *least* we can ask,
To secure us on sundry occasions;
When with this they comply,
Our utmost we'll try
To raise Lodges for Lady Freemasons!"

3.—"*Free born.*"

After slavery had been abolished in England by Act of Parliament the old demand that a candidate be "free born" was changed to "free man." In this country, and owing to the longer continuance of slavery, "free born" has been longer retained, and is still found, I believe, in several Constitutions. But now the term is given a more liberal interpretation and is made to mean that the man is not an inmate of a penal institution, and that his mind is free from enslaving superstitions. As we may read in Gibson's "Masonic Problem": "Is he free? Not free in common law only, but also free from hostile and absorbing interests subversive to Masonic influence?" Of this, more anon.

4.—"*Of mature and discreet age.*"

"Regarding the question of age," remarks MacBride, "the old Manuscripts do not, so far as we have noticed, particularise. They, in some cases, use the phrase 'of full age,' but nothing beyond that. Each lodge, in the old days, evidently settled this point for itself." As the operative custom varied in England, so has the speculative. The Grand Lodge Regulations made it 25 years in 1721; this was changed to 18 and thus remained "until a very recent period"; it is now 21, though some other countries have clung to 18. "Under these circumstances," MacBride comments, "the practice of obligating a candidate not to be present at the initiation of any one under the age of 21 years, is most reprehensible. It debars him while visiting a lodge working under a constitution in which the full age is 18, from remaining during the ceremony of initiation, if the candidate is under 21 years." The point is well taken. It would be well if Grand Lodges were to specify that by "full age" is meant the minimum age required of a candidate by any given Grand Lodge, and thus the member of one jurisdiction, while visiting in another, would not be put to the annoyance described by Brother MacBride; and the Grand Lodge itself could set its own minimum at the age declared legal by the state in which it operates. It must be remembered in these premises that a lodge sustains legal relations with a candidate; this makes it absolutely necessary that a candidate be of legal age.

V

The matter of physical qualifications has long been a storm-centre, and that for the reason that the "doctrine of the perfect youth" appears to be a landmark, and Masons are obligated to maintain inviolate the ancient landmarks.
Since the ancient builders performed difficult manual labour it is easy to understand why they found it necessary to demand of a candidate soundness of limb; besides, an infirm member was supported usually out of "the common chest" and that worked a hardship on his fellows. Accordingly, one may read in the Regius Manuscript—it was cast in poetic form—as follows:

> To the craft it were great shame,
> To make a halt man and a lame,
> For an imperfect man of such blood
> Should do the craft but little good.
> Thus you may know every one,
> The craft would have a mighty man;
> A maimed man he hath no might,
> You must it know long ere night.

After the speculative régime came into full blast in England these physical qualifications were greatly modified, so that we find lodges initiating the blind, deaf, and dumb, and persons otherwise defective or maimed. In this land, on the contrary, a majority of the jurisdictions still cling to the ancient doctrine of "the perfect youth," for what reason it is difficult to understand, seeing that what was so necessary in operative days is no longer needed in a symbolic Craft which requires of its members work with head and heart rather than with hands and feet. "It would be better for us," as Brother Louis Block, P.G.M., of Iowa, once exclaimed, "to admit a man with a wooden leg than with a wooden head!"

It would be quite easy to fill a book with quotations from eminent Masonic leaders and from Grand Lodges which have argued in behalf of a modification of the ancient rule. Three such quotations will suffice as being typical:

In 1875 the Board of General Purposes of the Grand Lodge of England issued a circular in which the writer said: "I am directed to say that the general rule in this country is to consider a candidate eligible for election who although not perfect in limbs is sufficiently so to go through the various ceremonies." It was left to the masters and members of subordinate lodges to determine whether the candidate was thus able.

Dr. George Oliver, who was once the mightiest influence in Masonic literature and whose influence is still felt everywhere, and who was always conservative, writes to this effect in his "Treasury": "It would indeed be a solecism in terms to contend that a loss or partial deprivation of a physical organ of the body could, by any possibility, disqualify a man from studying the sciences, or being made a Mason in our own times, while in possession of sound judgment, and the healthy exercise of his intellectual powers."

The veteran Masonic scholar of Iowa, Theodore Sutton Parvin, was of similar opinion, as when he contended that "it is the sole right of each and every lodge to act upon these qualifications, even as it is universally conceded that they are the sole judges of the 'moral' qualifications of all candidates."

VI

Such other qualifications as are required will receive consideration in later connections; there remains here only to remark that perhaps, after all, the chief essential qualification in any candidate is a right motive; that is, a full and sincere inward determination to take Freemasonry seriously. "The vast increase of late years," wrote Brother W. J. Hughan, one of the giants of modern Masonic scholarship, "both of lodges and members, calls for renewed vigilance and extra care in selecting candidates, that numbers may not be a source of weakness instead of strength." The man who enters out of mere curiosity, or to gain social standing, or business advantages, the "watch-fob Mason," he is the real cowan, and a subtle source of weakness inside the body of the Craft, which will surely sap the life from the Fraternity if we do not have a care!

CHAPTER V

THE HOODWINK

I

"Where were you prepared?" The answer made to that question opens for our vision a way into one of the secrets of Freemasonry. We must prepare ourselves in order to receive any teaching whatsoever, for we see only, as Goethe has expressed it, "that which we carry in our hearts." For this reason many of the Ancient Mysteries insisted on a long period of preparation, as do many churches to-day. For the same reason the Masonic lodge should see to it that the candidate is as fully prepared in mind as he is in body before he is given admittance to the door. In some parts of Europe, I have been told, an experienced Master Mason is appointed sponsor, or godfather, to a candidate; and lodges of instruction are held in which the petitioner is taught something of the history and principles of the Order. Surely this is a wise custom! Many a man—you yourself, perhaps, were one, as was I—has stepped into the First Degree without the slightest inkling of what "it was all about," with the consequence that he has been too bewildered to know whether to laugh or to cry. And how often it happens that a candidate passes from one degree to another as rapidly as he can learn the lectures, moving all the while in too great haste to comprehend the simplest rudiments of the great ideas and teachings that are dramatically presented to him moment after moment! To be "prepared in the heart" means that within one's own mind and feelings he is experiencing the meaning of that which he does and sees; if a candidate is hustled along too rapidly to be able to have any such understanding of the degrees, how can it be said that he is duly and truly prepared to be a Master Mason?

The Ritual itself is wise in these connections because it recognises the fact that a man must be prepared in the heart as well as in the preparation room. Except a man's mood be right, except his will be in the appropriate attitude, except he act from true motives, and in a reverent prayerful frame of mind, the "work" will be to him as meaningless as an old wives' tale. It is necessary that every lodge arrange to prepare the candidate's mind by previous instruction; and it is equally necessary that it build about the preparation room a wall of secrecy and sanctity in order to ward off the jest or careless word that may lead a candidate to approach the door in light or flippant mood.

II

Being in Masonic ignorance, a seeker after light, and a representative of the natural untaught man, it is fitting that the candidate be made to walk in darkness by wearing the hoodwink which Mackey has well described as "a symbol of secrecy, silence, darkness, in which the mysteries of our art should be preserved from the unhallowed gaze of the profane." The use of the blindfold goes far back among secret societies, even to the Ancient Mysteries, in which the candidate was usually made to enter the sanctuary with eyes covered. The Cathari, whom Innocent III tried so hard to annihilate, and who were at bottom Christian mystics, were accustomed to call those seeking initiation into their mysteries "hoodwinked slaves," implying that the eyes of the soul were still blind in ignorance and lust. Our own use of the device is in harmony with these old customs and ideas. The purpose of the hoodwink is not to conceal something from the candidate, for it has another significance: it symbolises the fact that the candidate *is yet in darkness*, like the babe lying in its mother's womb. Being in darkness the candidate is expected to prepare his inmost mind for those revelations that will be made to him after the hoodwink is removed.

III

I have used the word "revelations" advisedly in this connection because the entire symbolism of the hoodwink is a beautiful and pregnant suggestion of the methods of revelation, and of the part played by it in the larger life of man. Literally signifying "an unveiling," revelation carries within itself the meaning of something that is hidden behind a veil, and of the removing of the veil. If one stands before a blinded window a great sweep of the Sierra Madres may stretch before him but he will not see them any more than if they were not there; but the moment the blind is lifted the mountains appear, lifting their eternal sheaves of snow, and the apparition is like a piece of magic, as though they had been suddenly created. "The lifting of the blind"—that is revelation, whether in religion, science, art, or in Freemasonry.

In the Volume of the Sacred Law we read of Jesus that he "brought life and immortality to light"; these words do not mean that Jesus brought life and immortality into existence, as though before him they were not: the true life had been knocking at the hearts of men from the beginning, and immortality had always awaited them beyond "the narrow house"; Jesus was among the first to open the eyes of men to see these realities. Men had always been brothers; God had always been the All-Father; love had always been the law of the world, and purity the law of the heart: it was the great mission of Jesus to be one of the way-showers of men who could lift from their eyes the hoodwink of unseeing. He was an unveiler, and therefore a revealer.

It is ever thus with revelation. Gravitation existed before the first man came to be, but it was not until Sir Isaac Newton came that men saw this thing that had been about them always: he lifted the blind, and men saw gravitation. The sidereal universe is from eternity, but nobody "saw" it until Copernicus, after gazing at the stars from his narrow cell for many years, uncovered the majesty and meaning of the heavens. Steam had always been at work along with fire and water, like an unknown genie, but it took an Isaac Watt to discover ("discover" means to uncover, and is very similar to "reveal") its presence. And so it ever is. Realities more wonderful than gravity, steam, or stars are, perhaps, playing about or within us all the while, but we, wearing the hoodwinks of ignorance, are blind to the great presences. The prophet, the leader, the mighty teacher of the race is one who, born into blindness as are we all, somehow has been able to get the hoodwink from his eyes and is then able to cause us to see. He does not create; he confers the power of vision.

IV

It is in the sense thus explained that we may describe Freemasonry as standing among men to reveal to them the real brotherhood lived in the bonds of eternal life. It has created neither brotherhood nor eternal life, for these have always been facts; it reveals them to its adepts and thus enables them to avail themselves of the powers and privileges thereof. Brotherhood is a reality; it is a law of the race; but there are many, alas too many, who have not discovered that fact. They are like those who lived in the days before Watt learned to harness steam; steam was about them but they made no use of it. So with the uninitiated (using that word in a very deep sense); brotherhood is at their side but they do not see it and therefore can make no use of it. When Masonry comes into them, it is not that brotherhood has for the first time been created, but that for the first time the man is made to see it and to avail himself of it.

The kingdom of heaven may be defined as, "Mankind living happily together." The one way in which mankind can live happily together is through the use of brotherhood. This was true when the first savages ran naked about the forest, some of them, perhaps, eating each other. It was true then, but the primitive folk could not discover or see it, just as electricity was about them without their knowing of it. But know it or not, brotherhood was the fixed law of human association, and they progressed toward harmony with each other only in so far as they learned to discover and to practise brotherhood. And so is it to-day. It is not brotherhood that is in question, but ourselves; brotherhood is a law, a reality, like gravitation; it is in proportion as we recognise and make use of it that we progress. Until we learn and practise it we shall be unhappy in our living one with another, for happiness is impossible where brotherhood is not.

Freemasonry does not exist in a world where brotherhood is a mere dream flying along the sky; it exists in a world of which brotherhood is the law of human life. Its function is not to bring brotherhood into existence just as a hot-house gardener may at last coax into bloom a frail flower, though the climate is most unfriendly, but to lead men to understand that brotherhood is already a reality, a law, and that it is not until we come to know it as such, and practise it, that we can ever find happiness, together. Freemasonry does not create something too fine and good for this rough world; it "reveals" something that is as much a part of the world as roughness itself. In other words, it removes the hoodwink of jealousy, hatred, unkindness, and all the other myriad forms of unbrotherliness in order that a man may see and thus come to know how good and pleasant a thing it is for brethren to dwell together in unity. The hoodwink of cloth or leather that is bound over a man's eyes is not the real hoodwink at all, but only the symbol thereof; the real hoodwink, and it is that which Freemasonry undertakes to remove from a man's eyes, is all that anti-social and unhuman spirit out of which grow the things that make life unkind and unhappy. "Brotherhood is heaven; the lack of brotherhood is hell."

CHAPTER VI

THE CABLE TOW

I

The cowboy who "lassoes" a pony and the Laplander who throws a noose about the neck of a reindeer are making use of a device for fettering and controlling animals that was discovered by man long before the beginnings of history. Because of the many uses to which he put the rope, or noose, and because it was a natural thing for his imagination to play about simple every day implements and experiences man early made a symbol of the noose. It may be that the emblematic use of the rope could be traced to yet other sources, but that given is reasonable enough and may stand in our mind for a suggestion of the manner in which symbols and emblems often come into existence. The candidate in a number of the Ancient Mysteries was led into the place of initiation at the end of a rope; Brahmins and Dervishes continue to make a similar use of it at the present time. In every such case the noose, rope, or cable tow has been used to signify control, obedience, and direction. (See "Ars Quatuor Coronatorum," Vol. I, p. 264. Hereafter, in referring to these familiar volumes, which contain the published transactions of a great Lodge of Masonic Research of London, England, I shall use the well-known initials, A.Q.C.)

This symbol, as every candidate has learned, is used in Masonic ceremonies. When, by whom, and in what manner it was introduced there is still an open question, though our scholars have searched far and wide to discover. Its use may have been borrowed from earlier fraternities; or it may have been inherited from the Operative Lodges who may have used it for the purely practical purpose of maintaining bodily control of the candidate. The latter supposition receives a certain amount of support from the fact that English lodges still give the cable tow a non-symbolical function, and then in the First Degree only; and there are echoes of such a meaning in the First Degree as practised here in the United States.

II

Mackey defines a cable tow as "a rope or line for drawing or leading" and suggests that it may have been derived from the German "Kabeltau," which has that significance. Mackey adds that "the word is purely Masonic" but this is not quite true because it is found in the Standard Dictionary of 1913 and there defined as "a rope or line for drawing or leading; in Freemasonry, symbolising in the Second and Third Degrees the covenant by which Masons are bound." This last-named point is inaccurate, as the reader will have instantly noted, because the cable tow is used in the First as well as the other two degrees; this is one more example of the woful ignorance of Freemasonry displayed by profane editors of encyclopædias and dictionaries and reminds one how careful a student should be to make sure of the authenticity of his sources of information. Albert Pike traced the word back to the Hebrew "Khabel," which meant variously "a rope attached to an anchor" and "to bind as with a pledge." J. T. Lawrence finds its origin in two languages: "cabel," a Dutch word "signifying a great rope, which, being fastened to the anchor, holds the ship fast when she rides"; "tow" he believes to be a Saxon word "which means to hale or draw and is applied, nautically, to draw a barge or ship along the water."

III

What does this symbol mean? Many have contended, Albert Pike among them, that the cable tow is nothing more than a device for the bodily control of the candidate; but this interpretation is not borne out by the Second and Third Degrees in both of which it carries an undeniably symbolical meaning. Others see in it an emblem of the natural untaught man's bondage to ignorance and lust, which bondage it is the mission of Masonry to remove. Of such an opinion is Arthur Edward Waite, who, seeing in the rope a suggestion of the cord that binds the unborn babe, or the babe newly born, to its mother's body, finds in the symbol a representation of the gross earthly ties that hold unregenerated men to their appetites and passions. In view of the fact that the symbolism of rebirth runs through the Ritual this interpretation is not at all far-fetched. Paton finds in the cable tow a "simple and natural tie which unites the Fraternity": Lawrence sees it as "the Mystic Tie binding the initiate to God, to the Order, and to Righteousness; a tie which both binds and draws, and which holds a man fast, lest he drift like a ship at sea." Churchward, who loves to go far afield, traces the symbol back to ancient Egypt, where he believed himself to have discovered so many Masonic origins, in whose Mysteries, some of them, the candidate wore a chain about the neck "to signify their belief in God and their dependence on Him." (See his "Signs and Symbols of Primordial Man.") Others have believed that the cable tow is the symbol of all bad obediences—obedience to lust, to passion, selfishness, worldliness, etc., and consequently must be removed from the emancipated finder of the Light: others have found in it the opposite symbol of all good obediences—the ties that bind a man to his fellows, to laws, to duty, and to ideals. The variety of these interpretations tends to confuse one, especially a beginner in symbolism, who is tempted to believe that where so many meanings are found there cannot be any meaning at all; it must be remembered that a symbol by its very nature says many things at once, things often the most diverse, a function which is not the least of its many advantages. Almost all great and simple words—love, patriotism, friendship, immortality, God, etc.,—are similarly prolific of meanings, and so are symbols or symbolical actions in every-day use, such as a flag, the wave of a hand, or the tipping of one's hat.

IV

To my own mind the candidate is as a child struggling for release from narrow environments and external restraints in order to enter into the larger life of liberty and self-direction. The cable tow about his neck symbolises all those external checks and restraints, such as conventionality, fear of the world, fear of the adverse opinions or displeasure of men, and of the control of teachers and parents on which a child naturally depends but which must be thrown off when one has reached full responsibility as a man "of mature age." The removal of the noose symbolises the attainment of inward light, judgment and the power of self-direction—in other words, real manhood, which has its centre and support in an inward power that is stronger than any pressure from without. Dr. Buck whom I have already quoted (I am not in agreement with him in his interpretation of Masonry as a whole) has given us in words of admirable simplicity a noble exposition of the true significance of this symbol:

"He [the candidate] is restrained now [after the removal of the cable tow] by the voluntary obligations taken, all of which indicate the necessity of constant vigilance and self-control. In place of the former command—'thou shalt not'—comes the voluntary pledge—'I will.' The result is to replace outer constraint by inward restraint, without annulling or altering a single moral precept. The slave who formerly obeyed a Master through fear, now voluntarily serves a Master through love. The difference is that between a bondman and a freeman, and the result to the candidate can hardly be put in words when it is once realised." (*New Age*, Vol. vii, page 159.)

The homely practical truth and usefulness of all this interpretation may be made instantly discernible by a simple example. In human society in general, law, written or unwritten, is the cable tow that holds fast every man. The good man cannot escape from it any more than a bad man, and he who walks about his own yard, a free and respectable citizen, is quite as much held fast by the law as he who sits sullenly in a prison cell, denied the right of seeing the sun or of walking upon the grass. But while these two men are equally held by law, the manner in which law holds them is as different as day is from night; for whereas the prisoner is held by it against his own will, the free man obeys it of his own choice. The hope of the world depends upon those who "have the law in their inward parts" and keep it because they love order and security. Men and women who must be forced to keep order are a source of social unhappiness; it is impossible to have a policeman at every man's elbow. A wise and good citizen is one who inwardly understands why law is necessary and what law is, and gives it a voluntary obedience, so that nobody needs to stand by to force compulsion. Moreover, such a man has learned that freedom is nothing other than the inward and voluntary obedience, glad obedience, to wise and just laws. People of a low order must be held fast by external force; in proportion as men and women become advanced, external force becomes increasingly unnecessary, so that in a truly civilised state, order rests on the inward character of men. The savage has the rope about his neck; the civilised man has it in his heart. It is not a question of tie or no tie; but of what kind of a tie it is that holds a man to his fellows, to the state, and to his duty.

V

As to the meaning of the expression "length of my cable tow" it is somewhat difficult to speak, owing to the great variety of interpretations that have been offered, a few of the more typical examples of which may be here given. Pike sees in it "the scope and intent and spirit of one's pledge." Brother Rev. F. de P. Castello, writing on "The Geometry of Freemasonry" ("Author's Lodge Transactions," Vol. i, page 286), says, "The cable's length has always been understood to be one of 720 feet, which is twice 360, the measure of the circle"; making one circle to stand for the spiritual in man, and the other for the material, he believes the "length of my cable tow" to mean that, "I will go as far in assisting my brethren as my moral principles and my material condition will permit." In Mackey's Encyclopædia we may read: "The old writers define the length of a cable tow, which they sometimes called a 'cable's length,' to be three miles for an Entered Apprentice. But the expression is really symbolic, and, as defined by the Baltimore Convention in 1842 [a notable Masonic gathering], means the scope of a man's reasonable ability." With the Baltimore Convention one may very well agree.

CHAPTER VII

THE LODGE

I

Qualified in all ways necessary and prepared in body and mind, the candidate approaches the lodge, the symbolic significance of which may now claim our attention. The term itself has been traced back to early languages by word scientists. One Masonic writer, Pierson ("Traditions of Freemasonry"), asserts that its most ancient form was the Sanskrit *loga*, which had the meaning of *world*. Other writers find different origins for it, too many to be catalogued here, especially since the philology of Masonic words and names does not come within the range of this study. The reader curious of such matters will find an overwhelming abundance in the New English Dictionary, and similar works of reference.

The definitions of the word "lodge" are as numerous and almost as diverse as its derivations. It is found to mean a hut or cottage; the cavity at the bottom of a mining shaft; a miner's cabin; a collection of objects, such as a "lodge of islands"; a small house in a forest; any covered place or shelter, a bird's nest, even; but among Masons it has been used to signify the organised body of Masons, or the room in which that body meets. In eighteenth century English Masonry it was used also to describe a piece of furniture similar to the Ark. When first found among the records of the Operative Masons it meant the building, usually temporary, and often little more than a shed, which served as general headquarters for the Craft, being at the same time a meeting place, a banquet room, the "office" of the superintendents, and a store-house for tools and materials; occasionally it may have served for a sleeping place as well. As time went on the name of the building came gradually to signify the body of men using it, and thus arose our custom of speaking of the Fraternity itself as a lodge.

II

But over and above all this the lodge is used by the Ritual as a symbol, the chief, perhaps, among all our symbols, and as such it is understood as a mystical representation of the world. This use of it is more ancient than the others, for it connects up with ideas and customs of the early world. The peoples of antiquity who believed so thoroughly that power could be gained by imitating nature and the gods built their temples and the sanctuaries of their secret societies as miniatures of the earth, which they of course believed to be an "oblong square." Professor Breasted, who writes so fascinatingly of the Egyptians, says that the rich of old Egypt would even build their homes earth-shape, the floors made to represent plains and seas, the ceiling painted in imitation of the sky. This custom was of great value to the men of that day, for it threw something of the majesty of the universe and the sanctity of heaven about their daily tasks and their habits of worship. "All the most ancient temples were intended to symbolise the universe," writes Albert Pike, "which itself was habitually called the Temple and Habitation of Deity. Every temple was the world in miniature; and so the world was one grand temple."

Whether or not we stand in direct historical connection with this old custom we cannot know, but the fact remains that our lodge, like the Egyptian temple, is a symbol of the Universe; and only when it is thus interpreted can we understand its characteristics at all. Its form is ideally a double cube, of old considered the symbol of Deity, and now understood as containing the Rough Ashlar of the Apprentice and the Perfect Ashlar of the Master. This *form* includes the heaven above, in its height; and the earth beneath, in its being an oblong square. Its *situation* is on "the highest hills and the lowest valleys" because it includes men of all ranks in its membership. In *position* it lies East and West, its length in the path of the sun, its portals in the West in order that the member may enter facing the East, the place of light, hope, and power. In *dimension* it extends east and west and north and south to signify its universality. It is *supported* on the Three Pillars of Wisdom, Strength, and Beauty because these are the foundations of noble life; and its covering is the "cloudy canopy" of the heavens, which is connected with the earth by the mystic ladder of Faith, Hope, and Charity. Its furniture, its ornaments, and its jewels are flooded with a Light that shines through the windows of the East, the South, and the West; and an "All-Seeing Eye" keeps watch above it all. What a world is this into which the candidate is born, a visible representation of those invisible Truths and Spiritual Realities in which the pure of soul alone can live!

III

In this symbolic world, preserved in law and order as the real universe is, an otherwise discordant number of men become organised into a harmonious body, each member performing his appropriate function, and all co-operating in harmony. Through this co-operation the influence of the individual is multiplied many times over, and what these men could not do separately they easily accomplish through united effort. The member who finds the eternal verities growing dim from absorption in the heat and burden of his daily task has them made real to him again as he sits in this sanctuary surrounded on all sides by the impressive symbols of God, of Truth, and of Immortality. Truly, the body of men thus living and working becomes itself an eloquent prophecy of the far-off coming of the Universal Brotherhood, and stands in the midst of a warring humanity as an earnest of the good time coming when the engines of war and the implements of all contention will be laid aside forever.

> "God hath made mankind one vast Brotherhood,
> Himself their Master, and the world His Lodge."

CHAPTER VIII.

THE ENTRANCE

I

Bearing in mind all this manifold significance of the lodge and all that is implied by membership therein we can understand that entrance into its precincts is a step having something of the importance and the dignity of birth. Accordingly the candidate is placed in the care of trusty friends who will see that he is duly prepared; and he is given necessary instructions by one of the Officers of the Craft who is careful to ascertain that he comes with no unworthy motive. When he steps inside the door and enters for the first time into a tiled Masonic lodge he may well feel a certain awe, or even tremble a bit with apprehension; for he is about to participate in a rite, and to stand in the presence of symbols, over which hovers the awful impressiveness of centuries. The badges of rank, the tokens of distinction, the costumery of the world, the manifold ties of the temporal and external order now stand him in no stead, and he is thrown back on the resources of his own naked and essential humanity. The will to do, the mind to know, the heart to love, the imagination to conceive—these and these only can serve as the materials out of which his own Masonic temple can be built.

If he must knock for entrance into this world it is to remind him that everywhere and always he must knock for entrance into any of the great worlds of existence. God in His unsearchable wisdom has ordained that, except for the involuntary entrance into physical existence, every birth comes from our willing to have it so. The world of nature, the various worlds of literature, of science, of art, of religion, lie about man, but the doors leading therein never open except a man knock once, twice, thrice. It is only after the blows of his hammer, after his tireless, patient study of details, that the heavy portals of the rocks open their secrets to the geologist; it is only after the student has a hundred times implored in toil and prayer that music can be persuaded to swing back her ivory wickets of sweet sound. Over the lintels of every realm of great achievement the Infinite has carved His irreversible law, "Knock and it shall be opened unto you."

II

At the time of his entrance the candidate is given a definition of Masonry. This definition is beautiful and true as far as it goes, and that in the nature of the case cannot be far, but we shall be wise to press toward a more complete understanding of the matter than the Ritual makes possible. If such a definition as may be fashioned here falls far short of its purpose one can comfort himself by the reflection that the truer and more vital a thing is the less capable is it of definition, and that Masonry in this regard is in the same case as religion, or friendship, or art.

In discussing the "mission of Masonry," Brother A. S. MacBride ("Speculative Masonry," p. 1) defines mission as "the aim and purpose of anything." Of Masonry he writes, "The word carries with it through all the variants known to us, the idea of unity. To mass a body of men or troops, for instance, is to bring them into close touch or united action. From this view it appears that Masonry is the building together of various units, such as stones, bricks, wood, iron, or human beings, into a compact mass or structure." Speculative Masonry he defines as "the building morally of humanity into an organised structure, according to a design of plan."

Of similar purpose is the definition given by Thomas Green: "True Speculative Masonry teaches a man by the industrious application of the principles of Eternal Truth and Right to the untaught material of humanity, to shape its thoughts and actions so as to erect from it a spiritual building, on sure foundations, with intelligence and purpose, and admirable to contemplate."

The Royal Arch lectures give the definition a religious turn: "The glory of God is the grand object of our mysteries." Dr. J. D. Buck, who interpreted Masonry from the mystical point of view, states that "Masonry is really a school of instruction and preparation for the most profound wisdom ever opened to man." A. E. Waite, another mystic, albeit of a different school, says that "Masonry, in its proper understanding, is a summary of the quest after that which is divine." In connection with these it will be well to carry in mind the time-tried definition long accepted by the Craft: "Masonry is a beautiful system of morality, veiled in allegory and illustrated by symbols." These several definitions are all acceptable in their way as would be many others that might be cited.

For myself I have long thought of the Masonic life being, in one of its principal aspects, a quest for that which is divine in the universe and in the human soul; this purpose is expressed, it seems to me, in all our symbols, now in subdued whispers, and again in eloquent, ringing voices. And, because our ceremonies represent the combination of at least three streams of symbolism, it would be possible to set this purpose forth from as many points of view.

III

If we study the matter from the point of view of the architectural symbolism we may say that Masonry is the attempt to release in us those materials of our nature which are most divine and to build them into a temple fit for the indwelling deity; and that, in turn, the individual is to be used as a living building stone in that larger temple of human brotherhood which is now building, sometimes in the day and often in the night, among the children of men.

There is also in our Ritual a stream of symbolism representing the Mason as on a quest after that which is lost. This may be understood as a secret once in our possession but now escaped; or it may be known as the ultimate Truth, Goodness, and Beauty which lie behind the veils of time and sense. Of this latter significance of the quest, Brother MacBride has given us an illustration of rare appropriateness: "There is an ancient Gaelic poem called 'The Poem of Trathal' part of which describes a mother playing a harp to her children, and which translated runs thus: 'Two children with their fair locks rise at her knee. They bend their ears above the harp as she touches with white hands the trembling strings. She stops. They take the harp themselves but cannot find the cord they admired. Why, they ask, does it not answer us? Show us the strings where dwells the song. She bids them search for it until she returns. Their little fingers wander among the wires. And so with the children of men. Their fingers wander among the wires of the harp of life. They say 'show us the string where dwells the song.' We search for the lost song, the lost harmony of the soul."

Again, we have in our Ritual a symbolism that hints of a death, and a rising again to life. Let this not be understood as a rising up after the death of the body; the raising is done in the present. It signifies that there is in each of us, here and now, that which is truly Eternal, that which the old Christian Mystics called the divine spark in the soul. "Within thyself," declares the Bhagavad-Gita, and truly, "thou hast a sublime friend thou knowest not. God dwells within all men." To this heart-subduing truth all the seers have borne witness, and all the Ancient Mysteries, and all religions. It is Masonry's chief mission also to hear that same witness, for Masonry is, I believe, a drama of regeneration.

IV

Let us consider this a moment! There is that in a man which serves only his private, his physical, and his present temporal needs; food, clothing, drink, riches, these have almost wholly a reference to the body, and the body's desires, and for that reason are transient only, for "the flesh passeth away and the lust thereof." But there is also that in a man which has reference to the needs of his spirit, which craves Goodness, Truth, and Beauty. For these the spirit will be searching long after the body lies a heap of dust within its narrow house, will be searching and finding in all the worlds and in all the Eternities. It is the misfortune of the merely natural man, of him whom the prophets have called the unregenerate, that in his life the merely physical, the merely temporal, are in command; it is the great privilege of the new-born man, the regenerate, that in him the Good, the True, and the Beautiful, that is, the Spiritual, have full control, so that in the midst of the fleeting days, while he walks through the shadows of the earth life, and everything about him is steadily falling away into oblivion, he is already living "the life that shall endless be." To teach men the secret of this present Eternal Life is, I am convinced, Masonry's chief and greatest mission; and I may say that this interpretation can carry with it the weight of the authority of Albert Pike, whose brain was made like a continent, and whose soul towered like a Himalayan range: a farther-reaching, a deeper-going definition of Masonry than the following was never written:

"Freemasonry is the subjugation of the Human that is in man by the Divine; the conquest of the Appetites and Passions by the Moral Sense and the Reason; a continual effort, struggle and warfare, of the Spiritual against the Material and Sensual. That victory—when it has been achieved and secured, and the conqueror may rest upon his shield and wear the well-earned laurels—in the true Holy Empire."

CHAPTER IX

THE SHARP INSTRUMENT

After the candidate has effected his entrance a "certain sharp instrument"—(which should never be one of the working tools)—is applied in a peculiar manner, and a certain hint of the meaning of this is given, as the initiated reader will clearly remember. On all this there is no reason to comment save in brief manner, and then only on the meaning given as aforesaid. This meaning has especial significance to us because it sets forth the only *real penalty* that a Mason ever suffers for violating his obligation. (On "Obligation," see p. 53.)

It is accurate to say that a majority of the attacks on Freemasonry have been occasioned by the "Penalties" which are supposed to be enforced on oath-violating members. Of these Penalties it is manifestly impossible here to speak, though there is much that could be said, orally, in a tyled lodge. It seems that their present form was derived from the seventeenth century English Treason laws, though certain particulars may be elsewhere traced. It is certain that we have not inherited them from the operative Masons, for we have many of their OB's in print, and a comparison of our own form with theirs is not altogether to our advantage, as witness the following passage from MacBride's "Speculative Masonry":

"It seems to us, with these OB's before us, there is only one course open to all Masons desiring the welfare of our ancient institution, and that is to insist that a simpler, more sensible, and consequently, more solemn and binding form shall be substituted, wherever the corrupt form now prevails. The latter has neither the sanction of age, of law, of reason, nor of good taste."

This, it may be emphasised, is but a criticism of the *form* of the Penalties; I am very sure that neither Brother MacBride nor any other wise Mason will advocate the abandoning of Penalties else we leave out of our Symbolism a symbol of the everywhere present moral law that "the wages of sin is death." Truth dies out in the liar, Beauty dies out in the vulgar, Goodness dies out in the wicked, and the way of the transgressor is hard. Would ours be a complete *moral* science if it ignored this Divine law built into the spiritual structure of man?

There is more to be said. He who violates the laws of an art will lose out of his mind the power of that art. The pianist who occupies himself wholly with tin-pan rag-time loses the ability to play, and even to appreciate, real music. The author who descends to the "Diamond Dick" level of literature forfeits his ability to write nobler pages. The architect who scamps and cheats in his building will soon lose the skill of erecting structures that deserve the name of architecture, a fact brought out with convincing power by Robert Herrick in his great novel, "The Common Lot." So is it with him who deliberately transgresses the laws of the Royal Art of Freemasonry, the Art of noble brotherhood lived in the bonds of the Eternal Life; its skill and its influence will die out within him as if an instrument of torture had been plunged into his heart.

CHAPTER X

INVOKING THE BLESSING OF DEITY

I

It is of the highest import that in the ceremony of initiation the candidate kneel at the altar of prayer, for this is nothing other than a symbol of the fact that all right life, inside and outside of the Lodge, is established in our relationship with God. It is of further significance that in the early degree he has another to pray for him while at a later time he must pray for himself because this is a recognition of prayer as an art to be learned gradually, as all other arts are learned.

Brother J. T. Thorp, the veteran English student, has suggested that the Apprentice prayer has come to us from the old custom of beginning each Old Charge with an Invocation; this is a reasonable, historical inference, but perhaps it does not go deep enough. The prayer is in the Masonic ceremony because it must be in the Masonic life, and the important point here is not how we came to pray, but why we do pray; and the reason we do pray is that we cannot help it. Man is a praying creature because of the way he is made, and not all the arguments of the naturalist or all the sophistries of the sceptic can cure him of the habit.

Prayer is more "than the aspiration of the soul toward the absolute and Infinite Intelligence"; it is more than meditation; it is more than the soul's dialogue with its own higher self; it is more than soliloquy: prayer is a force which accomplishes real work in its own appropriate realm. When a forester wishes to fell a tree he uses an axe; when a farmer desires a crop he ploughs the soil and sows the grain; the merchant who seeks money applies himself to his trade: by token of the same universal law of cause and effect the soul that would get spiritual work done must apply the instrument of prayer.

II

If it be said that God is all-knowing and all-powerful and does not need our praying we reply that there are some things which God *will not* do, whether He *can* or not, without the assistance of man. Working by himself God produces the wild dog-rose; working with man He produces an "American Beauty"; working by himself He produces the wild wheat, unfruitful and inedible; working with man He carpets the prairies with heavy-seeded grain, enough to feed a nation; working by himself He brought forth the first man, half animal, half human, slinking in his mildewed cave and killing his prey with his hands, like the wild bear; working in co-operation with man they two have brought forth this human world of netted highways and thrumming cities—literature, art, beauty, the temple, and the home, the Iliad, The Tempest, the Bible, Homer, Shakespeare, and Christ. Man co-operates with God in transforming nature by the use of his hands; he co-operates with God in transforming the spirit by the use of prayer. Besides, God has not shut himself out of the soul that He has made, and prayer itself may well be His own activity, His Divine handclasp with the human heart.

This is not an argument to justify the use of prayer—there is no need of that; it is its own justification. After all is said pro and con, the fact remains that the great souls have been praying men. It is not for us to twist this *fact* about to suit our theories; it is for us to adjust our theories to the fact. Prayer widens our horizons, purifies our motives, disciplines the will, releases us from the gravitations of the material, sets a new light in the face, and links us to heaven in an ineffable fellowship. It is a stairway let down by God into the inmost chambers of our hearts up and down which the better angels of our nature pass and repass in their healing ministries.

"Upon this earth there is nothing more eloquent than the silence of a company of men and women bowed in the hush and awe of a House of Prayer. Through all the groping generations the soul of man has never ceased to seek a city unseen and eternal. No thoughtful man but at some time has mused over this great adoring habit of our humanity, and the marvel of it deepens the longer he ponders it. That instinct for eternity which draws together the stones of a stately cathedral, where the shadow of the Infinite is bidden to linger, tells us more of what man is than all else besides. So far as we know, man is the only being on our planet that pauses to pray, and the wonder of his worship is at once a revelation and a prophecy.

"Man sits here shaping wings to fly:
His heart forebodes a mystery;
He names the name Eternity.

"That type of Perfect in his mind
In Nature he can nowhere find,
He sows himself on every wind.

"He seems to hear a Heavenly Friend,
And through thick walls to apprehend
A labour working toward an end."

CHAPTER XI

CIRCUMAMBULATION

I

We come now to the Rite of the Mystic Journey wherein the candidate travels from the East to the West by way of the South, a ceremony of much interest and many meanings. How it found its way into our Ritual is, I believe, a mystery, though some have sought its origin in the Operative custom of leading the initiate from one station to another for examination; but this origin seems unreasonable because such a journey would have been conducted in a very different manner. It is more probable that Circumambulation ("walking around") is one of our inheritances from ancient times.

Primitive people firmly believed that they could wield influence over a god by imitating his actions. They believed the sun to be a god, or the visible embodiment of a god, who made a daily tour of the heavens, beginning in the east (in the northern hemisphere), and progressing toward the west by way of the south; it was most natural, therefore, that they should evolve a ceremony in imitation of this. Accordingly, in India, in Egypt, in Greece, and in Rome we early find the practice of circumambulation.

In Greece, the priest, or the priest leading the worshippers, would walk three times around the altar, always keeping it to the right, sprinkling it the while with meal and holy water. (See Mackey's "Symbolism," ch. 21.) The Romans employed a similar ceremony and called it "dextroversum," meaning "from the right to the left." Being so often used in connection with the rites whereby a person or an object was "purified," circumambulation became, after a time, the Roman equivalent of purification. Also "among the Hindoos," says Mackey, "the same rite of Circumambulation has always been practised," in illustration of which he cites the early morning ceremonies of a Brahmin priest who first adores the sun then walks towards the west by way of the south saying, "I follow the course of the sun." Mackey likewise refers to the Druids as having performed the same rite, and to the fact that even in recent years it has been a custom in the remoter portions of Ireland. Some have seen in the circular row of stones at Stonehenge a huge altar built for the purposes of Circumambulation, and others have seen in the various processions of the early Christian church an example of the same custom. It will be interesting, further, to note that the Greeks accompanied the journey with a sacred chant, divided into three parts, the *strophe*, the *antistrophe*, and the *epode*, on which Mackey makes a significant comment: "The analogy between the chanting of an ode by the ancients and the recitation of a passage of Scripture in the Masonic Circumambulation will be at once apparent."

II

What is the meaning of Circumambulation for us as Masons, and in our daily lives? Circumambulation is sometimes understood, among older Masonic writers especially, as a symbol of the progress of Masonry itself, which, according to the old Legends, was supposed to have originated in the East, in Egypt more particularly. This is hinted at in certain of the Old Charges in which we find the following scrap of dialogue: "When did it [Masonry] begin? It did begin with the first men of the East."

Other writers, Pike among them, see in this symbolism a figure of the progress of the civilisation of humanity. Whether that civilisation began in Egypt as some argue, or in Babylonia as others contend, it did begin in the Orient and travelled thence, along the Mediterranean, to the Occident, for, "all knowledge, all religion, and all arts and sciences have travelled according to the course of the sun from east to west."

Again, some writers see in Circumambulation a drama of the development of the individual life, which begins in the young vigour of the Rising Sun, reaches its climax in the meridian splendour of the South, and declines to the old age of the West.

Pierson sees in it an analogy of the individual's Masonic progress ("Traditions of Freemasonry," ch. 2): "The Masonic symbolism is that the Circumambulation and the obstructions at the various points refer to the labours and difficulties of the student in his progress from intellectual darkness or ignorance to intellectual light or truth."

III

Yet again, others see in it an allegory of the pilgrimage of the soul through the shadows of this earth life. We are born in darkness and walk all our days in search of That which is Lost, "the lost harmony among the strings." Believing that somewhere there exists the Absolute Life we make a continual search and transform our days into a long Pilgrim's Progress.

These various interpretations, you will have observed, have their point of departure, one and all, in the thought that Circumambulation is a journey; with this one cannot quarrel, but may one not also be permitted to fashion an explanation which builds on the fact that the candidate walks in harmony with the sun? To my mind this is its point of greatest significance, even as it was evidently the original idea embodied. Let the sun represent the powers and laws of nature as in the ancient ceremonies: let Circumambulation be understood as an attempt to work in harmony with those powers and laws, and we see at once that the Rite gives us the secret of human accomplishment. To fight nature is suicide; to work in co-operation with her is power. To keep step with her cycles, to move in sympathy with her vibrations, that gives us fulness of life. The sailor clasps hands with her winds, the farmer adjusts himself to her chemic processes, the artist vibrates with the pulses of her beauty, the poet weaves her rhythms into his lines, the saint harmonises himself with her laws as they rise in the soul. It is thus and thus only that we mount the stairs to Life.

CHAPTER XII

APPROACHING THE EAST

I

This portion of the ceremony has many things to tell us, which, for the sake of simplification, we may break into three divisions: (1) The Symbolism of the Cardinal Points; (2) Orientation; (3) The Meaning of the Candidate's Approach to the East.

Symbolism of the Cardinal Points, North, South, East and West. Mackey uses as an illustration of this the fact that the sun in its summer journey never passes north of 23° 28´, and that a wall built anywhere above that will have its northern side entirely in shadow even when the sun stands at his meridian. As this fact became known to early peoples it led them to look upon the North as the place of darkness. Accordingly, in all ancient mythologies, that portion of space was regarded with suspicion and even with terror. This prejudice was carried over into the Middle Ages, and traces of it, often dim and vague, survive to this day in popular customs. In his "Antiquities of Freemasonry," Fort writes that the "North by the Jutes was denominated black or sombre; the Frisians called it 'Fear corner.' The gallows faced North, and from these hyperborean shores beyond the North everything base and terrible proceeded." To the churchmen of mediæval times it carried a like sinister meaning, as we may read in "Animal Symbolism in Ecclesiastical Architecture" (E. P. Evans, p. 258): "The north is the region of meterorological devils, which, under the dominion and leadership of the 'Prince of the power of the air' produce storms and convulsions in Nature and foster unruly passions and deeds of violence in man. The evil principle, as embodied in unclean beasts and exhibited in obscene and lascivious actions, was properly portrayed in the sculptures and paintings on the north side of the church, which was assigned to Satan and his satellites, and known as 'the black side.'" Milton connects Satan with the North, and Shakespeare speaks of demons "who are substitutes under the lonely monarch of the north." This cardinal point has a similar meaning in Masonry, and the portion of the lodge on the northern side should contain no furniture or lights.

By token of the same symbolic reasoning the South stands for all that is opposed to the North; in that direction the sun reaches his meridian to pour out light, warmth, and beauty. Accordingly, church builders of old time were wont to depict on the South wall of their churches the triumphs of Christianity, and the millennial reign of Christ. In the lodge the Corinthian column, type of beauty, is placed in the South at the station of the Junior Warden. It is the place of High Twelve, and the scene of the labours of the Craft.

As the West is the place of the sun's setting and of the closing of the day it stands for rest, for darkness, and for death. In Operative Lodges it was the place set apart for finished work. In Greek mythology it was the place of Hades, that is, darkness and death. As we may read in Sophocles

"Life on life downstricken goes
Swifter than the wild birds' flight,
Swifter than the Fire-God's might,
To the westering shores of Night."

Tennyson makes Arthur to go into the West and Ulysses to travel beyond the baths of the setting sun; and at this day, it is said, soldiers in the trenches of Europe speak of a dead comrade as having "gone West." To the West all men come at last, men and Masons, to the beautiful, tender West, and lay them down in the sleep that knows no waking.

If there is one symbol that recurs again and again in our Blue Lodge Ritual, like a musical refrain, it is the East; of this I almost despair to speak, save in crudest outline, so rich and so many-sided is the truth enshrined in it. As the centre of gravity is to the earth, and all things thereon, so is the East to a Masonic Lodge; the Master sits there, the representative of a complete humanity; the Blazing Star shines there, the mystic "G" at the centre of the rays; it is the bourne, the goal, the ultimate destination, towards which the whole Craft moves. How it came to have this significance for early societies, as well as for our own may be made clear as we turn our attention to Orientation.

II

In early Egypt, as Norman Lockyer tells us in his "Dawn of Astronomy," the most brilliant of all works on Orientation, and as authoritative as it is readable, it was the custom to dedicate a temple to some planet or star, to the moon in one of her phases, or to the sun at one of his various periods. Originally, perhaps, a majority of the temples were dedicated to the rising sun; in that event the building was so situated that on a given day in the year the light of the sun would pass between the pillars at the entrance and fall upon the altar at the moment of his first appearance above the horizon. This placing of the temple so as to face the dawn gave rise to the term "Orientation," which means "finding the east." However, other temples were directed toward the moon or some star, and this also, by an accommodation of language, was called Orientation. The term was further used, in after days, when a building or a city was laid out in harmony with the cardinal points; according to this usage the City of Rome was oriented, for its first form was a quadrangle with a gate facing in each direction. ("A.Q.C.," vol. iv, p. 87.) This custom was practised by the Jews, and indeed may be considered as universal throughout the ancient world. Moreover it was carried over into Christian customs, for all the early churches were oriented to the sun, the Apostolic Constitutions specifying that a church must be "an oblong form, and directed to the east."

Inasmuch as the orienting of a temple was chiefly for the purpose of permitting the light to fall on its altar on a given day, the altar was necessarily placed in the west end of the building. This arrangement must also have been often used by the Jews, even though they did reverse so many "heathen" customs, for Dr. Wynn Westcott tells us that, "It is clear that both Mosaic Tabernacle and the Temple of Solomon had the Holy Place at the west." But, he goes on to say, and this is a point especially deserving of our attention, "it is equally certain that churches from the earliest Christian development have always reversed the positions when possible." This is to say that, though Christian houses of worship were placed east and west as heathen temples had been, they were built with their altars in the east end instead of in the west. It is from the Christian churches of Mediæval times, perhaps, that the Operative Masons derived their practice of placing the Master's station in the East.

The pagans saw in the sun a symbol of Deity, its rays an emblem of the Divine forth-shining; accordingly they had the sun, or a representation of the sun, in the East. We also worship a Deity whom we have clothed with Light, but in our East is no longer the natural sun, or even a representation thereof, but a man, the Master. To my mind this is a thing of significance, though I can not place the weight of the name of any one of our authorities behind the interpretation. Ancient peoples, like ourselves, were in search of God, even as are we. They hoped to find Him in nature, among the things that He had made, even as the Wise Men followed a star in their search for Him; but whereas they went "through Nature to God," we go "through man to God," and believe that His completest unveiling will be found in the perfected human soul, even as the Master of Masters said, "He that hath seen ME hath seen the Father."

III

If this interpretation of the East is valid, as I believe that it is, the candidate's "approach to the East" is a symbolic art of far-reaching meaning, for it signifies nothing less than that he has tuned his will toward the perfecting of his own human nature in order to enter into communion with the Divine; if he is compelled to advance by a certain regulated manner it is in token of the fact that the soul itself is a realm of law and that he who would reach the soul's highest development must walk in harmony with the spirit's laws; and if, in the succeeding degrees, his manner of approach approximates more and more toward a perfect step it is in recognition of the necessity of gradual and orderly progress in the highest growth. Always and everywhere, in whatever condition or task a man finds himself, if he would "go up into the seer's house," he must mount by those virtues of Purity, Beauty, and Truth which are the hidden laws of the heart.

CHAPTER XIII

THE ALTAR

I

In the centre of the lodge stands the Altar. It should be cubical in shape, and about three feet in height, and it should have horns at each corner to suggest, in light of a hoary usage, that it is a place of refuge. On the East, the South, and the West should be placed one of the representatives of the three Lesser Lights, but never on the North, for that is the place of darkness. On its top, in due arrangement, should lie the three Grand Lights. Thus arranged it may well be considered "the most important article of furniture in a lodge room," and the ground whereon it stands as "the most holy place." Too universal in its use, both through space and time, to admit of our tracing its history here we must content ourselves with some reference to the ideas embodied in it. To this end let us remember, here and everywhere, that the Masonic life is not that which occurs in the lodge rooms alone, for that is but its allegorical picture, its tracing-board; but it is that which a Mason should do and be in all circumstances, under the inspiration of the Fraternity and its teachings. Thus understood the Altar standing in the centre of the Masonic lodge is the symbol of something that must operate at the centre of the Masonic life.

Often serving as a table whereon the worshipper may lay his gifts to God, the Altar may well remind us of the necessity of that human gratitude which leads us to return to Him the gifts He has showered upon us. This is that teaching of stewardship found in all religions to remind us that our very lives are not our own, having been bought with a price, and that our talents are held in trusteeship to be rendered again to Him to whom they belong. Thus stated, I know, the matter may sound bald and even unappealing, but once we encounter a man who lives his life as a stewardship held in the frail tenure of the flesh, we see to what high issues the character of man may ascend; such personalities carry an atmosphere about with them as of another world, and radiate influences that are light and fragrant. Surely, a man who denied this in his practices can never serve as a living Building Stone in Masonry's Temple!

II

In its proper sense also the Altar serves as a sanctuary, a place of refuge, and this too has much to tell us, though I am aware of the dangers of moralising. In the earlier centuries of our era, before the complete development of common law, the hunted criminal, fleeing from his pursuers, would escape to a church and there lay hold of the horns of the Altar; in that he found safety, and an opportunity to prove his innocence, if innocent he was. Out of this arose the beautiful customs of "sanctuary," the chivalrous unselfish harbouring of the weak, the sorrowful, and the afflicted. Is there not a sanctuary in Masonry? Certainly there is, for in the Fraternity itself, in the privacy of its inner fellowships, a brother will often find rest for his heart and relief from the bruisings of the world; and a man is no true Mason in whose nature there is not at least one inner chamber in which the weary may find rest and the weak may have protection.

More than a table for gifts and a place of sanctuary the Altar has from of old served as the station of sacrifice, and this usage also is recognised in our symbolism, for therein we are taught that the human in us, our appetites, our passions, yea our life itself if need be, must be laid down in the service of man and the glory of God. How otherwise could Masonry remain Masonry if it is "the subjugation of the human that is in man, by the Divine?"

III

Of the Altar as a place of prayer we have already spoken, but in this connection we may well ponder a paragraph from Dr. J. F. Newton, composed of those lucid sentences of which he is a master:

"Thus by a necessity of his nature man is ever a seeker after God, touched at times with a strange sadness and longing, and laying aside his tools to look out over the far horizon. Whatever else he may have been—vile, tyrannous, vindictive—the story of his long search after God is enough to prove that he is not wholly base. Rites horrible, and even cruel, may have been a part of his early ritual, but if the history of past ages had left us nothing but the memory of a race at prayer, they would have left us rich. And so, following the good custom of the great ones of former ages, we gather at our Altar lifting up hands in prayer, moved thereto by the ancient need and aspiration of our humanity. Like the man who walked in the grey years of old, our need is for God, the living God, whose presence hallows all our mortal life, even to its last ineffable homeward sigh which men call death."

CHAPTER XIV

THE OBLIGATION

I

The turning point in the ceremony of each degree is the Obligation, for it is that which marks the Apprentice an Apprentice, the Fellow Craft a Fellow Craft, and the Master Mason a Master Mason; consequently the subject is worthy of careful consideration in this connection, especially as there will be no need of a repetition of the discussion in our study of the Second and Third Degrees.

Obligation, being a Latin word, literally means a "binding to"; it is more than an oath, and more than a vow, for it combines both, and it has been used, in one form or another, from antiquity. Philo described it as "the most sure symbol of good faith," and Cicero defined it as "an affirmation under the sanction of religion." Brother Twining (*American Tyler-Keystone*, vol. xviii, p. 423), writing in our own day, gives it a similar meaning: "An oath may be defined as an asseveration or promise made under non-human penalty or sanction." Some oaths have an imprecation attached but others do not.

The widespread use of oaths, in ancient and in modern times, has been well described by J. E. Tyler: "Through all the diversified stages of society from the lowest barbarism to the highest cultivation of civilised life—where the true religion has been professed, no less than where paganism has retained its hold, recourse has been had to oaths as affording the nearest approximation to certainty in evidence, and the surest pledge of the performance of a promise."

In the England of Operative days, oaths were taken as a matter of course, as witness Gould's "Concise History": "From the time of Athelstan down to the Norman Conquest, and from the Conqueror to Edward I and later, the oath of allegiance was annually administered to every free man." Gould suggests that this oath of allegiance to the king may have been the original of the Masonic Obligation: "The wording of this oath, as given in a publication of 1642; 'you shall be true and faithful to our Sovereign Lord the King,' is substantially the same as that of the corresponding 'charge' or inculcation which is met with in Masonic Constitutions. The two obligations . . . virtually stand on the same level as regards antiquity, and, as survivals of still earlier forms, their close resemblance is very suggestive of their common origin." It must be remembered, however, that the guild of that day could enforce its oaths only within narrow limits; grave offences were necessarily turned over to the courts which administered the common law. At the present day oaths and obligations are in very common use, from the crowning of a king to the "swearing in" of a juror. "The world is held together by oaths and affirmations, administered by the proper authorities, to all rulers and officials of a high and low degree in State and municipalities, and in every phase of human society. Without official oaths the country would undoubtedly lapse into a state of disorder, confusion, and finally anarchy." (*Trestle Board*, vol. xx, p. 247.) This right Freemasonry also enjoys, and for the same reasons, as another writer has expressed it: "In Freemasonry a number of men form themselves into a society, whose main end is to improve in commendable skill and knowledge, and to promote universal beneficence and the social virtues of human life under the solemn obligations of an oath. This liberty all human societies enjoy without impeachment or reflection."

II

It is difficult to believe, in the light of all this, that any sane person could attack Masonry for being an oath-bound Fraternity, especially since its oath is itself a symbol of those ties and obligations which everywhere bind men together; but such has been the case. The Roman Catholic attacks, from 1738 when Pope Clement the Twelfth issued the first papal bull against us, until the present year of grace, have all been principally aimed at our Obligation, a very inconsistent course in a society that authorises such a secret fraternity as the Jesuits. A few other churches and sects have followed suit, usually on the ground that Christ's saying that "whatsoever is more than yea or nay cometh of evil," makes oaths unchristian. Laying aside the false interpretations thus made of the Gospel text, this position is difficult to explain on the part of such organisations, for they use an obligation in the marriage ceremony of the most solemn kind, and their members often do not refuse to take oath when entering public office. The attack on Masonry made in America early last century, which used the Morgan affair as its subterfuge, and which was really a political scheme in disguise, grew savage in its condemnation of the Masonic Obligation, as is made clear by the words of one of its leaders, John Quincy Adams:

"The whole case between Masonry and Anti-Masonry, now on trial before the tribunal of public opinion, is consecrated in a single act. Let a single lodge resolve that they will cease to administer the oath, *and that lodge is dissolved.* Let the whole Order resolve that this oath shall be no longer administered, *the Order is dissolved; for the abolition of the oath necessarily imports the extinction of all other landmarks.*"

Of the penalties supposed to be attached to the Obligation, and which have especially aroused the animosity of the Anti-Masons, we have already spoken but more may be said in the present connection, with due reserves of secrecy; and I may say that I am herein much indebted to the illuminating article published in *The Builder* (vol. n, p. 135) by my friend and Colleague, Brother Robert I. Clegg.

III

Commenting on one phase of the matter he writes: "Death by slow drowning was once by legal authority [in England—H.L.H.] established as a proper punishment. . . . Consider the following: In the curious ordinances of Henry VI. for the proper conduct of the Court of Admiralty of the Humber, are enumerated various offences of a maritime connection and their due punishments. To adhere closely to the character of the Court, and to be within proper jurisdiction of the Admiralty, the punishments were generally inflicted at low-water mark." This court, he says, being composed of "Masters, merchants, and marines, with all others that do enjoy the King's stream with hook, net, or any engine" (or implement), was addressed, when assembled, as follows:

"You, Masters of the Quest, if you or any of you discover or disclose anything of the King's secret counsel or of the counsel of your fellows (for the present you are admitted to be the King's Counsellors) you are to be, and shall be, had down to the low-water mark, where must be made three times, O Yes! for the King, and then and there this punishment, by the law prescribed, shall be inflicted upon them; that is, their hands and feet bound, their throats cut, their tongues pulled out, and their bodies thrown into the sea."

In the England of the seventeenth century the death penalty, and that in its most terrible forms, was often inflicted because of comparatively small offences such as petty theft. Oaths were so freely given and taken that every little organisation had its own, even the brotherhood of pig drivers! If certain far-off echoes of these practices seem to be heard now and then in our own form it is because the Obligation was probably cast in its present mould in the early eighteenth century. This contention that the Penalties are thus of comparatively recent origin is apparently borne out by the fact that such Obligations as are found in the Old Charges are very brief and of quite a different character. I may cite, as one specimen of these, that found in the Harleian Mss. No. 2054, of the seventeenth century:

"There are several words and signs of a Freemason to be revealed to you which as you will answer before God at the great and terrible day of Judgment, you keep secret and not to reveal the same to any in the hearing of any person whatsoever but to the Masters and fellows of the said society of Freemasons. So help me God." (Spelling modernised.)

As to the agitation for the simplification of the Obligation, the Penalties more especially, much may be said pro and con. Archaic usages and obsolete terms, often unintelligible to the modern Mason, may be often found in the Ritual. Many are contending that these should be eliminated or modernised, as witness the following from Brother MacBride: "There are many errors in our ceremonies to be corrected, and not a few rude customs should be abolished, before our lodges can become what they ought to be, schools, in which men may learn the ways of right living and high thinking." With the spirit of this I am in sympathy, but I have often felt, while witnessing the work in lodge, that these very "errors" and archaisms are valuable in that they link us up to a long past and thus give us the feeling, so much needed in a hasty age too often irreverent of the past, of historical continuity. But, on the other hand, other considerations connect up with the Obligation, and other issues are at stake, and I have long believed that the Penalties should be changed to conform, not only with common sense and practicality, but with the modern spirit of humanitarianism, of which Masonry itself was one of the first exemplars.

IV

After all, the one object of the Obligation, aside from its official function of legally binding men to the Craft, is to secure secrecy, is it not? And there is one little word often used by Masons which carries all this within itself. This word is often spelled as it is pronounced, "Hail," but it is properly the Anglo-Saxon word "hele" ("hell" is derived from it!) and means "to bury, or to cover up." If "I hail" it means that down in the underground of my memory, far out of reach of the profane, I hide away all the affairs of my lodge, and all the secrets of my brother.

Too much, perhaps, has already been written on the subject, but there is yet another angle of it which deserves a word. We use all our arts and influences to make the member realise his obligation to the Craft; should we not do as much to make the lodge realise its obligation to the member? A man spends a sum of money he can sometimes ill spare to join the Fraternity; he devotes much time to learning the lectures; he is admitted and entered as a member; and very often—very often indeed—the lodge itself does not do one thing to explain to that man its symbolism or to instruct him in its history! Is this right? I do not believe it is. I believe that every lodge should do its utmost to place the right type of literature in the hands of its members; that it should conduct courses of lectures and Masonic schools; that it should encourage and support study classes whenever possible; in short, that it should as completely fulfil its duties to the candidate as it asks the candidate to do for it.

CHAPTER XV

THE THREE GREAT LIGHTS

The first objects to greet the candidate's unblinded eyes are the Three Great Lights, an appropriate arrangement, for they symbolise his duty to himself, to his neighbour, and to his God. Sending their rays into every nook and cranny of the lodge, they are fit representatives of those high realities of the spirit which are indeed the *Great* Lights, the master lights of all our seeing. In these three symbols, the Holy Bible, the Square, and the Compass, we shall find inspiration, as well as instruction, one as much as the other, and they may be studied in order.

I

Without the open Bible on its altar a lodge can neither receive nor initiate candidates, nor can it transact its own business, for the Book is a part of its indispensable furniture. So much of the Ritual is drawn from it that students have traced to it some seventy-five references, while almost every name found in the work is a Biblical name. The teachings of the Craft are based upon it as a house is built upon the ground, and it is fitting that the candidate should salute it in recognition of this fact. This salutation of the Book was much used by the church of mediæval times; from the ecclesiastics the courts derived the custom; and it is probable that early Masons adopted their usage from the courts. Some, basing their theory on references scattered among the Old Charges, believe that in Operative days the candidate sealed his oath by placing his hands on the open Bible, but of this we cannot be certain. At any rate we do know that the V.S.L. was considered a part of the furniture of the lodge long before the Revival, though it was not made a Great Light until 1760, or thereabouts.

Our Masonic forefathers were led by a wise instinct in this for they could have found no other book or object capable of sending out so many rays of healing and of revelation; at least so we of the western world believe. A library of sixty-six books of the most diverse character, drawn from many peoples and conditions, the Bible is yet one Book, its miscellaneous chapters being linked one to another by a single, pervading spirit, as pearls are strung upon a silver wire. The most recent of its pages are almost two thousand years old, while other portions go back a thousand years beyond, yet is its force unabated, and it seems to speak as though written yesterday. The history of the collecting of its books together is so marvellous that many have deemed it miraculous. That which "drew from out the boundless deep" of racial experiences makes its appeal to men of all races. It has been translated into more than five hundred languages and dialects, and read by men of the most opposite cultures and traditions to whom it seems as if it had been written especially for them. Truly such a literature is inspired if anything can be, and we Masons may well believe it to be the perfect symbol of the mind and will of God. We do not permit ourselves to be "carried to that extreme of fetichistic bibliolatry that has been such a serious obstacle to the spread of knowledge and to the progress of the race and is now just beginning to be set aside by scientific research and sound criticism," yet we may reasonably hold it to be mankind's divinest Book to date. The Bible was not written to be a textbook in history, or science, or philosophy, and as such it should not be judged; it was written to show us what manner of God God is, and what is the way of the soul.

With this, men of all faiths and of little faith may well agree. Goethe confesses that "it is a belief in the Bible, the fruit of deep meditation, which has served me as the guide of my moral and literary life." Huxley can give a similar testimony, agnostic though he is: "Take the Bible as a whole; make the severest deductions which fair criticism can dictate, and there still remains in this old literature a vast residuum of moral beauty and grandeur. By the study of what other book could children be more humanised!" To these ascriptions we may add a tribute spoken in a Masonic Lodge by Brother J. F. Newton:

"My brethren, here is a Book whose scene is the sky and the dirt and all that lies between—a Book that has in it the arch of the heavens, the curve of the earth, the ebb and flow of the sea, sunrise and sunset, the peaks of mountains and the glint of sunlight on flowing waters, the shadow of forests on the hills, the song of birds and the colour of flowers. But its two great characters are God and the Soul, and the story of their life together is its one everlasting romance. It is the most human of books, telling the old forgotten secrets of the heart, its bitter pessimism and its death-defying hope, its pain, its passion, its sin, its sob of grief and its shout of joy—telling all, without malice, in its Grand Style which can do no wrong, while echoing the sweet-toned pathos of the pity and mercy of God. No other book is so honest with us, so mercilessly merciful, so austere and yet so tender, piercing the heart, yet healing the deep wounds of sin and sorrow."

While holding to all this with the tenacity of our minds we must nevertheless remember that to Masonry the Bible itself is a symbol and stands for something larger than itself, even the whole race's "Book of Faith, the will of God as man has learned it in the midst of the years—that perpetual revelation of himself which God is making mankind in every age and every land."

"Slowly the Bible of the race is writ,
  And not on paper leaves nor leaves of stone;
Each age, each kindred, adds a verse to it,
  Texts of despair or hope, or joy or moan.
While swings the sea, while mists the mountain shroud,
  While thunder's surges burst on cliffs of cloud,
Still at the prophet's feet the nations sit."

Accordingly, our Craft permits lodges to use as the Great Light the book held sacred by the land in which they may be situated—the Old Testament to the Jews, the Koran to the Mohammedans, the Zend-Avesta to the Parsees, the Bhagavad-Gita and the Vedas in India. Also, we are not asked to accept any given interpretation of the Book, but are left free to fashion our own creed out of its materials, which is a privilege that theologians themselves have always enjoyed.
The members of the Operative Lodges were Trinitarians, as the invocation set at the head of the Old Charges will testify, but at the formation of the first Grand Lodge, the Fraternity ceased to be specifically Christian, though Hutchinson in an early day (see his "Spirit of Masonry," a volume of beautiful spirit and rich insights), and Whymper at a later time ("Religion of Free Masonry") have undertaken to interpret it in the terms of that faith. A Deputy District Grand Master of Burma wrote, in a letter to G. W. Speth: "I have just initiated Moring Ban Ahm, a Burman, who has so far modified his religious belief as to acknowledge the existence of a personal God. The W.M. was a Parsee, one warden a Hindu, or Brahmin, the other an English Christian, and the deacon a Mohammedan." This is wholly in harmony with the principles of a society that asks of its members only that they hold to that religion in which all men agree, and longs for the time, when, "high above all dogmas that divide, all bigotries that blind, all bitterness that beclouds, will be written the simple words of the one eternal religion—The Fatherhood of God, the Brotherhood of Man, the Moral Law, the Golden Rule, and the hope of Life Everlasting!"

The Fraternity does not even seek to impose upon us any given conception of the S.G.A.O.T.U., its position being that each must fashion for himself his own conception of Deity. On this Albert Pike has spoken for us all: "To every Mason there is a God—One, Supreme, Infinite in Goodness, in Wisdom, Foresight, Justice and Benevolence; Creator, Disposer and preserver of all things. How, or by what intermediate Powers or Emanations He creates and acts, and in what way He unfolds and manifests Himself, Masonry leaves to Creeds and Religions to inquire."

II

In our Blue Lodge Ritual the square has three distinct and different symbolisms: it serves as an emblem of the W.M., as a working tool of a Fellow Craft, and as the second of the Great Lights. Being concerned with it here only in its last-named capacity, I shall postpone until a future page much that may be said about it, asking the reader, meanwhile, to remember that it is a try-square and not a carpenter's square, as it is often depicted; and that it must not be confused with the square as a four-sided figure of right angles and equal sides, which is a very different symbol.

Until some four hundred years ago all men, save for a few isolated scholars, believed the earth to be an "oblong square." In consequence of this, figures of square-form were generally used as having reference to the earth, or to the earthly; and as the try-square was an instrument used for testing angles, or squareness, it came to serve as a symbol of that which is mundane or human, as opposed to the Divine. But as it was used to prove that angles were right, it received the further significance of true character, of conformity with righteousness, of duty done, etc. The ancient Chinese, to give one example of this, built their temple to the earth in square form, and called a person of rectitude, a "square man." This, I believe, is the meaning of the square when serving as one of the Great Lights; it is the symbol of right character in its human relationships.

III

The compasses are used in the entrance ceremony of the Second Degree, and in another connection in the Hiram Abiff drama, but here we are to interpret them as one of the Great Lights, and then in close connection with the exposition of the square as just given. The same crude observations that led the men of antiquity to see the earth as an oblong square caused them also to believe that the heavens were circular. Was not the sky itself a dome? Did not the heavenly bodies move in curved tracks? Were not the sun and the moon discs in shape? Was not an astronomical chart an assemblage of curves and circles? By an inevitable association of ideas the compasses, which were used to test or to draw curves and circles, were made to stand for the heavenly or the divine in man, and this is their meaning still, as they lie on the altar of the lodge.

In the First Degree the candidate is an Apprentice, a representative of crude, natural man, his earthly nature dominating or covering the spiritual; in the Fellowcraft Degree he has advanced halfway, and the nobler elements are struggling for control; when he has become a Master, as symbolised in the Third Degree, the "divine in him has subjugated the human." If you will carefully examine the relative positions of the square and compasses in the various degrees you will find an eloquent hint of this.

Right human conduct, right spiritual aspirations, and the revealed will of God; fitting is it that the lodge place the symbols of these principles at its very centre, for the Mason who walks in their light continually will never wander far from the paths of life.

CHAPTER XVI

THE LESSER LIGHTS

I

The Sun, Moon, and Master of the lodge, is, according to our best authorities, a Hermetic symbol and must be interpreted accordingly. The sun throws out light from itself, it dispenses energy, and in the physical sense is the creator of life. In view thereof the Hermetists made the sun to signify the active principle in nature. By a peculiar coincidence it is still a popular custom to speak of the sun as *he* or *him* and this suggests that the Hermetic theory was not very far-fetched.

By virtue of a similar kind of reasoning the moon was accepted as the symbol of the passive forces of nature, and here again we find the popular custom in agreement, for we all speak of the moon as *she* or *her*. The moon has no light of her own but merely reflects to us that which she has received from the sun; therefore she may be understood as symbolising the receptive, passive, and feminine principles.

This cleavage between masculine and feminine, active and passive, goes down to the roots of the world; it is a distinction found in all nature's processes and in every man and woman. Work and rest, ruthlessness and pity, hardness and tenderness—everywhere are these qualities found, mingling in various proportions; and the secret of the full-orbed life is to hold them in equilibrium. John Woolman was so tender that he grieved for days over a robin's death; Friedrich Nietzsche looked upon pity as a weakness, and taught men to flee it as a disease and urged his disciples to be hard. Too much of John Woolman in human nature would people the world at last with a race of sentimentalists too soft for the mastery of the hard, grey facts of nature; too much of Nietzsche would give us a world full of blond beasts, preying on each other, like the dragons in the slime; but when Woolman and Nietzsche balance each other, the one correcting the extravagances of the other, man will be tender with little children, chivalrous to women, patient with his fellows, and he will have strength to wage the warfare against death, disaster, and destruction. Out of Isis and Osiris, comes Horus, the master of life. Out of the woman and the man, comes Christ, "the man-woman." Out of the Sun and the Moon comes the Master, even the Master of a Lodge, for the Master of the Lodge, in our symbology, is nothing other than a representation of the Complete Man.

II

This, I have said, is the Hermetic explanation of the symbolism of the three Lesser Lights; but with this reading of the matter some scholars will not agree, preferring to trace it to usages in the old Operative Lodges. The hut, or the lodge, they say, was always erected "against the southerly wall of the church," and could therefore receive no light from the north, or "dark side"; accordingly the windows of the workroom were necessarily on the east, south, and west sides. Steinbrenner, who traces the Order to the German Steinmetzen, argues that windows were known as *lights*, and quotes Cicero and Vitruvius in support of his contention. He holds that these windows were the origin of the Great Lights, while others of the same school of thought believe them to have been the prototype of the Lesser Lights.

This interpretation of the matter is on the side of simplicity, and makes unnecessary that one go afield into occultism, but to some of us it is not convincing, and that for more than one reason. That Operative Lodges always, or even *frequently*, built their temporary headquarters on the south side of the church is not supported by evidence, and may well be questioned; besides it is difficult to understand how these windows could ever have become identified with the Holy Bible, Square and Compass, or with the Sun, Moon and Master. Moreover, the last-named symbolism was in use by occult fraternities long before lodges were built, as many authorities have testified, and it seems most reasonable to believe it to have been introduced into our Ritual by the Speculatives accepted into the Craft in the latter part of the seventeenth century.

CHAPTER XVII

"LUX E TENEBRIS"

I

"All great minds love the light," writes Brother J. F. Newton. "It is the mother of beauty and the joy of the world. It tells men all they know and their speech about it is gladsome and grateful. Light is to the mind what food is to the body; it brings the morning, when the shadows flee away, and the loveliness of earth is uncurtained. This is the mystery of light. It is not matter, but a form of motion; it is not spirit, though it seems closely akin to it; it is the gateway where matter and spirit pass and repass. Of all that is in nature it the most resembles God, in its gentleness, in its beauty, and in its pity."

This passage, so beautiful to read, and so revealing, would have met with a still more cordial response from the men of ancient days, for it seems that the first great religion of the world was the worship of light. As we read in Norman Lockyer's "Dawn of Astronomy": "Sunrise it was that inspired the first prayers of our race, and called forth the first sacrificial flames." After telling how large a place this light worship occupied among the remote peoples of India, the same author goes on to say, "The ancient Egyptians, whether they were separate from, or more or less allied in their origin to, the early inhabitants of India, had exactly the same view of Nature Worship, and we find in their hymns and in the lists of their gods that the Dawn and the Sunrise were the great revelations of Nature, and the things which were most important to man; and therefore everything connected with the Sunrise and the Dawn was worshipped." Knowing little of the cure return of nature's cycles, the Egyptians were fearful lest, the sun having disappeared at dusk, he would forget to return; accordingly, the night was a season of foreboding and fear, while the Dawn was an occasion of rejoicing. Out of this alternation of fear and gladness, of the sun's apparent death, and his apparent return to life, arose that ancient Egyptian Light Religion, so many echoes of which remain with us in our Masonic symbolism.

II

The ritualism of light and darkness occurs and recurs throughout the Bible like a refrain. When Jehovah would bring the world out of the dripping chaos He is made to say, "Let there be Light"; of Him the Psalmist cried, "Thy word is a lamp unto my feet, and a light unto my path"; the Evangelist says of Him that "God is Light, and in Him is no darkness at all"; and the Book of Revelation promises the faithful that in the Great Life beyond, there will be no more night.

Jamblichus wrote that "Light is the simplicity, the penetration and the ubiquity of God." Zoroaster made light to stand for all the good of life, and darkness for its evil. In the Ancient Mysteries the candidate, clothed in white, went into the caverns of the night to issue thence into a place of illumination. The Kabbalist's great book was the "Zohar," which means light, and it is an exposition of the saying, "Let there be Light." Similarly one of the great mottoes of Masonry is "lux e tenebris," light out of darkness, while Masons, true Masons, are justly called the "sons of light"; and in all the ceremonies there is not one more eloquent act than the "bringing of the candidate to light."

What is this Light that has been shed abroad in our lives? It is sometimes explained as Knowledge, and it is that; but it is more than that, for it is also Truth. Knowledge is the mind's awareness of a fact, while truth is the mind's understanding of the meaning of that fact. Facts may heap themselves up like the grains in a pile of sand; they may have little or no apparent relations with each other; and the man who is said to have knowledge of them may know little more than their number and their names. But when he has learned the hidden connections of these facts, how they bear upon each other, and what import they have for human life, he has learned Truth.

III

With this in mind, consider the world of men. Individuals jostle each other, they love and fight, events come and go, and the facts of life make and unmake themselves like summer clouds; thus considered the world is a jumble of unrelated happenings enough to bewilder the mind and freeze the heart. But Masonry says to this world, "Each and all of your facts are mystically bound together, your individuals are linked by unseen ties, and all your apparently warring forces are steadily at work to build a Temple in the world." Consider, also, the individual, himself. He finds in himself an array of feelings, thoughts, impulses, experiences, existing side by side, but apparently making for no end. To this man Masonry says, "The deepest forces in you are making toward Goodness, Beauty, Truth; far withdrawn in your nature is a Buried Temple; at the core of your being is the hidden Master; you are a potential Christ." When Masonry utters this word, which is more than a word, to the world and to the man who lives in the world, it is revealing the hidden unity that binds the jangling facts together; it is finding the song among the strings; it is discovering the Lost Word; it is bringing truth, that is to say, Light, into the race of men; it says, "Let there be light, and there is light." To this end every symbol speaks; of this mission the Ritual is eloquent more than the tongues of men and of angels, from the first of it unto the last.

CHAPTER XVIII

WORDS, GRIPS AND TOKENS

I

The candidate is now a member of an Entered Apprentice Lodge; accordingly he is given the words, grips and tokens whereby he may prove himself to his fellows, whether in the day or in the night. "These signs and tokens are of no small value," wrote Brother Benjamin Franklin: "they speak a universal language and act as a passport to the attention and support of the initiated in all parts of the world. They cannot be lost so long as memory retains its power. Let the possessor of them be expatriated, shipwrecked, or imprisoned; let him be stripped of everything he has in the world; still these credentials remain and are available for use as circumstances require.

"The great effects which they have produced are established by the most incontestable facts of history. They have stayed the uplifted hands of the destroyer; they have softened the asperities of the tyrant; they have mitigated the horrors of captivity; they have subdued the rancour of malevolence; and broken down the barriers of political animosity and sectarian alienation.
"On the field of battle, in the solitude of the uncultivated forests, or in the busy haunts of the crowded city, they have made men of the most hostile feeling, and most distant religions, and the most diversified conditions, rush to the aid of each other, and feel a social joy and satisfaction that they have been able to afford relief to a Brother Mason!"

Some historians believe this sign language to have existed before oral speech; its use is so ancient that we find men thus communicating when they first appear in history. The laconic Spartans preferred a gesture to a word; there is no doubt that the initiates of the Mysteries possessed a system of passwords and grips; indeed, the custom is referred to in the Bible, as in the instance where Ben-Hadad saved his life by making a sign. The Pythagoreans recognised each other by signs and tokens and so did the Essenes. In Rome the art of gesturing was once so cultivated that groups of players, the Pantomimus, were able to arouse any and every emotion without recourse to speech. In Mediæval monasteries, the monks were taught a sign language, "like the alphabet." Even among the American Indians, it has been shown (see Wright's "Indian Masonry") "the sign language is so well understood that tribes who have no common verbal medium of communication invariably and effectively use it." In the Orient, at this day, the language of the sign remains in use, and the Chinese employ a written language almost wholly composed of pictures or signs.

Of many other secret societies not mentioned above the same may be said, albeit there is little evidence to show that the Steinmetzen made much use of signs and words, though they were probably in possession of a grip. Brother Gould, in his essay on "The Voice of the Sign," writes that "signs and passwords, I think we may confidently assume, were *common features* [italics mine] of all or nearly all secret societies from the earliest times down to our own." The same authority further states, "That 'signs and tokens' were used by the Mediæval builders, nay, I think, be reasonably deduced as the result of legitimate inference or conjecture."

II

Brother Gould is careful to make it plain that his conclusion is a matter of inference because, strangely enough, our actual historical evidence of the Operative Mason's use of signs goes no further back than the seventeenth century. Randle Holme, in 1665, wrote of "several words and signs of a Freemason." Dr. Robert Plot, in his "Natural History of Staffordshire," published in 1686, describes the manner of admission into the "Masonic Society," "which chiefly consists in the communication of certain *secret signs*, whereby they are known to one another all over the *Nation*, by which means they have maintenance whither ever they travel; for if any man appear though altogether unknown that can show any of these *signs* to a *Fellow* of the *Society*, whom they otherwise call an *accepted* Mason, he is obliged presently to come to him, from what company or place soever he be in, nay, though from the top of a *steeple* (what hazard or inconvenience soever he run) to know his pleasure and assist him," etc. (Spelling modernised.) John Aubrey, in certain rough memoranda made in 1691 also says of the Masons that "they are known to one another by certain signs and watch words." Robert Kirk, in 1691, speaks of a grip and a word as being in use in Scotland, and Sir Richard Steele, writing in the *Tatler*, mentions "signs and tokens like Freemason's." If signs were thus in general use by Freemasons in the seventeenth century it is a fair inference that the practice was in vogue much earlier; just how early, or from what source derived, is still a mystery, though it may be mentioned that so high an authority as Dr. Krause traced the use of signs back to the Mediæval monasteries, in co-operation with which the early Builders so often worked.

Being members of a secret society, and often obliged to travel in strange places, it would seem that the Operative Masons were obliged to invent some form of recognition known to all their fellows. This conjecture is supported by Mr. Fergusson, "an architectural historian of the first rank"; for we find in his "History of Architecture," the following significant paragraph:

"At a time when writing was unknown among the laity, and not one Mason in a thousand could either read or write, it was evidently essential that some expedient should be hit upon, by which a Mason travelling to his work might claim the assistance and hospitality of his brother Masons on the road, and by means of which he might take his rank at once, on reaching the lodge, without going through tedious examinations or giving practical proof of his skill. For this purpose a set of secret signs was invented, which enabled all Masons to recognise one another as such, and by which also each man could make known his grade to those of similar rank, without further trouble than a manual sign, or the utterance of some recognised password. Other trades had something of the same sort."

As Operative passed into Speculative Masonry many of the old usages became lost, but secret modes of recognition were retained, and that because Speculative Masonry is always a secret society. Being modes of secret recognition it is manifestly impossible to discuss them in print, but a few hints, easily interpreted by the initiated, may safely be given.

III

"Due Guard." This, it is probable, was not used in early English Masonry, but came into practice in this country. Mackey calls it "an Americanism." It is a perpetual reminder to the member of his OB., and it is always given in entering or retiring from the lodge.

"Words." In eighteenth century Scotland "the only degree known . . . was that in which the Legend of the Craft was read, and the benefit of the Mason Word conferred." This seems to indicate that the Word meant more than a "pass," but it is in this latter sense that it seems to have been used by Operative Lodges, and other secret societies, generally. With us, however, it has become a symbol, and that of a high character, as will be learned in the study of the Third Degree, but at the same time it retains, it may be added, something of its original usage as a password.

"Grips." It is probable that the earliest form of a secret mode of recognition among Operative Masons was the grip, but what it was we may not know, the nature of the secret having made written descriptions impossible. Robert Kirk, a Scotch minister, who published a book called "Secret Commonwealth" in 1691, wrote that the Masons of his day "had some signe delyvered from Hand to Hand"; an entry in the minutes of the Haughfoot Lodge for 1702 gives a brief description of an initiation, in which it is noted that "they then whisper the word as before, and the Master grips his (the candidate's) hand in the ordinary way"; but in neither case are we told what the grip was.

"Tokens." This word, long in vogue among English and American Lodges, is used to describe a sign or grip when given as a brotherly recognition. It signifies an outward act as evidencing an inward pledge. When one Mason grips another by the hand it is as if he said, "This physical act is the outward sign, or token, of the union of our minds and hearts." In popular use it has the same meaning, as when we speak of a little gift as "a token of our regard."

This custom of having a secret mode of recognition among Masons has often been misunderstood, and sometimes derided, as when a friend remarked to me that "Masons act like children, with their signs and grips, and such nonsense." Had my friend known something of the Fraternity he would have spoken differently, for signs and grips are as necessary as secrecy, and for the same reasons. Masonry is a world within itself; Masons are as a hidden race among men; and there is nothing more natural than that they should have a language of their own. Besides, secret recognitions are on the side of gentle charity, for they often enable one brother to help another without undue injury to self-respect.

CHAPTER XIX

THE RITE OF SALUTATION

I

The Rite of Salutation, during which the candidate pays his respects to the various stations, is in one sense only the lodge's recognition of the membership of the candidate, he having now been received by the Master as a brother and fellow workman, and encouraged to make himself at home in his new fellowship; in another sense, and one of much greater importance, I believe, the salutation is the candidate's recognition of the constituted authority of the Craft as vested in the Master and Wardens. Of this there is need to speak at some length as it is a lesson to be learned by the citizen of a state as well as by a member of the Fraternity, since it is nothing other than the old and badly needed teaching of true Liberty, and of the relationship between Liberty and Law, a teaching to which Masonry has always borne testimony by its actions as well as its words.

"No part of its history has been more noble," writes Dr. J. F. Newton ("The Builders," p. 273), "no principle of its teaching has been more precious than its age-long demand for the right and duty of every soul to seek that light by which no man was ever injured, and that truth which makes men free. Down through the centuries—often in times when the highest crime was not murder, but thinking, and the human conscience was a captive dragged at the wheel of the ecclesiastical chariot—always and everywhere Masonry has stood for the right of the soul to know the truth and to look up unhindered from the lap of earth into the face of God. Not freedom from faith, but freedom of faith, has been its watchword, on the ground that as despotism is the mother of anarchy, so bigoted dogmatism is the prolific source of scepticism—knowing also that our race has made its most rapid advance in those fields where it has been free the longest."

True to this spirit, always, Masonry has everywhere fought as a champion of human freedom, in civil life, in art, and in religion. It worked as a leaven in France long before the Revolution set that country aflame; it was one of the secret forces that made for Italian nationality; it was a power behind the scenes in the American colonies' struggle for independence. Truly, as Albert Pike has said, it "is devoted to the cause of Toleration and Liberality against Fanaticism and Persecution, political and religious, and to that of Education. Instruction and Enlightenment against Error, Barbarism and Ignorance."

II

But this Freedom, be it noted—it is my point here—is freedom *in*, not freedom *from*, the law. This is nature's way, and law is never anything else, if it be truly law and not conventionality, than the open path along which Life walks to ample power. He that keeps the laws of hygiene enjoys the vigorous liberty of health; he that keeps step with the seasons reaps the first fruits of the fields; he that thinks in accordance with fact and evidence is given the sceptre of truth. It is our loyalty that sets us free; it is our keeping the rules of the game that yields us the joy and spontaneity of the game.

All just civil law partakes of this character, for its purpose is to relieve a man from the bondage of caprice, the dominance of the brutal, and the superciliousness of the tyrant, making it safe for children to play along the streets and for women to walk in the dark. It is the friend and protectress of the human. It guards our property and our limbs, it arbitrates our quarrels, it secures to us the fruit of our toil, and night and day stands watch above our lives. Always the best country is that where the head is held high, the heart is free, and men walk in that liberty which is "inbound in law."

If there is one danger lurking in our midst to-day it is the spread of that subtle civil scepticism that flouts authority and makes light of order. The rich would prostitute the statutes of the land to the support of ill-gotten gains; those that have nothing would shape them into means of wresting what they want from those that have; and the anarchists, of whom there are many in fact if not in name, whisper that law itself is bondage and every officer a tyrant. Masonry's word to this condition is that the evil of law is to be remedied only by making laws wiser and more just and that the one cure for bad authority is good authority. Accordingly, the candidate is no sooner released from his cable tow than he is told to salute the Wardens; this act may be a contradiction in appearance but is not in fact.

CHAPTER XX

THE APRON

I

Having been privileged to read up and down a great deal of Masonic literature I may say that on no other one symbol has so much nonsense, in my opinion, been written. The apron has been made to mean a thousand and one things, from the fig-leaf worn by Adam and Eve, to the last mathematical theory of the fourth dimension; and there is little to cause wonder that the intelligent have been scandalised and common men bewildered. If an interpretation can be made that steers a safe course between the folly of the learned and the fanaticism of the ignorant it will have some value, whatever may be said of its own intrinsic worth. Warned by the many who have fallen into the pit of unreason we shall be wise to walk warily and to theorise carefully.

The wildest theories concerning the apron have been based on its shape, a thing of comparatively recent origin and due to a mere historical accident. The body of it, as now worn, is approximately square in shape and thus has suggested the symbolism of the square, the right-angle and the cube, and all arising therefrom; its flap is triangular and this has suggested the symbolism of the triangle, the forty-seventh proposition, and the pyramid; the descent of the flap over the body of the apron has also given rise to reasonings equally ingenious. By this method of interpretation men have read into it all manner of things;—the mythology of the Mysteries, the metaphysics of India, the mysteries of the Kabbala, and the phantasies of Magic. Meanwhile it has been forgotten that the apron is a *Masonic* symbol and that we are to find out what it is intended to mean rather than what it may, under the stress of our lust for fancifulness, be made to mean. When the Ritual is consulted, as it always deserves to be, we find that it treats the apron (1) as an inheritance from the past, (2) as the badge of a Mason, and (3) as the emblem of innocence and sacrifice.

II

For one purpose or another, and in some form, the apron has been used for three or four thousand years. In at least one of the Ancient Mysteries, that of Mithras, the candidate was invested with a white apron. So also was the initiate of the Essenes, who received it during the first year of his membership in that order; and it is significant that many of the statues of Greek and Egyptian gods were so ornamented, as may still be seen. Chinese secret societies, in many cases, also used it, and the Persians, at one time, employed it as their national banner. Jewish prophets often wore aprons, as did the early Christian candidates for baptism, and as ecclesiastical dignitaries of the present day still do. The same custom is found even among savages, for, as Brother J. G. Gibson has remarked, "wherever the religious sentiment remains—even among the savage nations of the earth—there has been noticed the desire of the natives to wear a girdle or apron of some kind."

From all this, however, we must not infer that our Masonic apron has come to us from such sources, though, for all we know, the early builders may have been influenced by those ancient and universal customs. The fact seems to be that the Operative Masons used the apron only for the practical purpose of protecting the clothing, as there was need in labour so rough. It was nothing more than one item of the workman's necessary equipment as is shown by Brother W. H. Rylands, who found an Indenture of 1685 in which a Master contracted to supply his Apprentice with "sufficient wholesome and competent meate, drink, lodging and aprons."

Because the apron was so conspicuous a portion of the Operative Mason's costume, and so necessary a portion of his equipment, it was inevitable that Speculatives should have continued its use for symbolical purposes. The earliest known representatives of these aprons, so we are informed by Brother J. F. Crowe, who was one of the first of our scholars to make a thorough and scientific investigation of the subject ("A.O.C.," vol. v, p. 29), "is an engraved portrait of Anthony Sayer. . . . Only the upper portion is visible in the picture, but the flap is raised, and the apron looks like a very long leathern skin. The next drawing is in the frontispiece to the 'Book of Constitutions,' published in 1723, where a brother is represented as bringing a number of aprons and gloves into the Lodge, the former appearing of considerable size and with long strings." In Hogarth's cartoon, "Night," drawn in 1737, the two Masonic figures, Brother Crowe points out in another connection (see his "Things a Freemason Should Know") "have aprons reaching to their ankles." But other plates, of the same period, show aprons reaching only to the knee, thus marking the beginning of that process of shortening, and of general decrease in size and change in shape, which finally gave us the apron of the present day; for since the garment no longer serves as a means of protection it has been found wise to fashion it in a manner more convenient to wear, nor is this inconsistent with its original Masonic significance. It is this fact, as I have already suggested, that has made the present form of the apron a result of circumstances, and proves how groundless are interpretations founded on its shape.

According to Blue Lodge usages in the United States the apron must be of unspotted lambskin, fourteen to sixteen inches in width, twelve to fourteen inches in depth, with a flap descending from the top some three or four inches. The Grand Lodge of England now specifies such an apron as this for the First Degree, but requires the apron of the Second Degree to have two sky-blue rosettes at the bottom, and that of the Third Degree to have in addition to that a sky-blue lining and edging not more than two inches deep, "and an additional rosette on the fall or flap, and silver tassels." Grand officers are permitted to use other ornaments, gold embroidery, and, in some cases, crimson edgings. All the evidence goes to show that these ornate aprons are of recent origin. The apron should always be worn outside the coat.

III

"The thick-tanned hide, girt around him with thongs, wherein the Builder builds, and at evening sticks his trowel" was so conspicuous a portion of the costume of the Operative Mason that it became associated with him in the public mind, and thus gradually evolved into his badge; for a badge is some mark voluntarily assumed as the result of established custom whereby one's work, or station, or school of opinion, may be signified.

Of what is the Mason's badge a mark? Surely its history permits but one answer to this—it is the mark of honourable and conscientious labour, the labour that is devoted to creating, to constructing, rather than to destroying. or demolishing. As such, the Mason's apron is itself a symbol of a profound change in the attitude of society toward work, for the labour of hand and brain, once despised by the great of the earth, is rapidly becoming the one badge of an honourable life. If men were once proud to wear a sword, while leaving the tasks of life to slaves and menials, if they once sought titles and coats of arms as emblems of distinction, they are now, figuratively speaking, eager to wear the apron, for the Knight of the present day would rather save life than take it, and prefers, a thousand times over, the glory of achievement to the glory of title or name. Truly, the rank has become the guinea's stamp, "and a man's a man for a' that," especially if he be a man that can *do;* and the real modern king, as Carlyle was always contending, is "the man who can."

If this is the message of the apron, none has a better right to wear it than a Mason, if he be a real member of the Craft, for he is a knight of labour if ever there was one. Not all labour deals with things. There is a labour of the mind, and of the spirit, more arduous, often, and more difficult, than any labour of the hands. He who dedicates himself to the cleaning of the Augean stables of the world, to the clearing away of the rubbish that litters the paths of life, to the fashioning of building stones in the confused quarries of mankind, is entitled, more than most men, to wear the badge of toil!

IV

When the candidate is invested with the garment he is told that it is an emblem of innocence. It is doubtful if Operative Lodges ever used it for such a symbolic purpose, though they may have done so in the seventeenth century, after Speculatives began to be received in greater numbers. The evidence indicates that it was after the Grand Lodge era, and in consequence of the rule that the apron should be of white lambskin, that Masons began to see in its colour an emblem of innocence and in its texture a suggestion of sacrifice.

In so doing they fell into line with ancient practices, for of old *white* "has been esteemed an emblem of innocence and purity." Among the Romans an accused person would sometimes put on a garment of white to attest his innocence, white being, as Cicero phrased it, "most acceptable to the gods." The candidate in the Mysteries and among the Essenes were similarly invested, and it has the same meaning of purity and innocence in the Bible which promises that though our sins be as scarlet they shall be white as snow. In the early Christian church the young catechumen (or convert) robed himself in white in token of his abandonment of the world and his determination to lead a blameless life. But there is no need to multiply instances because each of us feels by instinct that white is the natural symbol of innocence.

Now it happens that "innocence" comes from a word meaning "to do no hurt" and this may well be taken as its Masonic definition, for it is evident that no grown man can be innocent in the sense that a child is, which really means an ignorance of evil. The innocence of a Mason is his gentleness, his chivalrous determination to do no moral evil to any person, man, or woman, or babe: his patient forbearance of the crudeness and ignorance of men, his charitable forgiveness of his brethren when they wilfully or unconsciously do him evil; his dedication to a spiritual knighthood in behalf of the values and virtues of humanity by which alone man rises above the brute, and the world is carried forward on the upward way.

It is in token of its *texture*—lambskin—that we find in the apron the further significance of sacrifice, and this also, it seems, is a symbolism developed since 1700. It has been generally believed until recently that the Operatives used only leather aprons, and this was doubtless the case in early days, but Brother Crowe has shown that many of the oldest lodge records evidence a use of linen as well. "In the old Lodge of Melrose," he writes, "dating back to the seventeenth century, the aprons have always been of linen, and the same rule obtained in 'Mary's Chapel' No. i, Edinburgh, the oldest Lodge in the world"; whilst Brother James Smith, in his history of the old Dumfries Lodge, writes, "on inspecting the box of Lodge 53, there was only one apron of kid or leather, the rest being of linen! As these Lodges are of greater antiquity than any in England, I think a fair case is made out for linen, versus leather, originally."

Brother Crowe has not entirely made out his case to the satisfaction of all, for other authorities contend that the builders who necessarily handled rough stone and heavy timbers must have needed a more substantial fabric than linen or cotton. But in any event, the Fraternity has been using leather aprons for these two centuries, though cotton cloth is generally substituted for ordinary lodge purposes, and it is in no sense far-fetched to see in the lambskin a hint of that sacrifice of which the lamb has so long been an emblem.

But what do we mean by sacrifice? To answer this fully would lead one far afield into ethics and theology, but for the present purpose, we may say that the Mason's sacrifice is the cheerful surrender of all that is in him which is *un-Masonic*. If he has been too proud to meet others on the level he must lay aside his pride; if he has been too mean to act upon the square he must yield up his meanness; if he has been guilty of corrupting habits they must be abandoned, else his wearing of the apron be a fraud and a sham.

Carrying with it so rich a freightage of symbolism the apron may justly be considered "more ancient than the Golden Fleece or Roman Eagle, more honourable than the Star and Garter," for these badges were too often nothing more than devices of flattery and the insignia of an empty name. The Golden Fleece was an Order of Knighthood founded by Philip, Duke of Burgundy, on the occasion of his marriage to the Infanta Isabella of Portugal in 1429 or 1430. It used a Golden Ram for its badge and the motto inscribed on its jewel was "wealth, not servile labour"! The Roman of old bore an eagle on his banner to symbolise magnanimity, fortitude, swiftness, and courage. The Order of the Star originated in France in 1350, being founded by John II. in imitation of the Order of the Garter. Of the last-named Order it is difficult to speak, as its origin is clothed in so much obscurity that historians differ, but it was as essentially aristocratic as any of the others. In every case, the emblem was a token of aristocratic idleness and aloofness, the opposite of that which is symbolised by the apron; and the superiority of the latter over the former is too obvious for comment.

CHAPTER XXI

DESTITUTION

I

Before a man can be persuaded to learn an art he must realise his ignorance thereof; before he can be made to enter into a new life he must be made to feel that he is in a natural state of ignorance in regard to that life. There is a certain method by which the candidate is prepared in our ceremonies that is designed to cause the Apprentice to know that, whatever may be his title and possessions in the world, he is poor, and naked, and blind as regards that new life which is Masonry. There is in this method no desire to humiliate him, as that word is understood, but there is every need that he experience humility, a very different thing.

Humiliation may come from disgrace, or some check of adverse fortune; humility is that lowliness of mind in which one becomes aware of his real position in the universe. To know one's self is to be humble, for in the presence of the infinities of the universe an individual, be he the greatest of the great, is pitiably small and weak; "what is man that thou art mindful of him" is his cry, and he will be the last to strut with pride. A mere sense of humour alone would preserve a man against vanity, did he not also know that he is a frail creature, compounded of dirt and deity, hemmed in by ignorance, and weak every way. When a man compares himself with his fellows he may find cause for pride but when he stands in the midst of that lodge which is itself a symbol of the cosmos, surrounded by emblems and images on which rests a weight of time more than that which lies upon the pyramids, where the All-Seeing Eye, symbol of omniscience, looks down upon all, he can but feel how frail, how unspeakably helpless and frail, he is. The worldling may eke out a modicum of pride in considering how much wealthier he may be, or more learned than another, but the Mason, acknowledging a law that demands he be perfect as the Father in Heaven is perfect, will be more inclined to cry, "Depart from me, for I am a sinful man, O Lord."

"Among the ancients," writes Pierson, "the ceremony of discalceation, or the pulling off a shoe, indicated reverence for the presence of God." The Pythagorean rule, that an initiate must "sacrifice and worship unshod" applied throughout the religious customs of antiquity. The priest removed "his shoes from off his feet" before entering the place of worship even as does the Mohammedan of to-day. Of this Mackey gives an interpretation as simple as it is wise! "The shoes, or sandals, were worn on ordinary occasions as a protection from the defilement of the ground. To continue to wear them, then, in a consecrated place, would be a tacit insinuation that the ground was equally polluted and capable of producing defilement. But, as the very character of a holy and consecrated spot precludes the idea of any sort of defilement or impurity, the acknowledgment that such was the case was conveyed, symbolically, by divesting the feet of all that protection from pollution and uncleanness which would be necessary in unconsecrated places. . . . The rite of discalceation is, therefore, a symbol of reverence. It signifies, in the language of symbolism, that the spot which is about to be approached in this humble and reverent manner is consecrated to some holy purpose."

II

In the beginnings of the moral life of man a place was made holy by being set apart, as the word literally means; the Sabbath was kept separate from other days, the Temple from other buildings, the altar from all other spots of earth. This was a necessary teaching to cause men to recognise the mere existence of sacredness. But the floor of a Masonic lodge room is not made sacred in order to render other places defiled by contrast; rather is it to convince us that as the lodge is a holy place so also should the whole world be, of which the lodge is a symbol. When men walk the common ways of life with bare feet, when they undertake every daily task with clean hands, when they seek out their fellowships with a pure heart, then will all life shine with the sanctity God intended, and the Universe be in fact, as well as theory, the Temple of Deity.

In the days before our era when astrology and alchemy were seriously received by great minds, the planets were believed to rule variously over the fates of life, and each planet was supposed to be in some wise linked up with a corresponding metal. Lead was Saturn's metal, iron belonged to Mars, copper to Venus, gold to the sun, etc. To keep one of these metals in one's possession was to invite the influence of the planet to which it was sacred. Consequently, as a Candidate came to the Mysteries, he was divested of metals lest he bring some unwelcome planetary influence into the sanctuary.

If we find a far-off echo of this custom in our own ceremonies we may understand that the lodge would thus symbolically exclude every jarring element from its fellowship. We may further understand it in another sense, as meaning that the possessions which secure us the services of the world have no potency in the lodge. Of this, as we may read in his booklet on "Deeper Aspects of Masonic Symbolism," A. E. Waite has written with characteristic insight. His words have a finality of wisdom that may fitly conclude a study of destitution:

"The question of certain things of a metallic kind, the absence of which plays an important part, is a little difficult from any point of view, though several explanations have been given. The better way toward their understanding is to put aside what is conventional and arbitrary—as, for example, the poverty of spirit and the denuded state of those who have not yet been enriched by the secret knowledge of the Royal and Holy Art. It goes deeper than this and represents the ordinary status of the world, when separated from any higher motive—the world-spirit, the extrinsic titles of recognition, the material standards. *The Candidate is now to learn that there is another standard of values*, [italics mine] and when he comes again into possession of the old tokens, he is to realise that their most important use is in the cause of others. You know under what striking circumstances this point is brought home to him."

CHAPTER XXII

THE NORTHEAST CORNER

I

When the candidate, reinvested with that of which he had been divested, is made to stand in the Northeast Corner of the lodge as the youngest Entered Apprentice, both the position in which he stands and the posture of his body have reference to such laws of the "new life" in Masonry as are deserving of careful consideration. It has long been observed, and that for the most obvious reasons, that Northeast is neither North nor East, but a midway situation partaking of both. If we recall that the North is the place of darkness, the symbol of the profane and unregenerated world, and that the East is the place of light, the symbol of all perfection in the Masonic life, you will see that it is fitting that an Apprentice be made to find his station there; for by virtue of being an Apprentice he is as yet neither wholly profane nor wholly initiate, having yet much light to receive in Masonry. It is unfortunate that some Masons, in all the deep senses of the words, never move beyond this position but remain, through indifference to the influences of the Order or sluggishness of spirit, in that halfway place.

His standing in an *upright posture* is at once a hint and a prophecy; it is a hint because it is indicative of the plumb which will be offered him as one of the working tools of a Fellow-Craft; it is a prophecy because it is an anticipation of that raising up which will be made in the Sublime Degree. Inasmuch as these completer unfoldings of this symbolism will come in due time, and under their appropriate circumstances, I have elected to defer a study of moral perpendicularity to subsequent pages.

Meanwhile we may be reminded that the Northeast Corner is also the place, at least ideally, of the laying of the Cornerstone, a ceremony as ancient as it is significant. From of old the builders have ever attended the placing of the Cornerstone with elaborate ceremonies, often lasting many days, and the custom is still in use. If we stop to inquire the reason for this celebration of a constructing process we shall find that the Cornerstone is the most important stone in the building, and that it represents the sacrifices that have gone to the making of the structure.

"That is called the Cornerstone, or chief Cornerstone, which is placed in the extreme angle of a foundation," writes a seventeenth century commentator, "conjoining and holding together two walls of the pile, meeting from different quarters." Performing a function of such cardinal importance, the Cornerstone has always appealed to men with a meaning beyond its practical use, serving as the symbol of that which is the foundation and principle of consistency in a structure. The Apprentice, standing upright and ready for his working tools, a tried and trusty brother, is, accordingly, the Cornerstone of the Fraternity, even as youth is the Cornerstone of society.

But there is a meaning in it even beyond this. Before the influence of civilisation banished many barbarous usages from the rites of men it was no uncommon custom to bury a living human being under the cornerstone. This was at first, probably, intended to mollify the gods of the ground on which the building stood, and later a recognition of those sacrifices always required of mere when they would build. (See Speth's "Builders' Rites.") As time went on effigies or statues were used in lieu of human beings, and this was in time refined away into the custom of placing metals, jewels, and other valuables in the cornerstone, even as we Masons now use Corn, Wine, and Oil.

II

In keeping with all this we may see in the Apprentice standing in the Northeast a dedicated and consecrated man who offers *himself* as a building stone in the spiritual Temple which the lodge is making of itself and striving to make of all human society. This symbolism, wholly divested of every vestige of the inhuman practices of which it is a far-off reminder, is beautiful and wise every way, for until men, the individual as well as the mass, do offer their own lives to the service of the Brotherhood and the State both Brotherhood and State will ever remain as imperfect as they are now.

Moreover, it seems to me that when the Craft says to the Candidate, "*You* are the material of which I am builded, and of which the kingdom of Heaven is being builded" it pays a tribute to the essential dignity, and even divinity, of human nature itself. We humans may be crude and barbarous, we may be of the earth, earthy, but it is out of us, out of that very nature we often affect to despise that all the noble stately things of the future must be made. There is no need that we call angels to our assistance, or any celestial beings whatever; in us, as we now are, are those qualities which, would we let them rule in us, would bring the will of God to pass in the earth. It is not beyond reason that the reigning religion of this western world dares to link God to Man in the Person of its Founder, for in a man there is that which is at once Human and Divine. This is the ancient faith of the Builders, and it is above all things fitting that it should have been set to music by Edwin Markham, who is both poet and Mason, as gifted in the one as he is enthusiastic in the other:

"We men of earth have here the stuff
Of Paradise—we have enough!
We need no other thing to build
The stairs into the Unfulfilled—
No other ivory for the doors—
No other marble for the floors—
No other cedar for the beam
And dome of man's immortal dream.
Here on the paths of every day—
Here on the common human way—
Is all the busy gods would take
To build a heaven, to mould and make
New Edens. Ours the stuff sublime
To build Eternity in time."

CHAPTER XXIII

WORKING TOOLS OF AN ENTERED APPRENTICE

I

"Man is a Tool-using Animal; weak in himself, and of small stature, he stands on a basis, at most for the flattest-soled, of some half-square foot, insecurely enough; has to straddle out his legs, lest the very wind supplant him. Feeblest of bipeds! Three quintals are a crushing load to him; the steer of the meadow tosses him aloft, like a waste rag. Nevertheless he can use tools, can devise tools; with these the granite mountain melts into light dust before him; he kneads glowing iron, as if it were soft paste; seas are his smooth highway, winds and fire his unwearying steeds. Nowhere do you find him without tools; without tools he is nothing, with tools he is all."

Thus writes Thomas Carlyle, who was not always as Masonic as he is here. It would be difficult to state in language more forceful the whole philosophy underlying the Working Tools of Masonry, albeit reference might also be made to Henri Bergson, who wrote his "Creative Evolution" many years after Carlyle had penned his "Sartor Resartus," and when new light had come, and men had grown wiser in science. In his book, which is the most original discussion of Evolution since Darwin's "Origin of Species," Bergson shows that nothing more distinguishes the man from the brute than his use of tools. The brute has his tools built into his own body and consequently can neither modify nor change them; the beaver's teeth, the spider's spinnet, the eagle's talons, the lion's claws, in all these and similar cases the brute's tool is a part of the brute's anatomy, with the result that its operations are confined within very narrow limits. But man makes his own tools, can modify or change them at will, and is always free to adapt himself and his work to ever-changing needs; from this has arisen man's superiority to the brute creation, for he can use his tools upon himself and thus change his own nature as well as the external world. Accordingly, Bergson defines man as "the animal that makes things," and he is careful to show that man's superiority lies in his power to work upon *himself* as well as upon *things*.

Here, in this last clause, is the key to Masonry's use of Working Tools. In no case are they instruments to be used on external things, though they are symbolised by the tools of the Operative Builders; in every case they are mental or moral forces with which a man may reshape himself into a masterful man and help reshape society into a great Brotherhood. With the implements thus understood, no man or Mason can ever hope to build except he be equipped with his kit of tools.

But some tools are simpler in use than others, and better adapted to simpler work; therefore the Craft has wisely distributed the implements among the Degrees, in recognition of the candidate's increase of skill and responsibility; in the First Degree the Apprentice is given the Twenty-four Inch Guage and Common Gavel; in the Second the candidate is allotted the Plumb, Square and Level; while the Master Mason, in token of his task in completing the building work, is given the Trowel.

II

The Twenty-four Inch Gauge.

This is nothing other than an ordinary two-foot rule such as may be found in use among stone-masons of to-day; as such we need not go far to seek its origin or dive deep to find its meaning. Our Monitors make it the symbol of time well systematised, and our older writers have often referred to Sts. Ambrose and Augustine, and to King Alfred, as exemplars of the wisdom of devoting eight hours to the service of God and distressed worthy brethren, eight hours to their usual vocation, and eight to rest and to refreshment. This reading of the symbolism may be accepted without reserve, but is not this right use and dividing of time itself suggestive of that wider use of law and order so necessary in the life of the individual and the world?

What time is in itself we do not know, perhaps we shall never know. But in every-day life it is nothing other than our opportunity to live and work. We have our allotted span of existence; we have our allotted task; our wisdom consists in making one fit the other. Time flows over some men as water flows over a stone; to others a single hour may bring a new depth of experience and open out new vistas of vision. It is not the least among the secrets of genius that it understands the value of the odd moment or the spare hour. Many Illinois lawyers between 1840 and 1860 found their days eaten up by their practice; Abraham Lincoln was as busy as the others but he managed in his *spare time* to learn White's Geometry by heart, to study the technique of politics, and to master every phase and angle of the slavery question. There were only twenty-four hours in one of Albert Pike's days even as in ours; he made of himself, in spite of a thousand handicaps, one of the profoundest scholars of his day—antiquarian, linguist, jurist, philologist, what not; he "found the Scottish Rite a log-cabin and left it a palace"; he ploughed his influence into America, and all because he knew how to apply the guage to his time.

Much of the waste and confusion of human existence arises from men's failure to measure their work by some standard or rule; they float down the stream like chips, take things as they come and go, and suffer themselves to be blown this way and that like a derelict at sea. Their days are as mere heaps of stone to which no quarryman has ever brought his tools. He who has learned how to transform time into life, deals with circumstances as an artist uses his materials; he has ever before him a plan laid out on his mind's tracing-board; he selects his materials and appoints each to its appropriate function, fitting and shaping all according to his design.

What is the standard by which we may test our work? What is the measure of rightness? For many centuries we have been dividing our actions into two opposing tables, one made up of *good* actions, and one of *bad*. When we have desired to learn whether or not some proposed action was good or bad we searched for it in the two lists. But this *morality by code* is rapidly breaking down, for we find that a deed will be wrong under some circumstances, right under others. If I shoot a man for assaulting my family I may do right; if I shoot a friend in a quarrel I do evil. The one test which we can apply to any and every action is, "What is its effect on life?" If it enlarges, exalts, ennobles, if it makes life more musical, more worthful, more rich, it is good; if it cramps, corrupts, debases, defiles, it is evil. This is *life morality* and every evidence indicates that it is to be the morality of the future.

And it is also, I believe, the morality of Masonry, as symbolised by that Working Tool which would teach us how to transform time into life. He who learns this use of it need never regret the passing of "every year," for every year will but add honour to his head and riches to his heart until the end comes when time will lead him to eternity.

"Old time will end our stay,
But no time, if we end well, will end our glory."

III

In the Middle Ages the Gavel was a symbol often made use of by religious bodies to signify possession, a meaning derived, perhaps, from the ancient custom of throwing a gavel (or hammer) across a field to claim ownership. In the Scandinavian mythology it was Thor's hammer and stood for power, often seen in the thunderings and lightnings by which that dread god split the rocks and destroyed the trees. It is similarly used, we learn from H.G.M. Murray-Aynsley ("A.Q.C.," vol. VI, p. 51) by New Zealanders, the Maoris, and Channel Island savages. In Masonry it has other meanings, being derived from the tool used by the workmen in dressing a stone to the desired shape.

As a Working Tool it must not be confused with the Master's hammer which, because it stands for his authority, is often called "Hiram," in commemoration of the authority wielded by the First Grand Master. The Gavel is a tool with one sharp edge and combines the functions of the hammer and the chisel. When looked at from the end, with the cutting edge turned up, it has the appearance of the gable of a house, and this suggested to Mackey that it may have been derived from the German "gipful," or gable. However that may be, it is a tool for shaping and not for breaking and is therefore not an emblem of *force*, as some have fancied, though it is obvious that force must be employed to use it.

According to the Monitorial explanation, "The *common gavel* is an instrument made use of by Operative Masons, to break off the corners of rough stones, the better to fit them for the builder's use; but we, as free and accepted Masons, are taught to make use of it for the more noble and glorious purpose of divesting our minds and consciences of all the vices and superfluities of life, thereby fitting our bodies, as living stones, for that spiritual building, that house not made with hands, eternal in the heavens." In other connections we are told that the Gavel was used by Operative Masons to break off the knobs and excrescences of stones in order to shape the Rough Ashlar into the Perfect Ashlar, or finished building stone.

PART TWO: THE SECOND STEP

CHAPTER XXIV

AN INTRODUCTION TO THE SECOND STEP

I

The term "Fellow Craft" as a compound word was first used by Scotch Masons and it so happens that our earliest detailed picture of the old manner of passing an Apprentice to the Fellow Craft grade is found in the Schaw Statutes, an old Scottish document. Brother Gould has given so complete a summary of the matter that I shall quote his paragraph in full as found in his "Concise History" p. 253:

"The most complete picture we possess of the early Masonry of Scotland is afforded by the Schaw Statutes of 1598 and 1599. These are Codes of Laws signed and promulgated by William Schaw, Master of the King's Work and General Warden of the Masons, the one directed to the Craft in general, the other to the Lodge of Kilwinning. From these two codes we learn very little with regard to the entry of Apprentices—simply that in each case it was booked—but on other points they are more communicative. Thus a Master (or Fellow Craft, which was a term importing the same meaning) was to be received or admitted in the presence of six Masters and two Entered Apprentices; his name and mark [each Mason had a private mark which he chiselled or painted on his finished work just as a painter will place his name or initials in one corner of his picture.—H.L.H.] were also to be booked, together with the names of those by whom he was admitted, and of his Intenders [or instructors]. No one was to be admitted, according to the earlier Code, without an Essay [a specimen of his work] and sufficient trial of his skill and worthiness in his vocation and craft; or, according to the later one, without a sufficient essay and proof of memory and art of craft. A further regulation requires an annual trial of the art of memory and science thereof, of every Fellow Craft and Apprentice, according to their vocations, under penalty if any of them shall have lost one point thereof."

This manner of Passing was in vogue in Scotland; evidence shows that a similar usage obtained in England as well. The term "Fellow Craft" was first introduced into the English Lodges by the Constitutions of 1723, but even then, it still meant, so far as the grade was concerned, the same thing as Master. It was not until some years later that the two names came to have their present import.

"Fellow Craft" literally means fellow, or companion, of the Craft. In language other than English it is usually derived from some form of the word companion and the meaning is always as that given above. Brother Gould, along with other authorities, believed that the Operative First Degree was broken in two by the Speculatives some time between 1723 and 1738, and that the former half of the ceremony was made into the new First and the latter half into the new Second. This Second became known as the Fellow Craft Degree, while the old Second became, after sundry additions, the new Third, or Master Degree. In this manner *Fellow Craft* and *Master Mason* came to have their present meanings.

II

The Operative Apprentice was compelled to prove his proficiency by a *masterpiece* or essay before being passed to the higher grade. This means that the Apprentice was one learning to use his tools, and that the Fellow was one who had achieved, at least in part, that knowledge. In our present Ritual this old distinction is still observed so that the key word to the Second Degree is knowledge, just as the key word to the First Degree was obedience. This knowledge is at once a knowing about things, and a knowing how to do things, and the entire Fellow Craft ceremony is a kind of treatise on the functions played by enlightenment, information, and mental development in the life of man. We know that while Operative Masons were men of trained minds they did not incorporate into their simple ceremonies any such elaborate treatment of knowledge as that found in our present degree. We owe this enlargement of the Rite to a Scotchman, William Preston.

Preston was born in Edinburgh on August 7, 1742. At twelve years of age he was compelled by his father's death to leave school at which time he was apprenticed to a printer. In 1762 he moved to London where he found employment with the king's printer. During his first year or so in London he was made a Mason, becoming a member of a Lodge of Scotchmen situated in London, and later, at the age of twenty-three, a Master. Accepting the obligations of the office with more than usual seriousness he set out to master the history and symbolism of the Order. Preston found that the usual ceremony of initiation consisted of a reading of the Old Charges to the candidate followed by oral expositions. These expositions were often hasty and superficial to a degree, and they seemed a very unworthy form of Lecture to Preston, who had studied hard and mastered "a notable literary style." Accordingly he set out to write a new system of lectures more in harmony with the dignity of the Fraternity and with the real value of the initiation ceremony. After many delays and much criticism these Lectures were sanctioned by Grand Lodge and "diffused throughout England." But, owing to an unfortunate state of affairs, Preston's Lectures were replaced by Hemming's at the time of the Union of Ancients and Moderns in 1813. Meanwhile Preston had organised a band, or club, of disciples and it was through the influence of this group that his lectures "came to America, where they are the foundation of our Craft lectures," the fact that has led me to this biographical sketch of the man. To this day most states are using the Prestonian system as modified by Philip Webb.

Brother Roscoe Pound, whose "Philosophy of Masonry" I am never weary of recommending, and whom I am following herein, has pointed out that Preston's age was one in which "finality was the dominant idea"; that "it was the period of formal over-refinement in every department of human activity;" and that it was the century of intellectualism when "reason was the central idea of all philosophical thought" and "knowledge was regarded as the universal solvent" of all problems. True to the spirit of his day and awake to the necessity of education in a land without a free public school system Preston undertook to transform Masonry into an academy of learning. Accordingly we find in the Second Degree, which most carries his impress, a complete system of education, covering the Five Senses, the Liberal Arts, and the Sciences. "To-day this seems a narrow and inadequate conception, but the basis of such a philosophy is perfectly clear if we remember the man and his time."

III

"One need not say (I am quoting Pound) that we cannot accept the Prestonian philosophy of Masonry as sufficient for the Masons of to-day. Much less can we accept the details or even the general framework of his ambitious scheme to expound all knowledge and set forth a complete outline of a liberal education in three lectures. We need not wonder that Masonic *philosophy* has made so little headway in Anglo-American Masonry when we reflect that this is what we have been brought up on and that it is all the most Masons ever hear of. It comes with an official sanction that seems to preclude inquiry, and we forget the purpose of it in its obsolete details. But I suspect we do Preston a great injustice in thus preserving the literal terms of the lectures at the expense of their fundamental idea. In his day they did teach—to-day they do not.

"Suppose to-day a man of Preston's tireless diligence attempted a new set of lectures which should unify knowledge and present its essentials so that the ordinary man could comprehend them. To use Preston's words, suppose lectures were written, as a result of seven years of labour, and the co-operation of a society of critics, which set forth a regular system of modern knowledge demonstrated on the clearest principles and established on the firmest foundation. Suppose, if you will, that this was confined simply to the knowledge of Masonry. Would not Preston's real idea (in age of public schools) be more truly carried out than by our present lip service, and would not his central notion of the lodge as a center of light vindicate itself by its results."

Brother Pound's idea of modernising the educational element in the Second Degree appeals to me as one of eminent sanity and desirability. However, few of us can afford to wait for such a time; we are in the Fraternity now, and we must have its services now or never. But we do not need to fear that if we throw ourselves into a thoroughgoing study of the degree as it now is that we shall be disappointed, for it will richly repay the most laborious examination. Besides, there are many elements in it, as we shall see, that derive from the customs of the Old Builders centuries before Preston was born. With these elements, and with Preston's great conception of the function of knowledge in the life of man, we shall now have to do.

CHAPTER XXV

PASSING

I

In Operative days the Apprentice was compelled to spend a series of years, sometimes five, usually seven, in mastering his trade. During this period he remained indentured, or bound, to some Master Mason; at its termination he was examined in an assembly of the lodge, usually on St. John's Day, and if found proficient was *passed* to the grade of Fellow Craft. In our Speculative system there is no necessity that so much time be spent between the two degrees, but many of our best experienced men believe we have gone to the opposite extreme. In at least three jurisdictions in the United States the candidate may be passed from the First to the Second in *two weeks;* in nine jurisdictions he may pass as soon as proficient; in a majority one month must intervene. Of course, the candidate may take longer than necessary in every case, but the point is that he is almost never *required* to spend more than one month in preparation for passing! Surely, no man can become fully prepared for advancement, which means that he has *mastered* the teachings of the preceding degree and is made ready for the next, in so brief an interval, especially if he be engaged in daily work! Surely one thing to explain the indifference of many members to the order is just this habit of hurrying through the degrees!

When the Apprentice passed to the Fellow Craft grade in Operative Masonry he was given a distinguishing mark, which was usually a crude figure having something of the appearance of a letter of the alphabet, though some of these marks were pictures, and others were symbols or emblems. "It is very remarkable," writes Gould, in his "Concise History," (p. 239) "that these marks are to be found in all countries—in the chambers of the Great Pyramid at Gizeh, on the underground walls of Jerusalem, in Herculaneum and Pompeii, on Roman walls and Grecian temples, in Hindustan, Mexico, Peru, Asia Minor—as well as on the great ruins of England, France, Germany, Scotland, Italy, Portugal and Spain. Some of the foundation stones of the Haram Wall of Jerusalem are cut in the surface to a depth of three-quarters of an inch, but most of the characters are painted with a red colour like vermillion. . . . To use the words of the late Professor Hayter Lewis, they seem to give at least strong presumptive ground for the belief that in these splendid foundation stones *we may see the actual work of the Phœnician Hiram for his great Master, Solomon.*" (Italics mine.) Similar marks were used by Mediæval guilds, among them the Masons. By the latter they were employed to identify each man with his own work in order that responsibility for ill-done tasks might be easily traced. In early days these marks were chiselled or painted in plain view and often, evidently, carried a symbolic significance; in later days they were placed on a side of the stone that was hidden from sight. Each mark was a worker's own private possession which another could copy only at his peril; consequently the receiving of an authorised mark by an Apprentice when passing to be a Fellow Craft was a token of his assumption of full responsibility for his work and must have been to him an occasion of pride and rejoicing. It would be easy to comment on this from our Speculative point of view, did space permit, for every Mason, even to-day, is leaving his own mark on his work, whether it be a visible mark or not, and the All-Seeing Eye beholds it when men cannot.

In order to be passed the Operative Apprentice had also to produce an *essay*, or masterpiece, the latter word literally meaning, *Master's piece.* It was a proof of his ability to handle his tools and to understand his materials, and it was a token to the Craft of his mastery of its trade secrets. We have a parallel to this in the present custom of colleges in demanding of a student some treatise or book to prove his worthiness for a degree. A lodge of Masons might also take up a similar rule again; if a candidate were compelled to study the Craft and its history enough to enable him to write a paper about it, or if he were required to give some signal of genuine service in its behalf, his earnestness therein would enable him to get more out of Masonry, and Masonry to get more out of him.

One test we still employ in advancement that was used by Operatives of old—the memory test, a thing I am very sure you will remember as vividly as I do myself! Some radical critics are advocating that the letter-perfect learning of the lecture be abandoned, but this, I believe, would be a catastrophe, for this work is the only form of Masonic study *demanded* by the lodge, and that, surely, when we remember all that Masonry has to offer its votaries, is little enough.

II

It may be noted, in conclusion, that it was often the custom in old lodges to appoint an *Intender*, or instructor to have responsibility for teaching the candidate. Our present system of Custodians of the Work, or other similar standing committees, to instruct District Lecturers and Masters in the proper methods of ritualism, is roughly analogous to the ancient custom, but it has only a remote influence on the candidate. It would be a wise thing as I have already more than once suggested, if every lodge maintained a permanent school in which to expound to the initiates the Mysteries of our Craft. The Masonic Study Club is a step in the right direction; may they multiply in number, and increase in power!

Up to this point I have been interpreting the *passing* in the light of Operative customs and you may be wishing to remind me that in our present Speculative system we have added a Third Degree, and that to-day the Fellow Craft is no longer a master of the trade. All this I admit, but is not this true, that if so much preparation was once required for passing to one higher degree, that we should require all the more preparation for advancing to two higher degrees? If our candidates are caused more thoroughly to master the Fellow Craft teaching all the more will they be ready for the *sublime* degree; besides, the Second Degree is so rich in material that it is many times worth a candidate's labour to make it his own; and furthermore, the better a man has prepared for the Fellow Craft work, the more completely will he have digested the teachings of the Apprentice Degree, and that is always a consummation devoutly to be wished!

CHAPTER XXVI

SQUARE ON THE BREAST

I

In the earliest of the Old Charges we find fifteen "points" or rules set forth for the regulation of the conduct of the Fellow Craft; these were the "perfect points" of his entrance to the Order as well as in his transactions with mankind, and it is worthy of note that this code of ethics was far in advance of the standards of the fifteenth century. There is no need to analyse these requirements except to say that they consisted, in essence, of *acting on the square*, that is, the candidate was to deal squarely with the Craft, with his masters, his fellows, and with all men whomsoever. In his relations with the Craft he was expected above all else to keep an *attentive ear* to his instructors, to preserve carefully the secrets of his Order and his brethren in a *faithful breast*, and to be evermore ruled by the principle of virtue in his behaviour. If such qualifications were demanded of Apprentices in an Operative trade, how much more may they be reasonably required of a Fellow Craft in a speculative, or moral, science!

In its original form *virtue* meant valour; to-day it means rectitude. But the rectitude which is virtue is more than a passive *not-doing* of evil; it is the courageous *doing* of right. "Virtue is but heroic bravery, to *do* the thing thought to be true, in spite of all enemies of flesh or spirit, in despite of all temptations or menaces." The man of conventional morality is content *not to* steal, drink, gamble, swear, etc., but often it does not enter his head that there is an active, aggressive work to be done in cleaning up the world. Conventional morality is neuter; virtue is masculine; and the Craft that seeks to *build* the Temple of Humanity needs in its votaries something more than passive morality.

II

Many of the most vital organs are in the breast. A man can go without water for days; he can do without food, if necessary, for a month or more; but without breath in his lungs or blood in his heart he cannot live an hour. The breast, accordingly, is the symbol of the most essential things in personality,—love, faithfulness, purity, and character. If the square is applied to the breast it is to compel us to realise that virtue must rule in the very deeps of us, in the springs of conduct, and the motives of action, as well as on the surface. The man whose morality is on the outside of his skin is held up by external restraints and will often fall into evil if they chance to be removed, as the deacon of a church or the pillar of a community will sometimes wallow in vice while among strangers. But when virtue is the law of the hidden motives of the will, the man will walk as uprightly in the slum of a city as in the precincts of his home. Should Masonry trust to conventional morality alone it would build on sands; by demanding virtue of its members it lays its foundations in bed-rock, and the storm may come, the winds blow, the rains fall, but its house will not be moved. And the same virtue that it requires in the lodge room, it expects in all a Mason's transactions with mankind, else Masonic virtue itself becomes a lifeless conventionality.

CHAPTER XXVII

THE SCRIPTURE READING FROM AMOS

I

The Greeks, as we recall from our discussion of circumambulation, chanted an ode as the worshipper moved about the altar from left to right, for their odes were the most sacred literature in their possession; but the Master of the Masonic lodge reads from the Holy Bible as the Fellow Craft makes his mystic rounds, and that for the same reason. He on whose life's journey the Great Light sends its rays may walk confidently and cheerfully and not as those who stumble through the dark.

And it is fitting that in this connection the rays come from the prophecy of Amos, for that seer sought to bring order and light into the workaday world of men, one of the chief tasks of the Fellow Craft, who receives knowledge that he may become a social builder. Amos wrought his great work during the days of Jeroboam II, in whose reign religion had grown hard and formal, pleasure had rotted into vice, luxury had become a disease, and the aristocracy fattened on the poor. Against these conditions Amos set himself, though he was "no prophet, nor the son of a prophet," and he lashed the abuses of his people with such effective fury, that the high-ups had him banished from the kingdom. "The first great social reformer in history" Amos was no mere denunciator, but one who condemned things as they are by setting before them a picture of things as they should be.

In the graphic visions recorded in his book, Amos sets before us a picture of Israel being judged by a plague of locusts; then follows a fire that "devoured the great deep, and had begun to devour the tilled land;" these visitations are stayed by the supplication of the prophet, and then Jehovah brings a new kind of judgment to bear on his people. As we may read in Amos' own words; "Thus the Lord shewed me; and behold, the Lord stood upon a wall made by a plumbline, with a plumbline in his hand. And the Lord said unto me, Amos, what seest thou? And I said, a plumbline. Then said the Lord, behold, I will set a plumbline in the midst of my people Israel; I will not pass by them any more."

II

This was no mere dramatic way of saying, The people had been bad; they must now be good. The lesson is no such banality as that, but cuts deeper into things. It is really a vision of an entirely new kind of judgment, for consider:—At first Jehovah chastised his people physically, as one may whip a child; later, he passed from external things into their hearts and said, In your conscience you will be judged and in your conscience you will be punished. It was just the Lord's method of plunging a sharp instrument into the naked left breast of Israel! External punishments came and passed, but when the inner standard was set up, it remained whatever came and went, and the Lord did "not pass by them any more."

Ever is this the truth of things, the law of life—that bad men are not always visited by physical evils, and that good men do not always receive material reward. This was a lesson learned by Job many centuries ago. But there is a harvest from wrongdoing that is always sure, as sure as the tides, and it is nothing other than inward corruption. To lie blunts the moral perception; to fall into impurity beclouds the heart; to live in selfishness puts out the eyes of love, for "the wages of sin is death." Like the path of the eagle the ways of the punishment of transgression may be viewless, but they are sure, as sure as a plumbline; the universe is just, and in its laws there is neither variableness nor turning, and he that is a skilled Fellow Craft in the building tasks of life will be wise to govern himself accordingly.

CHAPTER XXVIII

THE OBLONG SQUARE

I

Having discussed the Approach to the East in its First Degree connections there is no need that we go into the matter here, though the Fellow Craft's Approach naturally falls into this place. But there is one problem associated with this rite which was not touched on in the earlier section, and as it occurs in both the First and Second Degrees, it may be fitly studied here; I refer to the Oblong Square. This has long been one of the standing puzzles of Masonry, and that because "oblong square" seems a contradiction in terms, and because no scholar has thus far traced the origin of the Masonic use of this phrase. What it really means is still a mystery, though we may make our guess as other students have done before us.

Mackey defines it as "a parallelogram, or four-sided figure, all of whose angles are equal, but two of whose sides are longer than the others" (rectangle). Following Pierson he finds in it a reference to the ground plan of the lodge room and this, in turn, he sought to trace to the shape of the world as known to the Ancients. From this point of view, we may infer, he saw in the candidate's adjusting his feet to *an* (not *the*) angle of an oblong square an indication of his willingness to stand to and abide by all the laws, rules and regulations of the Craft.

Others have seen in the *oblong square* a reference to the try-square, one of the working tools, when made "gallows" shape, with one arm longer than the other. To this it may be objected, first that our working tool is properly a stone-mason's try-square with the two arms of equal length and not divided into inches; and secondly, that the "gallows" square interpretation can not explain the allusion to a "perfect square" in the Third Degree.

Others, again, find in it a suggestion that the stones of bricks used in a wall of masonry are almost never cubes, but bodies longest in their horizontal dimensions, the better to overlap; they say the candidate is to adjust himself to the Oblong Square because he is himself to be built into a wall that must stand while the ages last. But this seems a far-fetched explanation, and, also, does not explain the "perfect square" of the Master Degree.

II

Brother C. C. Hunt, Deputy Grand Secretary of Iowa, has given another interpretation, and one that seems to me most reasonable. "What, then, is the oblong square of Freemasonry? I believe it to be a survival in our ceremonies of a term once common but now obsolete. My reading has convinced me that at one time the word 'square' meant right-angled, and the term 'a square' referred to a four-sided figure, having four right angles, without regard to the proportionate lengths of adjacent sides. There were thus two classes of squares, those having all four sides equal, and those having two parallel sides longer than the other two. The first class were called 'perfect squares' and the second class 'oblong squares'. In time these terms were shortened to square and oblong respectively, and that is the sense in which they are used at the present time, so that when we speak of an oblong square, we are met with the objection that if it is a square it can not be oblong, and if it is oblong it can not be square. This is true in the present sense of the term, *but Freemasonry still retains the older meaning.*"

support of this, so far as America is concerned, at least, Brother C. F. Irwin of Ohio produced a letter written by a certain Dr. S. P. Hildreth, of Marietta, Ohio, on June 8, 1819, in regard to the fortifications near his city: "On the outside of the parapet, near the *oblong square*, I picked up a considerable number of fragments of ancient potter's ware." Brother Irwin contends that if this term was thus in use in Ohio in 1819 it must have been in use further east much earlier.

If Oblong Square was so used by Masons prior to the seventeenth century it may be that the Speculatives received at that time (they were accepted earlier but not in such numbers) brought with them, as an inheritance from other orders of symbolism, the Perfect Square; and it may be that the framers of our Ritual meant to signify that as the candidate in the preparatory degree is to try himself by an Oblong Square, the Master Mason, as befits the adept of perfection, must adjust himself to the Perfect Square. Thus read, the symbolism as found variously in the Three Degrees, is really a recognition of the fact that the Masonic Life is necessarily progressive, and that a Mason strives toward perfection.

CHAPTER XXIX

DUE FORM

Of the Obligation of the Fellow Craft there is no need to speak inasmuch as the general topic of Obligations was dealt with in an earlier section; but it may be wise here to add to the previous discussion a very brief comment on that "due form" in which the oath is made. As the details are necessarily secret they must be passed by though it may be said that all the postures seem to be arranged about the square thereby suggesting that in order to keep the covenant a candidate must be "square" through and through, in every limb of his body; so that not one faculty or organ shall be permitted to violate those principles and secrets of Freemasonry to which the candidate obligates himself.

In ordinary every-day life, we make a distinction between *form* and *formality*. The man who overvalues the manner of doing things, or who does not put his conscience into his forms, we call a formalist, and that rightly. He may have the veneer of a gentleman, but the heart of a cad; he may perform the external functions of morality but remain all the while like one of those white-washed sepulchres of which Jesus speaks. Formality is pretence, mockery, unreality. But our abhorrence of formalism must not blind us to the necessity of form, for the manner of our behaviour is itself a kind of language and speaks with "the voice of the sign" about the realities of character. I may love or admire you greatly, but if I do not express my regard through actions that you can understand you may live and die in ignorance of it. We lift the hat, shake hands, step aside for ladies, surrender our seats to the aged, observe the propriety of dress, etc., and all because *manners* are so essential a form of social communion that, as Emerson says, if they were lost to the world some gentleman would be obliged to re-invent them.

Now it needs to be observed that while Masonry must not become formal lest it die, and while it must ever be as clean and natural as the blowing clover and the falling rain, yet must it use forms, and nowhere are they more manifestly needed than in taking the Obligation. In that connection—as in others—we call them *due forms* because they are *due* to the Order in the nature of things, and they are nothing other than the candidate's manner of expressing to his brethren his whole hearted determination to keep to the last letter all the duties, principles and secrets to which he therein binds himself.

CHAPTER XXX

WORKING TOOLS OF A FELLOW CRAFT

The first operation of actual building is the quarrying of the stones; this is followed by dressing them into shape, with straight and level sides, and true angles. As the Gavel and the Guage are appropriately used in the first process they are allotted to the Apprentice; as the Plumb, Square, and Level are for testing perpendiculars, angles, and horizontals, they belong naturally, as being next in order, to the Fellow Craft.

I

"The line teaches the criterion of rectitude," wrote William Preston, "to avoid dissimulation in conversation and action and to direct our steps in the path which leads to immortality." The Webb Monitor of 1821 defines it in similar fashion: "The *plumb* is an instrument made use of by Operative Masons to raise perpendiculars . . . the plumb admonishes us to walk uprightly in our several stations before God and man." The idea embodied in each of these definitions is expanded by Mackey, in his "Symbolism of Freemasonry" as follows:

"The plumb is a symbol of rectitude of conduct and inculcates that integrity of life and undeviating course of moral uprightness which can alone distinguish the good and just man. As the operative workman erects his temporal building with strict observance of that plumbline which will not permit him to deviate a hair's breadth to the right or to the left, so the Speculative Mason, guided by the unerring principles of right and truth, inculcated in the symbolic teachings of the same implement, is steadfast in the pursuit of truth, neither bending beneath the frowns of adversity nor yielding to the seductions of prosperity."

By an inevitable co-incidence the central word in each of these three typical definitions is *rectitude*; and *rectitude* is from the Latin *rectus*, "signifying upright, not leaning to one side or another, standing as it ought." From *rectus* we have derived our word*right*, a term referring to a straight line, originally, even as *wrong* first meant a crooked line. Rectitude, therefore, is a straight line running up and down, and we find in it the very picture of the plumbline. In the Operative Mason's hand it is an instrument for making a wall stand straight up and down; in Speculative Masonry it is the symbol of that in us by means of which we may cause our characters to stand straight up and down.

Therefrom arises the question, What is this *"that"* which we find in human nature, and by which we can test our rectitude? This question must be answered lest we be trying to use a working tool without knowing what it is; but our answer, if it be adequate, cannot be packed into a sentence.

"By a necessity of our nature, it would seem, we must think in terms of time and space. Men in all ages have instinctively linked whatever is strong, noble and true with that which is above, and whatever is weak, base and vile with that which is below. This habit of thought is more hoary than the most antique custom, and no matter what science may tell us of how the world is made, the two dimensions of space will always describe the two orders of being. Indeed, it could hardly be otherwise, and until the end of things men will still look to the heights for the sovereign virtues and to the depths for the malefic and infernal vices. Nor does it matter what words we use, so long as we keep it in mind that such ways of thinking are only symbols which conceal as much as they reveal the truth which they try to tell."

In consequence of this manner of thought, to which we are thus instinctively led, we find ourselves constantly saying of things within our own character "This is lofty, or high; this is low, or base!" We may call this perception of different moral levels, taste, conscience, idealism, or what we will, but the power of such perception is in us every one, and *it is this which is our plumbline.*

By virtue of this same habit of judging we recognise that other men also are high or low in character, and we say that the saint lives on the heights while the sinner grovels in the depths; to one we look *up*, on the other we look *down*. "What the best man says is sweet, is sweet," says Walt Whitman, most democratic of mortals; and the *best man* must ever be to us an example and an ideal, to be followed as a teacher, and reverenced as a superior. All nations have had such guides and leaders, as Moses to the Jews, Buddha to the Hindoos, Mohammed to Islam, Confucius to the Chinese, and Jesus to the Christians. These great characters are the plumblines of society.

II

"The Level," says Mackey ("Encyclopedia"), "is deemed, like the square and the plumb, of so much importance as a symbol, that it is repeated in many different relations. First, it is one of the Jewels of the lodge; in the English system a movable, in the American an immovable, one. This leads to its being adopted as the proper official ensign of the Senior Warden [the plumb is the badge of the Junior Warden, and also an immovable jewel], because the Craft when at labour, at which time he presides over them, are on a common level of subordination."

When a building is being erected every stone in it must be so placed that the stress of gravity pulls on all portions of the structure in such a manner that its unity and consistency are preserved. This is accomplished by having the longitudinal axis of each stone made perfectly horizontal. As the level is used for this purpose it is properly said to "lay horizontals." And because of that mental custom of dividing things into higher and lower classes, described above, we naturally think of the level, in its figurative sense, as denoting equality and symbolising democracy. If we can discover that in us which unites us to our fellows on a common ground we shall have unveiled the principle in human nature which may be figured by the Level and may serve as a genuine symbolical working tool.

In a time when nations bowed before the divine right of kings and churches made obeisance to a pope, Masonry was teaching men to meet upon the level; indeed, as Albert Pike has said, "Masonry was the first apostle of equality." Before democratic governments were known in Europe an early Mason was justified in saying that "the chief glory of Masonry is that it brings together upon a plane of common equality men of the most diverse opinions, occupations, and interests. Here upon the level, the symbol of equality—the rich and poor, high and low, titled princes and sturdy yeomen, forget all differences of rank and station and unite their best endeavour for the highest good of each and all." So marked was the democratic character of the Order, even in the seventeenth century, that certain of its English critics declared it to have been secretly organised by Oliver Cromwell as an engine of republicanism!

What is this equality of which Masonry has ever been so ardent an advocate? We may answer, first, that it is a task. In ways without number men are unequal by birth and by circumstances; one man is born in a city slum, another in a circle of wealth: one is endowed with talent, another is condemned to mediocrity; one seems to be bound in by an iron wall of disabilities, while another finds the gates of opportunity opening out on all sides. Our Fraternity's solution of this problem of the inequalities of fate and fortune is to bring all the diverse men into a circle of Brotherhood, where each can share with the others, the learned giving his knowledge to his less enlightened mate, and the strong helping to bear the burdens of the weak. From this point of view the equality of Masonry is like that of a family in which the members may contribute little or much, but all share equally, and the law is "from each according to his ability, to each according to his need."

Again, the Fraternity recognises equality as a natural *fact*, contradictory as these two attitudes may seem. For, despite the sundering differences of talent, of possession, of opinion, race and creed, there is in each of us that which he holds in common with all, even as the sap flows in the roots of a tree as well as in the leaves. This is our universal human nature, our life in the one world of time and space, and our childship under the one God. These are the things that unite us, and ever are they more than the things that divide.

Thus understood there is no conflict in idea between the Plumb and the Level; for in one we have that aristocratic ideal which bids us grow as tall of soul as possible, and in the other the democratic ideal which bids us share our advantages with our fellows. To use one alone might lead us to pride; to use the other alone might debase us to the dead level; to use them in co-operation saves us from both extremes and rightly adjusts us to that sovereign will of the Grand Architect of the Universe, which is to the world of men what gravity is to the world of matter.

III

When a perpendicular is united to a horizontal a right angle results; this is embodied in the Square, which is therefore included with the Level and the Plumb as a working tool, and which may consequently be appropriately studied as the third member of this Fellow Craft triad. It is necessary to bear in mind that we have to do, not with a four-sided figure, or the measuring square of the carpenter, but with the Try-square of the Mason.

Of the Square it is difficult to speak under due limitations because its history is so varied and so ancient, and its use so universal; but perhaps, if we study it simply as a working tool, as the present connection only requires, we may uncover something of its secret.

In China's classic "The Great Learning," written some five centuries before our era, it is said that a man should refrain from doing unto others that which he would not want them to do unto him, a rule described by the writer as "the principle of acting on the square;" while Mencius, Confucius' great disciple, adjured his followers to apply the square and compass to their lives. (See Gould's History, vol. 1, ch. 1.) Brother John Yarker tells us that "one of the oldest words in the Chinese language is literally 'square and compass,' and signified right conduct." In the foundation of Cleopatra's Needle, the Egyptian obelisk removed to New York City, the Square was found carved in the stone, surrounded by other builder's emblems. Among the Egyptians the Square was evidently a sacred symbol from a remote period and some believe that it originally derived from an old form of the Cross. Among many other ancient peoples it was widely used and always for similar purposes.
In Brother Conder's "Hole Crafte and Fellowship of Masons" we read that a picture of William Warring-ton was engraved on that worthy's tombstone, showing him holding the square and compasses in his hand; the date was 1427. In 1830 a square was found in the foundations of an old bridge near Limerick, dated 1517, and bearing the inscription:

> "I will strive to live with love and care
> Upon the level by the square."

The emblem is also found in Shakespeare's "Antony and Cleopatra":

> "Read not my blemishes in the world's report;
> I have not kept my square, but that to come
> Shall all be done by rule."

The square played a conspicuous part in the symbolism of the Compagnonage and of occult fraternities of the Middle Ages.

The data thus thrown promiscuously together comprises but a fraction of the number of examples that might be given, but, even so, they show us how widespread has been the symbolic use of the Square, and how under all circumstances it has meant the same thing—*right conduct.*

What explains this universal usage? Some have suggested, and rightly I believe, that the square is a natural symbol and would deliver its message to a man utterly ignorant of its symbolic interpretations. Brother MacBride believes that it may have received its vogue from its obvious connection with the great transition of the building art from pyramid form to square form structures. Speaking of the early workman groping his way along the path of progress he writes, "Gradually, no doubt in the course of centuries of experience and through the lessons of repeated failures, he acquired a working knowledge of the Law of the Square in building. But it seems that it was only when he properly mastered the problem of forming a right angle that the day of civilisation really dawned. This was the chief cornerstone in his evolution. Progress, seemingly, would have been impossible without it. Art and science alike owe almost everything to it."

The same wise interpreter goes on to suggest the symbolic meaning of the tool: "Hence the importance attached to this instrument and the reason why Masons, Speculative and Operative, call it the great symbol of their Craft. But, however important it may be, it should not be forgotten that after all it is nothing more than an instrument. It has no power nor virtue in itself. Operatively, it derives its importance from being adjusted to the great central forces that dominate in the material world. Speculatively, it obtains its significance, because it represents the great faculty of conscience that governs in the moral world. . . . As the Square is applied by the operative to his work, so are we to apply our conscience to our work of life-building. It is true, theoretically, that neither Square nor Compass is perfect. But they are the best, and the only test we have, and are, in their respective spheres, indispensable to true building."

If we consider carefully the practical use of the Square we see that its function consists in the right adjustment of two lines which would otherwise oppose each other. In view of this a number of our scholars have seen in the implement a symbol of that Doctrine of Balance which Albert Pike expounded with such stately language, especially in the closing pages of his "Morals and Dogma." In this world of men, light and darkness, fatalism and freedom, dogmatism and agnosticism, sensuality and asceticism, etc., are ever in conflict. The true life of man consists in the right adjustment of one opposing force to another, so that one does not lapse into either extreme, but walks on a level in which the two hold each other in equilibrium. "The way of wisdom is to accept both facts in the case, as the Two Pillars of a Temple of Truth, and walk between them into the hush of the holy place." (See *The Builder*, vol. II, p. 268.)

CHAPTER XXXI

THE ASHLARS

I

A further meaning of the Square lies in the fact that it is the tool used by the workmen whereby to test the Rough and Perfect Ashlars. These should have been discussed, perhaps, in their usual position in the First Degree Lecture, but as space forbade a detailed examination of that Lecture, and as many of the symbols adverted to therein have been or will be explained in other connections, it may not be inappropriate to study the Ashlar symbolism in this connection, especially as the latter is so intimately related to the former.

"Not unnaturally," writes one author, "in times when the earth was thought to be a Square the Cube had emblematical meanings it could hardly have for us. From earliest ages it was a venerated symbol, and the oblong cube signified immensity of space from the base of earth to the zenith of the heavens." This world-old meaning was incorporated by the framers of our Ritual in the symbolism of the two Ashlars.

The Rough Ashlar is, according to the Monitor, "a stone, as taken from the quarry, in its rude and natural state"; a Perfect Ashlar is a "stone made ready by the hands of the workmen, to be adjusted by the working tools of the Fellow Craft." In connection with this, it must be remembered that even the Rough Ashlar is not a mere shapeless stone found by accident but a stone roughly shaped, suggesting thereby that the Craft is selecting its materials and not attempting to make something out of nothing.

If the Rough Ashlar signifies the Apprentice coming crude and unfinished from the quarries of mankind, then the Perfect Ashlar is the man made complete by the influence of Masonry. When thus understood we may agree with the words of Brother J. W. Lawrence, whose little volumes of simple exposition enjoy a popularity justly deserved:

"The Perfect Ashlar, as a symbol, is the summum bonum of Freemasonry. That is to say, everything else in Masonry leads up to it. The V. of S. L. describes it, the checkered pavement illustrates it, the Great Architect no less than the Grand Geometrician desire it and are satisfied with nothing less. When the Craft has fashioned the Perfect Ashlar it has nothing else to do."

II

The distinction between the Rough and Perfect Ashlars is an eloquent example of the power of refinement, for the latter does not differ from the former in its substance, being the same stone as *completed* for use. Indeed, the word *perfect* properly means *complete*, and suggests that while none of us may hope ever to become flawless, at least in the present world, each of us may grow symmetrical—a full-orbed man in body, mind and spirit—to achieve which is not the least among the ideals of a Fraternity that asks us to remove all knobs and excrescences that so often disfigure us and render us unfitted for Fellowship.

Another meaning of the Ashlar symbolism is set forth by certain of the Old Lectures, in one of which occurs the following paragraphs: "He that is truly square, well-polished, and uprightly fixed, is qualified to be a member of our most honoured society. He that trusteth such a person with any engagement is freed from all trouble and anxiety about the performance of it, for he is faithful to his trust, his words are the breathings of his heart, and he is an utter stranger to deceit." This is as well put as Emerson's description of a Perfect Ashlar man, whose character consists, he says, "in the power of self-recovery, so that a man cannot have his flank turned, cannot be outgeneralled, but put him where you will, he stands."

Albert Pike found in the Ashlar symbolism a picture of the true state. "The Rough Ashlar is the *people*, as a mass, rude and unorganised. The Perfect Ashlar, cubical stone, symbol of perfection, is the State, the rules deriving their powers from the consent of the governed; the constitution and the laws speaking the will of the people; the government harmonious, symmetrical, efficient—its powers properly distributed and duly adjusted in equilibrium." If a man objects that nowhere does such a social Perfect Ashlar exist, Masonry might make reply in the words of the late Josiah Royce, our noble apostle of the Gospel of Loyalty: "I believe in the beloved community and in the spirit which makes it beloved, and in the communion of all who are, in will and in deed, its members. I see no such community as yet; but none the less my rule of life is: Act so as to hasten its coming." This is a great truth greatly said, and as Masonic as it is true.

These interpretations of the Ashlar may seem to differ, but they harmonise one with another, like the parts of a fitly framed building. When the Fellow Craft adjusts himself to that which is above him by the Plumb; to that which is about him by the Level; and when he rightly adjusts the Plumb to the Level with the Square, he will make a Perfect Ashlar of himself; and when once thus made he will be ready to be fitted into the Great Temple of the Supreme Architect whose will is the genius of Masonry.

CHAPTER XXXII

THE MIDDLE CHAMBER

The ascent toward a place representing the Middle Chamber of King Solomon's Temple is the outstanding ceremony of the Second Degree; because of this, and because of the space devoted to it by the Ritual, we shall devote several sections to its study. In the present section we shall deal with the Middle Chamber itself, and with the truth of which it is a symbol.

That it is a symbol, and not a bit of history, there is every evidence to show. Sir Charles Warren, while Master of the Quatuor Coronati Lodge of Research, gave expression to the opinion of the best modern scholars in saying that, "There never was a Middle Chamber in the Temple. . . . As the Fellow Crafts were only employed during the building of the Temple, they could not have used this Chamber for the service mentioned [you will recall what this service is supposed to have been] even if it had existed. . . . Even if this Chamber had existed they would not have been allowed to desecrate it by use as a pay office."

Albert Mackey, one of the most conservative of Masonic writers, and who wrote his "Symbolism of Freemasonry" some twenty years before Brother Warren delivered his speech, took the same position. As we may read, p. 210: "The whole legend is, in fact, an historical myth, in which the mystic number of the steps, the process of passing to the Chamber, and the wages there received, are inventions added to or ingrafted on the fundamental history contained in the sixth chapter of Kings, to inculcate important symbolic instructions relative to the principles of the order."

The passage in the Book of Kings, to which Mackey here refers, is in the authorised version of the Bible as follows: "They went up with winding stairs into the middle chamber." Modern Biblical scholarship has shown that the term here translated "chamber" really means a "storey," and that there were three such storeys on one side of the Temple composed of small rooms in which the priests kept their vestments, utensils, etc. That workmen were paid their wages in this middle storey, or that Fellow Crafts were there prepared for a higher grade, there is not a hint in the record to show. This account of the matter, as Mackey has said, is "an historical myth."

A myth has been defined as "philosophy in the making." It is an allegorical piece of fiction designed to convey some abstract teaching. The purpose of our ceremonies is not to furnish truth rather than history, and that truth is nowise affected by the accuracy or inaccuracy of the narrative behind which it is veiled. To remember this in all connections will save one from those pitfalls of literalism into which so many Masonic students used to fall.

When understood purely as a symbol, the Middle Chamber stands for that place in life in which we receive the rewards of our endeavours. This is the broadest sense of it. Its narrower sense, as found in the Second Degree lecture, is that it represents the wages of education, of mental culture, for learning is described as the peculiar work of the Fellow Craft. Learning stores the mind with facts, preserves one from bigotry and superstition, offers to one the fellowships of great minds, quickens perception, strengthens the faculties, gives one, in short, a masterful intellect. It is into the possession of such riches as these that the Winding Stairs of the Liberal Arts and Sciences bring a man at last.

We may rejoice that William Preston gave this teaching so large a place in our lectures, for without it Masonry would have been wholly inadequate as a complete system of life. Ignorance is a sin, in most cases at least, and the sooner we thus regard it the better will it be for all of us, Masons and profane. In olden days when men had so few opportunities for learning it was inevitable that the common man should be ignorant; but in these days, with public schools, correspondence schools, cheap books and periodicals, and free libraries, a man who remains content with not possessing the best that has been thought and said in the world is wholly without excuse. Always and everywhere should men have in the house of life a winding stair of art and of science up which to climb into a middle chamber wherein to hold converse with the good and great of all ages!

CHAPTER XXXIII

OPERATIVE AND SPECULATIVE

In mediæval times the builders were organised into a secret fraternity composed of separate lodges, which was for the purposes of self-protection, and for preserving the secrets of the trade; and men were given words, grips, and tokens on their admittance to a lodge. This fraternity had an ancient traditional history, and it used its tools and trade processes as emblems and symbols whereby to teach a code of morality far above the average ethical standards of the time. This was called Operative Masonry because its followers were engaged in the work of actual building.

At the time of the Reformation ecclesiastical building, in which the Freemasons were mostly engaged, fell into a decline. During the sixteenth and seventeenth centuries the Operative Lodges began to receive a large number of members who had no intention of practical building, but were attracted by the history and symbolism of the Order. In course of time this Speculative element outtopped the Operative so that, at the Revival of 1717, Masonry became wholly a Speculative Body.

The details of this picture may be filled out by a remarkable paragraph in Brother MacBride's "Speculative Masonry" (p. 124): "The view we wish to consider is, that down through the Roman Collegia and the Mediæval Craft Guilds, along with certain traditions, there was probably transmitted some of the symbolism of the Ancient Mysteries; and that the great quickening of intellectual life in the sixteenth century, resulting from the social and political upheaval of the Reformation, gave new life and a more developed form to the speculative element within the old Craft Lodges. The mental activities of men had so long been 'cribbed, cabined, and confined' under ecclesiastical rule that, having burst its bonds, it fairly revelled and rioted in all sorts of ways. Hence we find Kabbalism, Theosophy, Alchemy, and Astrology receiving attention and support from the learned scholars of the age. . . . The spirit of inquiry was rampant, and ill directed as it was in many respects, it had on the whole a wonderfully stimulating effect. Science, in all its branches, expanded and developed; literature, art, and social and political life, acquired fresh vigour. It is from this period that we can mark the presence of the speculative element in the old Craft Lodges. Our view is, that the seed of our present Speculative System, lying latent in these old lodges, was quickened into life through the influence of the Reformation period, and, later on, in 1717, developed into the present organised form."

On another page of the same work Brother MacBride gives a more specific description of the moral and symbolic germ in the craft guilds which later expanded into Speculative Masonry: "Taking the Old Charges, and reading them over, no one can fail to be impressed with the moral precepts they contain, and how the speculative bulks over the purely operative parts. In every case the Mason is charged first of all to be true to God, the King and to his fellows. Stealing and vice are explicitly named to be avoided. Falsehood and deceit are condemned and the general impression left after reading these ancient documents is, that they are not those of a mere trades union or operative guild. There is an element in them, apart from and above the operative work, that refers to conduct and morals, and it is in this, more than anything else, that their relationship with modern Masonry shows itself. After all, what is the purpose of our speculative system but to shape life and conduct to noble ends."

In these passages Brother MacBride takes the position that Speculative Masonry is the expansion of a germ that lay in Operative Masonry. Other writers, while holding this view, also believe that the non-operatives who were accepted during the sixteenth and seventeenth centuries brought with them an entirely new element. Brother A. E. Waite speaks for these writers in his booklet, "Deeper Aspects of Masonic Symbolism":

"The interest in Operative Masonry and its records, though historically it is of course important, has preceded from the beginning on a misconception as to the aims and symbolism of Speculative Masonry. It was and it remains natural, and it has not been without its results, but it is a confusion of the chief issues. It should be recognised henceforth that the sole connection between the two Arts and Crafts rests on the fact that the one has undertaken to uplift the other from the material plane to that of morals on the surface, and of spirituality in the real intention. . . . My position is that the traces of a symbolism which may in a sense be inherent in Operative Masonry did not produce, by a natural development, the Speculative Art and Craft, though they helped undoubtedly to make a possible and partially prepared field for the great adventure and experiment."

On another page of the same book Brother Waite contends that among the men who were accepted into the Operative Lodges were many "Latin-writing" scholars who brought with them ideas and symbolisms from Kabbalism and Rosicrucianism. With this position Albert pike and many other authorities agree.

Brother Waite's argument, it seems to me, does not contradict, but rather supplements, Brother MacBride's position. If this be the case, we may say that from Operative Masonry our Speculative System has received an organisation, a moral element, and certain emblems and symbols derived from the building art; but that there is an element of philosophy and mysticism in it, in the Third Degree more especially, is derived from other sources.

Leaving for other pages a discussion of the mystical and philosophical element, we may examine here only the elements inherited from the Operative Guilds. The Operative Mason used actual tools to erect structures of wood and stone; for this he received material wages. The Speculative Mason uses moral, mental, and spiritual forces to erect himself into a nobler manhood, and society into a nobler Brotherhood; his wages consist in the enrichment of his own and his race's life.

These words are familiar enough to every Mason; indeed they have become almost hackneyed and threadbare; but familiarity must not be permitted to blind us to the radical, I had almost said, the revolutionary, character of this teaching. For it implies that human nature may be modified, reformed, regenerated; and the world likewise. The cry of the reactionary, the obstructionist, the ultra-conservative, has ever been, "As the world is so has it always been, so will it always be. Poverty, ignorance, vice,—these are fated things, built into the nature of the race, and can in no wise be improved." Against this position Masonry throws itself with all its weight, and contends that out of the stuff of the Present a nobler Future can be made; that a man's nature is plastic material out of which a better man can be fashioned; that the world of to-day is a rough quarry out of which may be hewn the stones for a Temple of To-morrow, in which a God may be found to dwell. If his philosophy of Masonry be true, as we Masons are most profoundly convinced that it is, it gives us the one Great Hope of Man, the one certain pledge of Progress.

"Man is not man as yet,
Nor shall I deem his object served, his end
Attained, his genuine strength put fairly forth,
While only here and there a star dispels
The darkness, here and there a towering mind
O'erlooks its prostrate fellows.

"When all mankind is perfected;
Equal in full-blown powers—then, not till then,
I say, begins man's general infancy,
Such men are even now upon the earth
Serene amid the half-formed creatures 'round."
(Robert Browning.)

CHAPTER XXXIV

THE TWO GREAT PILLARS

I

Of all objects to which the candidate's attention is called as he begins his ascent to the Middle Chamber, none are more conspicuous, or more deserving of the most thorough investigation, than the Two Great Pillars which stand at the entrance. At one and the same time they guard the Sanctum from the outer world, and invite the Initiate into its mysteries; so noble in proportion, so intricate in design, so beautiful to see, they seem to keep solemn watch above the scene, as if to throw a hush of awe about the soul that would mount to the Upper Room of the Spirit. If throughout our history students of Masonry have surrounded them with a host of swarming theories more intricate than the network, and more multitudinous than the pomegranates it is because so many hints of ancient wisdom and secrets of symbolism have of old been hidden within these mighty columns. And if our own studies of the matter lead us to meanings numerous and almost conflicting we need not worry about it, for a symbol that says but one thing is hardly a symbol at all.

It was the custom of many of the most primitive peoples, as Frazer describes so abundantly in his "Golden Bough," to set up stones about their huts, and their villages, and over the graves of their dead. In some cases these crude rock pillars were thought to be the abodes of gods or demons; in others, homes of the ghosts; and often as symbols of sex. Of the last-named usage one writer has said that "pillars of stone, when associated with worship, have been from time immemorial regarded as symbols of the active and passive, the generative and fecundating principles." In Egypt, Horus and Sut were regarded as two living pillars, twin builders and supporters of the heavens, and Sir Arthur Evans has shown that pillars "were everywhere worshipped as gods." "In India, and among the Mayas and Incas," we read in "The Builders," "there were three pillars at the portals of the earthly and skyey temple—Wisdom, Strength, and Beauty. When man set up a pillar, he became a fellow worker with Him whom the old sages of China used to call the first Builder. Also, pillars were set up to mark the holy places of vision and Divine deliverance, as when Jacob erected a pillar at Bethel, Joshua at Gilgal, and Samuel at Mizpeh and Shen. Always they were symbols of stability, of what the Egyptians described as 'the place of establishing forever'—emblem of the faith 'that the pillars of the earth are the Lords,' and He hath set the world upon them."

"In all countries," remarks another writer, "as the earliest of man's work we recognise the sublime, mysteriously speaking, ever recurring monolith": but by no people were pillars so venerated, or so variously used as by the Egyptians. Originally, perhaps, they served as astronomical instruments to mark the time, to denote the stages of the heavenly bodies, and to assist in the orienting of temples. Connected with the places of worship they were gradually associated with the gods, and became in time symbols of deity, as we may learn from Professor Breasted's "History of the Development of Religion and Thought in Ancient Egypt," in which delightful book he tells us that the obelisk, as Egyptians called the pillar, came at last to stand pre-eminently for the great Sun God.

This veneration of upstanding stones answered so deep a need in man's habits of worship that it proved to be one of the last forms of idolatry to give way before Monotheism, the worship of the One Invisible God. The Israelites, as the Bible witnesses, cling stubbornly to their "stocks and stones," reverence for which they may have learned in Egypt during their long sojourn there; and even in Christian countries the custom remained with such tenacity that the Lateran Council formally prohibited stone worship as late at 452.

From Egypt, it is said, the custom of placing Pillars before temples was borrowed by the Phœnicians, but this has been somewhat disputed; be that as it may, we know that Hiram of Tyre erected two great columns before his magnificent temple of Melkarth, where Herodotus saw them five centuries afterwards. It was these, perhaps, that served Hiram as models for the more famous Pillars which he erected before the Temple of Solomon.

Of these Pillars one description is in the Book of Kings, another in the Book of Chronicles. In the former record the height is given as eighteen cubits; in the latter as thirty-five; if a cubit be accepted as denoting eighteen inches, the former height would be twenty-seven, the latter fifty-two and one-half feet, a variation of twenty-five feet. To explain this discrepancy scholars have supposed Kings to give the height of only one, Chronicles the combined height of both, leaving allowances for the sockets of the head-pieces. Concerning these head-pieces, historians have differed, but none have given a clearer explanation than Mackey:

"Above the pillar, and covering its upper part to the depth of nine inches, was an oval body or chapiter seven feet and a half in height. Springing out from the pillar, at the junction of the chapiter with it, was a row of lotus petals, which, first spreading around the chapiter, afterwards gently curved downward towards the pillar, something like the Acanthus leaves on the capital of a Corinthian column. About two-fifths of the distance from the bottom of the chapiter, or just below its most bulging part, a tissue of network was carved, which extended over its whole upper surface. To the bottom of this network was suspended a series of fringes, and on these again were carved two rows of pomegranates, one hundred being in each row."

II

The Pillars were cylindrical in shape, probably, and were cast of brass, and the combined weight must have been not less than fifty-three tons. One of them was called Boaz, the other Jachin, and the former stood in the northeast corner of the Porch, the latter in the southeast; Jachin was the right pillar, Boaz the left, and this means that right and left have reference to one standing inside the Temple, which faced the East. According to the tradition, the Pillars were cast in foundries situated between Succoth and Zeredatha, about thirty-five miles northeast of Jerusalem, whose moulders and jewellers still use clay brought from that region.

The network about the chapiter was probably an ornamental lattice work of metal, though some think it was an interlacing of branches or vines. The lily-work, doubtless, was a formal design, made to represent a species of the Egyptian lotus, a sacred plant among the dwellers of the Nile and much used by them. There were no globes on these Pillars, though the chapiters themselves were spherical; the globes were added at a late date by some Masonic ritualist, Preston it may be.

Those Pillars, strange to say, were not often copied by mediæval builders, though they seem to have been imitated in the Cathedral of Notre Dame, at Poitiers, erected in 1161; and in the Wurtzburg Cathedral, in Bavaria, the work, it seems, of the Comacines. But at a very early date they were used by Masons for symbolical purposes, as testified by the history of the Compagnonage, and by the "Old Charges" of the Freemasons.

In the latter we find a curious legend. The Cooke MS. of about 1350 relates that before Noah's flood, Jabal, Jubal, and Tubal Cain knew that God was to destroy the world; "wherefore they wrote the sciences that they had found out on two pillars of stone. Hermes, that was son to Cush, afterwards found the two pillars, and the sciences written thereon; and Abraham taught them to the Egyptians." Inasmuch as it was supposed that Masonry had come from Egypt the old chronicles thus quaintly sought to link their traditions up to the very beginnings of the world. From these Old Charges, we may suppose, the legend crept into the symbolic lore of the Craft, and was thus preserved until Speculative days, when the Pillar symbolism became embodied in the Rituals as we now have them.

It has often been shown that in the descriptions and interpretations given in our work of the Pillars there are many inaccuracies and inconsistencies. Thus, only fourteen American jurisdictions use the Pillars as being eighteen cubits in height; one jurisdiction makes them thirty, and twenty-seven make them thirty-five! Thirty-five cubits is a lofty height indeed and would make the Pillars entirely out of proportion to a Temple that was only ninety feet long and thirty feet wide! But such inaccuracies as these, historical and architectural, need not trouble us if we will but keep in mind the fact that with us the Pillars have become symbols of truth, and that errors of fact do not touch the hidden meanings.

What are these hidden meanings? William Preston saw in them a reference to the Pillar of Cloud and the Pillar of Fire by which, it is said, the Israelites were guided, and accordingly made them to stand for Providence. This is ingenious but altogether out of harmony with the long historical use of the emblems, for no other interpreter had ever found such meanings in them. Caldecott believed that the Jewish king stood before one Pillar in public ceremonies and the High Priest before the other, and that the Pillars consequently stand for Government and Religion in society. Brother Covey-Crump, writing in the *Transactions of the Authors' Lodge*, vol. I, made them to stand for Space and Time, the two pillars through which the human mind passes into knowledge; of similar character is the other reading which sees in them the two tropics of Cancer and Capricorn. Mackey, reasoning from their names, Jachin, which means, "He shall establish," and Boaz, "In it is strength," makes them to mean the strength and the stability of Masonry.

Many of the old Jewish Rabbis, afterwards followed by the Kabbalists, found in them the symbolism of birth; as one wrote: "The names of the pillars signified potency and perpetuity; the pomegranates on their capitals or chapiters were symbols of generation." With this, after everything is taken into consideration, I am inclined to agree. Being properly stationed at the door of the lodge room, or on the Porch of the Temple, they signify entrance, for it is through them that the candidate passes to his initiation, and Initiation, as we have already seen, is birth into a new life.

When thus understood the Two Pillars represent a law that applies throughout the world of men, as well as in the lodge, and that in a sense not at all far-fetched. We have learned that many of our human ills spring from bad heredity and come to us in birth, and not until men are well born will they be well men, sound in body and soul. And what is true of birth into life is also true of any new birth into any of the realms of life. If the pillars at the door of the family be strong and clean the child will be wholesome and happy in its life therein. If wise men guard the doorways of the schools our youth will enter into the mind's world of light and power, but not otherwise. For always is it, that if one would anywhere become a Master he must make a right entrance into Life's Temple. And he who thus lives will himself become a Pillar, strengthened and strengthening, against which Kings and Priests may lean, and past which others may be enabled to enter into the life that is life indeed. Woe be it to human society, if ever it neglects to give, in any of its spheres, right birth to its children, its seekers and learners!

CHAPTER XXXV

THE GLOBES

On the top of each of the Two Pillars thus described stand two Globes, one, the Celestial, representing the heavens; the other, the Terrestrial, representing the earth. Whence came these? and what do they signify?

In answer to the first of these questions our scholars have offered two hypotheses: first, that they are of Egyptian origin; second, that they are a modified form of the chapiters, or head-pieces, of the Two Pillars. The first of these theories was evidently suggested by the ancient Egyptian symbol of the winged globe, often found on the entablature above a temple surrounded by a snake holding its tail in its mouth and flanked by two wide, outstretched wings. So common was this device that it became at last one of the national emblems, so that Isaiah speaks of Egypt as "the land of the winged globe." This globe was in all probability oval in shape, to suggest the egg, symbol of life; the serpent was the symbol of infinity; the wings, of power; combined, the figure stood for the infinite life-giving power of Deity. If it be supposed that the globe was a true circle, as some contend that it was, instead of an oval then it may have represented the Sun, the first great god of Egypt, but the meaning remains practically the same.

If our two Globes could be made to serve as a modern form of the Egyptian winged globe they might be enriched in meaning and interest, but there is no evidence whatever that the older symbol ever transmigrated into Masonry. The probability is all against it, for we have two globes instead of one, and we do not have the serpent or the wings; besides, as actually exhibited, our Globes manifestly refer to the earth and the heavens as modernly understood.

The chapiters on the Two Pillars were spherical in shape and always so represented. It would evidently seem, therefore, that the men who framed our present Ritual of the Second Step, among whom Preston was conspicuous, simply modified the chapiters into Globes. But why did they do this? Because Preston and his circle undertook to transform the lodge into a school and consequently required symbols for geography and astronomy, two very important branches of the curriculum they outlined. This theory is verified, it seems to me, by reference to the Prestonian lectures, in which we find the following paragraphs, as slightly abridged by Webb:

"The sphere, with the parts of the earth delineated on its surface, is called the Terrestrial Globe; and that with the constellations, and other heavenly bodies, the Celestial Globe.

"The principal use of the Globes, besides serving as maps to distinguish the outward parts of the earth, and the situation of the fixed stars, is to illustrate and explain the phenomena arising from the annual revolution and the diurnal rotation of the earth around its own axis. *They are the noblest instruments for improving the mind* [this was Preston's motive—H.L.H.], and giving it the most distinct idea of any problem or proposition, as well as enabling it to solve the same."

Some of our writers have ridiculed all this. They say that the use now made of the globes is schoolboyish. Perhaps! but even so, the idea behind it all is sound and worthy of serious consideration. It is good to think about this marvellous planet on which we live, and it is good to gaze into the heavens by which we are surrounded. The heavens and the earth together, this is the Universe, the All-Thing as the old Norsemen called it, the contemplation of which, as old Samuel Kant once confessed, fills one with unspeakable awe. If a man cannot feel reverence in the presence of all that which is represented by the Two Globes there is something lacking out of his nature.

CHAPTER XXXVI

THE ASCENT

I

The Three, Five and Seven Steps have long been a puzzle to the candidate and a problem to Masonic writers; in the present connection there is no need that we go into the erudite debates that have circled about the matter, because our main concern is with that living and practical truth of which the stairs are a symbol.

Whence came this symbolism? To that question many answers have been offered, some ingenious, but none very convincing. Any discussion of origin is valuable only as it throws light on the symbol itself.

Some scholars have contended, though not in recent years, that there was a winding stair of three, five and seven steps in Solomon's temple itself. It is thought that at the Gate Nicanor there was a semi-circular stairway leading from one court to another, and that it was on the successive steps of this stair that the Levites chanted the fifteen "Psalms of Degrees," specimens of which remain in the Book of Psalms. But the archæologists who have learned most about the Temple as it actually existed are generally agreed that this stairway could not have been the prototype of the three, five and seven steps as we find them in our Second Degree. Sir Charles Warren, as eminent in archæology as he is in Masonry, writes that "there was a winding staircase, certainly, but this led to little cells or chambers a few feet square in the thickness of the Temple walls, in which the functionaries [temple attendants] kept their stores for the votive offerings." ("A.Q.C.," vol. 1, p. 42.)

Other scholars have opined that the steps were originally the same in the Masonic system as the Theological Ladder, and had the same historical origin. This Theological Ladder, which appears on our Tracing Board, and represents by its seven rungs the three theological virtues of Faith, Hope and Charity, and the four cardinal virtues of Temperance, Fortitude, Prudence, and Justice, was introduced into the Ritual it is thought by Martin Clare in 1732. This ladder was made to stand for the progress of the soul from the earthly to the heavenly and it was looked upon as a Masonic type of a similar symbol used in several of the Ancient Mysteries (especially in Mithraism), in Brahminism, etc., and it was generally held to be, in its strictly Masonic form, a suggestion of that Ladder which Jacob saw in his vision, up and down which the angels came and went. Inasmuch as this Theological Ladder symbolised progress, just as does the Winding Stair, some have argued that the latter symbol must have come from the same sources as the former. This interpretation of the matter may be plausible enough, and it may help toward an interpretation of both symbols, but it suffers from an almost utter lack of tangible evidence.

Other scholars of more modern views believe that the Winding Stair symbol may have been devised by Operative Masons during the Saxon period in England. It seems that the numbers, three, five and seven were in the air, so to speak, at that time as is proved by Gould, who gives examples to show that these numbers were grouped together in laws, religious doctrines, superstitions, etc., "with startling frequency," especially during the years 449–1066. But this latter date, it will be seen, is some two centuries earlier than our oldest Masonic record, consequently there can be no hope of tracing the Winding Stair symbol to that time with any degree of accuracy.

Thus it is that we are thrown back upon conjecture. Accepting that alternative we may believe that the Stairway was first used simply because it was a necessary part of the symbolic temple of the Second Degree. Here were the pillars standing at the entrance on the porch; yonder was the Middle Chamber, on a higher level; some means of ascent was obviously needed to get the candidate from one to another.

II

But the difficulties in the way of accounting for the origin of the symbol need not perplex us while searching for an interpretation, for that is plain; the mystical use of numbers in the Ascent suggests to us that the climb itself is a divine task, worthy of the noblest in man; the stair as a whole is a symbol of the progress of a man from the low level of natural ignorance toward that high level of spiritual power and insight symbolised by the Middle Chamber.

The number Fifteen itself cannot have much mystical significance because it is another one of those dreaded "American innovations" which have given so much scandal to certain interpreters. In some eighteenth century tracing boards the stair is composed of only five steps, in others of seven. Preston divided them into one, three, five, seven, nine and eleven, making thirty-six in all. The Hemming lectures, which replaced Preston's at the time of the Union, struck out the group of eleven steps, thus reducing the number to twenty-five. The American Ritual, in turn, further reduced the number to fifteen by striking out the one and the nine. Albert Pike was of the opinion that the nine should have been retained because he believed that the series three, five, seven and nine had a very ancient and very precious meaning. "As long ago as the time of Zarathustra," he writes, "the Irano-Aryan Soldier and King of Bactria, five thousand years or more before our era, [this date is most certainly wrong.—H.L.H.] the *Barecura*, or bundle of twigs used in the sacrifices, were bound by three, five, seven and nine twigs, and even then the number seven had a peculiar significance." I consider it a fine thing that the architects of the House of the Temple at Washington, which is a monument to Albert Pike and headquarters of the Scottish Rite of the Southern Jurisdiction, have divided the steps that lead from the street to the entrance of that noble building into groups of three, five, seven and nine. But while it may possibly be true that the original symbolism should have contained the group of nine, the Winding Stair as it now exists in the Second Degree can never be changed; to do so would dislocate the entire structure of the Ritualism of the Second Degree, and it is doubtful if the additional group would give us any additional meanings.

From ancient times numbers have been much employed in symbolism as is proved by the records of all the ancient nations, philosophies, and religions. For one reason or another, too complicated to explain here, the even numbers were usually made to denote earthly or human things while the odd numbers were revered as expressions or suggestions of divine or heavenly truths. This was not the case invariably because the early Christians used 888 as the number of Jesus; but even they made 666 to stand for the human or demoniac and 777 to mean absolute perfection. It is now believed that the "number of the beast" spoken of in the Book of Revelation, and given as 666 in our Authorised version was really 616, which was the numerical value of the words "Kaisar Theos," or "God Cæsar," and referred to the worship of the emperor. At any rate, with few exceptions, number symbolism has always made the odd number to suggest that which is divine or very noble and as such we may understand the use of the odd numbers, three, five and seven. An old Roman historian of architecture notes that ancient temples were nearly always approached by an odd number of steps because they led to the divine precincts.

The Three, or triad, or ternary, is found scores of times throughout the Ritual, and it is bodied forth in the Triangle, the symbol of Deity. It would be impossible in the present space even to hint at the wealth of instances in which the Triad occurs in the various symbolic systems of the past; we must satisfy ourselves with the following paragraph from Pierson's "Traditions of Freemasonry.

"The ternary [or triad] is the first of unequal numbers. The triad, mysterious number, which plays so great a part in the traditions of Asia, the philosophy of Plato, the mysteries of all ages, an image of the Supreme Being, includes in itself the properties of the two first numbers [that is—1 plus 2, equals 3.—H.L.H.]. It was to philosophers the most excellent and favourite number, a mysterious type, revered by all antiquity and consecrated in the mysteries; wherefore there are but three essential degrees among Masons, who venerate in the triangle the most august mystery—that of the Sacred Triad, object of their homage and study."

III

Concerning the number five I cannot do better than give Mackey's interpretations, as found in his Encyclopædia, Volume I:

"Among the Pythagoreans *five* was a mystical number, because it was formed by the union of the first even number and the first odd, rejecting unity; and hence it symbolised the mixed conditions of order and disorder, happiness and misfortune, life and death. The same union of the odd and even, or male and female, numbers made it the symbol of marriage. Among the Greeks it was a symbol of the world, because, says Diodorus, it represented ether and the four elements. It was a sacred round number among the Hebrews. In Egypt, India, and other Oriental nations, says Gesenius, the five minor planets and the five elements and elementary powers were accounted sacred. It was the *pentas* of the Gnostics and the Hermetic Philosophers; it was the symbol of their quintessence, the fifth or highest essence of power in a natural body. In Masonry, five is a sacred number, inferior only in importance to three and seven. It is especially significant in the Fellow-Craft's Degree, where five are required to hold a lodge, and where, in the Winding Stairs, the five steps are referred to the orders of architecture and the human senses. In the Third Degree we find the reference to the five points of fellowship and their symbol, the five-pointed star. Geometry, too, which is deemed synonymous with Masonry, is called the fifth science; and in fact, throughout nearly all the degrees of Masonry, we find abundant allusions to five as a sacred and mystical number."

The number seven usually stands for perfection, and it may not be without meaning that in the V.S.L. it occurs, as one writer has said, "an incredible number of times." During the mediaeval period knowledge was usually divided among seven branches of learning; first was a group of three, called the trivium and composed of grammar, rhetoric, and logic; secondly was the quadrivium, which comprised arithmetic, geometry, music, and astronomy. It is interesting to observe how our monitorial interpretation of the third group of steps preserves this old idea. Gould says that during the same period these seven "sciences" were thought of as "a number of steps leading to virtue, and finally to heaven."

Let us now glance first at the group of three steps. The most familiar explanation of them is that they represent the Three Degrees or the three principal officers of the lodge. In either case the first three steps suggest to the candidate that he is being helped on his way by an organised fraternity, represented by the degrees or the officers. Does not this have much to tell us? Is not this one of the prime functions of Masonry? Instead of leaving the individual to climb on alone it surrounds him with its inspiration and its help, as the organised public school stands back of the child that begins the ascent to an education. No individual Mason need fail in his attempt to lead a manly life; a world-wide brotherhood, with its almost inexhaustible resources, is at hand to help him. Have you kept that in mind during dark days? No Mason climbs alone, even from the start; the entire Order, sensitive to his needs, and responsive to his call is ever ready to help him on and up.

If we glance at the next group of five steps we find another teaching, equally valuable and quite as practicable, a teaching that has more boldness in it than appears on the surface. Let us agree with the Monitor that this group of steps now represents to us (whatever it may have originally meant) the five senses; in other words, our physical body with its organs, functions, and faculties. What does this mean? Is it not this, that the very body itself, when kept in control by thorough discipline and when trained by education, may be a stepping stone toward the highest life? This was an exceedingly bold teaching when first promulgated, for it was at a time when religious teachers and moralists were telling people that the body was evil in itself and must be put under foot. Masonry does not despise the physical, but urges us to prepare it so as to serve as a stairway toward the noblest life.

The third group of seven steps is interpreted as referring to the liberal arts and sciences; in other words, we are told that right learning and culture of the mind will lead us up and on. This is a teaching as badly needed now as ever because so many men tend to make light of knowledge, or to excuse themselves for not having it. But Masonry condemns this attitude, teaching us as it does in other connections as well as in this that ignorance is a sin. If we lay our prejudices aside here and are brave enough to face the facts I believe that we must agree with Masonry. We may say that we have no time to read, or to learn; the fallacy of this is proved by the number of men about us who are as busy as we yet manage to get an education in odd moments. We may say that we have not the opportunities for securing an education, that we cannot go to school, or that we cannot buy books. We do not need to go to school; we can turn our bedroom into a school and be our own teacher, like Elihu Burritt, or Benjamin Franklin, or David Livingstone. Nor do we need to buy books; they can always be borrowed from public libraries or from our friends. When we remember how superstition, crime, fanaticism, disease, poverty, and kindred evils grow out of ignorance we can well afford to study again the lessons of the Winding Stairs.

The Winding Stair, as a whole, is a symbol of progress. When is a man progressing? Let Ruskin answer: "He alone is advancing in life whose heart is getting softer, whose blood warmer, whose brain quicker, whose spirit is entering into living peace." In spite of the Great War, which for so long dragged its bloody coils across the world, we may still believe that the race progresses, that

> "Step by step since time began
> We see the steady gain of man."

But we must not fall into the error of measuring progress by merely mechanical achievements as the custom is; the race as a race goes forward only as mankind as a whole becomes possessed of those qualities described by Ruskin. Do you not believe that Masonry has a leading rôle to play in this real progress of man? Can you think of a better recipe for advancement than Masonry's—to unite with others for co-operation, to control the passions and discipline the faculties, to enlighten the mind, and to keep ever before one a great ideal, as is suggested by the Holy of Holies?

CHAPTER XXXVII

THE BUILDERS

I

In the foregoing section I interpreted the group of five steps as alluding to the five senses, as the Monitorial lectures suggest; but these same lectures also make the five steps to allude to the Five Orders of Architecture, and it is to this that we must now devote our attention. In so doing we must remember that Preston's great idea in the formation of the lectures just here was to give to the candidate certain useful information which the average man of his day was unable to get elsewhere; in our times such matters are taught in the public schools and a man does not go to lodge for instruction. Some have criticised this lecture because the division of Architecture into Five Orders is no longer countenanced by Architects themselves; be that as it may, we need not quarrel over details, for it was a wise insight that led Preston to devote so much space to the builder's art, seeing that it is the one art that has given most to Masonry, even as it is still the art that furnishes Masonry with most of its symbols and illustrations. So while we may ignore a discussion of the Five Orders (though such a discussion would not be fruitless by any means and might be carried out by a Masonic Study Club with great profit) we cannot afford to omit from our study some reflections on architecture as a whole and its meanings for the Masonic life.

Perhaps the one man of modern times who, next to Ruskin, has written most beautifully of architecture, is William Morris, a great prophet who, though not a member of the Fraternity, blazed and throbbed with the spirit which is the soul of Masonry. One of his biographers (Clutton-Brook) says that "for him the great art was always architecture; for in that he saw use made beautiful and the needs of man ennobled by their manner of satisfying them." When we ask Morris to give us a definition of this "great art" we have the following as his reply:

"A true architectural work is a building duly provided with all necessary furniture, decorated with all due ornament, according to the use, quality and dignity of the building, from mere mouldings or abstract lines, to the great epical works of sculpture and painting, which, except as decorations of the nobler forms of such buildings, cannot be produced at all."

In this definition Morris contends that a building deserving of the name of architecture must satisfy physical needs and that it must also satisfy the need for beauty. Only a structure satisfying both needs can be called architecture; therefore a mere pergola which is ornamental only, or a pigsty, which is practical only, cannot be described as architecture.

When we turn to a study of the art of building we find that Morris' definition is borne out by facts, for always, from the first rude hut down to the last erected dwelling house or public building, men have made their buildings to house both the mind and the body. The stately structures of the ancient world were houses, books, monuments, statues, creeds, and dreams all in one; "the solemn colonades at Thebes, and the graceful dignity of the Parthenon," tell us what men hoped and believed as well as how they lived. In the Middle Ages it was the same, for throughout that long period architecture was the very mother of all the arts; "it stood above all other arts, and made all others subservient to it. It commanded the services of the most brilliant intellects, and the greatest artists." Always a great building is more than a building; it is a human document; and a man might recover the history of the life of man upon the earth from the records left us in the ruins and remains of his architecture, so completely has man embodied his soul in the work of his hands.

"For, whatever else man may have been—cruel, tyrannous, vindictive—his buildings always have reference to religion. They bespeak a vivid sense of the Unseen and his awareness of his relation to it. As you travel through Europe, what arrests you most are the glorious cathedrals which tell of the faith of the past. One can read the history of Christianity, of its bewildering varieties, of its contradictions and oppositions, of the secrets of its life, in its buildings. The story of the Tower of Babel is not a fable. Man has ever been trying to build to heaven, embodying his prayer and dream in brick and stone. And as he wrought his faith and vision into stone, it was but natural that the tools of the builder should become the emblems of the thoughts of the thinker. Not only his tools, but his temples themselves are symbols of that House of Doctrine, that Home of the Soul, which, though unseen, he is building in the midst of the years."

II

"That Home of the Soul." In these words we have the secret of Masonry's use of architecture. No longer are we, as Masons, interested in the building of material structures, but we are using the builder's tools and methods, hallowed by long use, enriched by ancient associations, and found appropriate through centuries of experience, as symbols and types of a building work of a different kind, even a great structure of truth and love wherein brethren may dwell in unity and joy. Not arbitrarily have we chosen these symbols, for men have so used them from the earliest times, as may be learned from very ancient books, the Holy Bible especially, which is full of allusions, references and metaphors, drawn from the builder's art. And this emblematic use of tools which was so instructive to early man is equally instructive now as one may learn from a study of our daily language. How often do expressions, words, and phrases, borrowed from architecture, spring to our lips! "Edification," "constructive," "solid foundation," "well founded," "roof of the world," "floor of the seas," "the walls of creation," "the windows of heaven," "erect," "construct," "raise," "edify": one could extend such a list indefinitely, for we use the ideas of building up or tearing down almost every day of our lives, and almost always, be it noted, we use the builder in a good sense, and the tearer-down in a bad sense. There is something appropriate, in the nature of things, in the intimate relation between the message of Masonry and the language of architecture. This is not to forget, of course, that there is also a historical connection between the two, for one grew out of the other; but even had there been no such actual relationships the two arts, that of the Builder and that of the Mason, respectively, have so much in common as to ideals and methods that the latter has a native right to employ the terms and symbols of the former.

What is a Mason, if not an architect of the mystical order? Insofar as he is true to his Royal Art he is one engaged in building up within himself a real, but viewless, Temple; its foundations laid deep in character, its walls formed of the solid stuff of genuine manhood, its roof the stately dome of truth, its spires the upreaching of that aspiration toward a Higher which was the original inspiration of every great cathedral. This is no fanciful picture or collection of high sounding words; you and I have both known of brethren, have we not, formed by their Masonic fellowships and inspired by their Masonic ideals to be with whom was itself an act of worship? Truly such men are Temples, Temples not made with hands!

What is Masonry itself if not a world-builder, a social architecture on the grand style? With its fellowships established in every nation under heaven, its activities never ceasing night or day, its message uttered in nearly all the languages of the race but always the same message, it is one of the mightiest, one of the most benign, one of the most constructive of all forces in the world. When its work is finished, which will not be until the end is ended, it will have proved itself a builder of an unseen cathedral more noble, more enduring, than any ever made of stone.

CHAPTER XXXVIII

THE FIVE SENSES

I

All the emotions and thoughts aroused in me on the night I took my "Second" are still fresh in my memory after these many years, but nothing remains more vividly than my surprise at the elaborate lecture about the Five Senses. "What," I kept saying to myself, "does all this mean? In what possible way can our sense apparatus have anything to do with the Masonic life?" I remained nonplused over the matter until I began to ask myself what part these senses play in life outside Masonry and then it dawned upon me that the Ritual would be incomplete were it to omit the Senses from the scope of its illumination. I began to see that an interpreter could write whole libraries about the senses from the Masonic point of view; and I began to believe that it would require a long lifetime for a man thoroughly to *Masonize* his Five Senses.

Consider the part played by the Senses in a Man's life! At the centre of the man is his consciousness, a lonely, isolated, invisible centre of awareness; outside the man, surrounding him on all sides, is the universe, with its limitless number of things and happenings; the senses are nothing other than the channels—perhaps the only channels—through which the outside universe gets into man's consciousness. He is an island; the senses are the bridges over which he passes to the mainland, and over which the mainland sends its messages into him. Every impression, every experience, every sensation, every word must pass by way of them. If you could control a man's senses then you would be able to determine how much of the universe gets into him and how much of him gets into the universe. This is the idea at the bottom of the great series of wall paintings in the Congressional Library at Washington wherein a picture is devoted to each sense. Since this is true it follows that the man who would make his mind the home of goodness, truth, and beauty, will be the one who sees to it that his senses are trained to do their work effectively, and that he permits nothing to travel back and forth over their bridges except that which is good, or true, or beautiful.

II

This, I take it, is the chief point made in the Second Degree lecture; a Mason is to make his five senses into five points of contact with his fellows by seeing to it that only good-will, kindliness, and all the fine things of brotherhood are permitted to travel back and forth between him and them. This implies the further point—and it is one that we shall need to elaborate—that the senses, like every other faculty of a man, may be trained and improved, so that the man who has been making a bad use of them can learn to make a good use. If this seems far-fetched or even impossible to us we need only direct our attention to each sense in turn to be convinced that it is always being done.

"What is more or less than a touch?" says Walt Whitman. Touch is the first, or original sense, and is employed in the lowest forms of life, such as the jelly-fish, long before separate organs are dreamed of. As the living creature grows more and more responsive to the world outside it the general sense of touch grows more and more defined until it gradually breaks itself up into the other senses of smelling, tasting, seeing, and hearing, and by so doing the creature rises in the scale of life. From one point of view, at least, it is not too much to say that the whole process of physical evolution consists of splitting up the general sense of touch and of refining and specialising each of the split-offs. Even when we get to man, the highest in the scale, this development and improvement of the sense of touch need not stop; a musician or an artist can carry the development of it to the utmost limit of refinement.

At the back of the tongue is a series of little organs, called taste-buds; when any object is brought against them they give to the consciousness a feeling of flavour. This sense, also, may be developed. Only a few days ago I watched a "tea taster" at work determining the quality of various kinds of tea. He sat at a revolving table on which were several cups of the beverage from each of which he sipped in turn; it was only a mouthful but it sufficed because his taste-buds were so accurate that he could tell where the tea had been grown and what it was worth.

In lower animals the sense of smell is often unimaginably acute. Henri Fabre describes a moth which can detect the presence of another rods away in a forest at night merely by the odour. This is the sense of smell raised to the nth degree of acuteness, for the naturalist himself was unable to detect the slightest odour even in a jar full of the insects. We cannot smell as the animals can because we do not need to; nevertheless, like the other senses, one can develop this faculty, as is demonstrated by the perfumery expert who can detect the various kinds and grades of perfumery quite as easily as my tea taster can judge of tea.

When we make sounds, either by speaking or by striking against some object, waves travel through the atmosphere in all directions; when these waves strike against the tympanum of the ear they give us the experience of hearing, so that hearing itself is a kind of touch. The extent to which hearing can be developed and educated is shown by the expert musician who can detect subtle variations of sound wholly lost on others of us.

III

"Seeing is touch at a distance." The sun, or some artificial light, sends waves through the ether; these strike against the retina of the eye and give us the sense of seeing. If the waves are of one length and speed we see one colour; if of another we see a different colour. The Indian who can see an antelope grazing afar off on the prairie, the pilot who can detect the smoke of a coming ship in the remote distance, are examples of men who have raised this sense to an extraordinary degree of perfection.

In this discussion, which may seem to some almost schoolboyish, I have had it in mind to emphasise the fact that we humans have a considerable degree of control over our senses, and that, if we choose, we can improve them by right training. From the point of view of general culture this means that we can greatly enrich our lives, and that is surely worth while; from the point of view of Masonry, which is necessarily our chief concern, it means that the senses may be so used as to Masonize our lives. The candidate is urged to touch, taste, or smell nothing that would injure himself or brethren: he is, in the language of the V.S.L., to "take heed how he hears," lest some word of slander against a brother be given admission to his mind; and he is to see nothing in his fellows except their better selves. How much it would mean to every lodge, by way of avoiding friction and of increasing brotherhood, if every Mason would train his senses to ignore the things that divide or injure, and to heed only those things that increase brotherly love! This is a high ideal, truly, but, then, Masonry itself is a high ideal!

CHAPTER XXXIX

THE LIBERAL ARTS AND SCIENCES

I

The educators of the Middle Ages taught seven branches of learning in their school and these were divided as I have already said, into two groups, the first of which was called the "trivium" (meaning "where three roads meet"), and the second, "quadrivium" ("where four roads meet"). Grammar, rhetoric, and logic, comprised the former group usually, and it was these subjects that the young student in college first studied: the latter group included arithmetic, music, astronomy, and geometry. When all of these subjects were mastered the man was said to have a "liberal education" and the school in which they were taught was called (as it still is) a "college of liberal arts."

This educational system was in vogue when the earliest Operative lodges were practising, and it was inevitable that the Masons, who refused to permit their guild to become a mere labour organisation, should incorporate the Liberal Arts and Sciences into their schemes of study and in their literature. Brother Conder informs us that as early as the fourteenth century the London Society of Masons "required the Master Mason to be acquainted with the seven liberal sciences." In the "Ahiman Rezon," a book of constitutions much used by the "Ancients" in the eighteenth century, we have a reminiscence of this in the following bit of doggerel:

"The grammer rules instruct the tongue and pen,
Rhetoric teaches eloquence to men;
By logic we are taught to reason well,
Music has claims beyond our power to tell;
The use of numbers, numberless we find;
Geometry gives measure to mankind.
The heavenly system elevates the mind.
All those, and many secrets more,
The Masons taught in days of yore."

This doggerel is really a free paraphrase of a few lines from the oldest of our Manuscripts, written about 1390, and it goes to show that for four or five centuries the arts and sciences had held a prominent place in the thought, as well as in the ritual and constitutions, of Freemasons.

In the beginning of the eighteenth century the Liberal Arts and Sciences were embedded in the First Degree after the revision of the ritual they were moved to the Second Degree, where they very naturally served Preston's scheme for making this degree a short course of instruction. There they still remain; if they can no longer fulfil Preston's great purpose they may still very fittingly serve to remind us of the place which such culture must have in the life of every complete and well-furnished Mason.

To enter into any detailed analysis of the seven subjects is obviously impossible here, though it might prove more interesting than we would think; but we may well ask ourselves, why are these arts and sciences set in the middle of the Ritual? Why do the Lectures devote so much space to them? What possible connection can they have with a man's Masonic life? I believe that we can find a satisfactory answer to these questions by recalling a bit of history.

During the so-called Dark Ages what few scholars there were in Europe devoted themselves almost entirely to studies that had little or no connection with human life; they debated such questions as, What are the attributes of Deity? What are angels? What are demons? What is being? What is existence? How many angels can stand on the point of a needle? etc. After the great Revival of Learning had come, with its rediscovery of history, of nature, of human life, and of classical literature, the scholars turned from the old subjects to themes that were nearer to life—history, the arts, science, politics, and so on. The men who took up these studies were called Humanists because they were more interested in questions related to the life and needs of humanity than they were to the dry-as-dust discussion of metaphysics; and they urged in favour of their new studies that they would "humanise" men who would pursue them.

II

I believe that Masonry is justified in retaining the Liberal Arts and Sciences in its Ritual just because they still have power to humanise us, to "improve us in social intercourse," to make us broader of mind, more tolerant in opinion, more humane in action, and more brotherly in conduct.

Besides, knowledge of them, even a little knowledge of them, can make us more useful to the lodge. The brother who understands enough grammar to write a paper to be read to his brethren; who has studied enough rhetoric to learn how to speak well in open lodge; who has so disciplined his mind by logic as to think straight and clear without prejudice or passion; who has an appreciation of a fine art like music so as to be mellowed and softened by the charm it throws about one's personality; who has had his mental outlook broadened and his store of knowledge enriched so as to have useful information to place at the disposal of the Craft; such a brother, it seems to me, is one who exemplifies the Masonic love of light.

We may go a step further. Suppose a lodge member is critical, captious, fault-finding, prejudiced, and ignorant; he adds nothing to the Brotherhood and he is a cause of trouble. If the lodge could persuade him to ascend the seven steps of the arts and sciences consider how it would affect him; his prejudice and vanity would drop away, for these are fruits of ignorance; his captiousness would vanish, for that comes from a lack of culture; his enlarged mind would make him more tolerant of others' opinions and more patient with others' faults, for great knowledge always begets humility. The man who has captured even a little vision of the wide world of knowledge can never be bigoted or vainglorious because he has learned how little he himself really knows. Masonry needs the Arts and Sciences for the sake of brotherhood itself!

CHAPTER XL

THE EPHRAIMITISH WAR, AND CORN, WINE AND OIL

I

For many years the Jewish tribes had been harassed on one side by the Philistines and on the other by the Ammonites, the latter a rude Bedouin tribe of crafty, fearless desert people. Made desperate by their losses the Israelites at last gathered behind a semi-barbarous chieftain from the land of Tob, a region just north of the Ammonites and full of folk almost as barbarous as they. This chieftain, whose name was Jephthah and who suffered the disgrace of illegal birth, easily bested the foes and was afterwards made one of the Judges of Israel. (See Book of Judges.)

On this, the men of the Jewish tribe of Ephraim became jealous of the new leader and undertook to destroy his power. They crossed over to the east side of Jordan where Jephthah lived and there engaged him in war. After he had thoroughly whipped them he set groups of his men at each of the Jordan fords to intercept the refugees. But Jephthah discovered that the Ephraimites were so much like his own soldiers in appearance that confusion would result so he hit upon the ingenious expedient of having every suspect undertake to say "shibboleth" as he waded across the river. The Ephraimites were as unable to frame the sound of "sh" as Englishmen are to pronounced the Scotch "och." The nearest they could come to the pronunciation was "sibboleth." This betrayed them, and forty-two thousand were slain.

II

Among all primitive peoples the gods were supposed to have need of food; from that idea arose the custom of placing gifts on the altar, a custom as universal as it was ancient. The nature of the gifts was determined, usually, by the occupation of a people; the shepherds, for example, offered a sheep or a lamb, while agricultural peoples appropriately gave fruits or grain. This explains why it was that the Greeks and Romans, in their early periods, so often brought to their altars gifts of corn, oil and wine.

The same people also were accustomed to offer similar gifts to the gods when they undertook the erection of a building. Thinking to appease the gods for taking possession of the soil they would place fruits and grains in the bottom of the foundation pits, a practice well described by Ovid in his mythical history of the building of Rome: "A pit is dug down to the firm clay," he writes, "fruits of the earth are thrown to the bottom, and a sample of earth of the adjacent soil. The pit is filled with the earth, and when filled an altar is placed over it," etc. The present-day habit of placing valuables in a cornerstone is a reminiscence of that ancient custom.

The Masonic reader will understand from this our custom of using corn, wine and oil in the dedication of Masonic buildings. But these things have a very different significance in the Fellow Craft lecture: there they symbolise the wages of the workmen, alluding to Nourishment, Refreshment, and Joy. This symbolism interprets itself. It is nothing more than a figurative manner of saying to the candidate: "If you actually put into practise the teachings of this degree you will receive a rich reward; you will be nourished in mind and body; you will be refreshed by the consciousness of work well done; you will know the joys of brotherhood, of achievement, of a life well lived." Compared with such wages money compensation is a very poor thing.

CHAPTER XLI

THE LETTER G

I

The letter "G" is so intimately related to the symbolism of the Middle Chamber and all connected therewith that it will be wise, just here, to attempt an explanation of that mysterious letter. "Mysterious" is used advisedly because there has been very little agreement among our scholars either as to its origin or to its meaning. Usually, we can hit upon the manner in which a symbol was introduced into the Ritual by studying the records of the early eighteenth century in England, at which time and place the Ritual was cast in its modern form, but such a study cannot help us here because the eighteenth century Masons were themselves confused about the matter. This confusion survives to our own day with some authorities holding to one theory, others to its opposite, and still others, like the Grand Master of one American Jurisdiction, inclined to throw the symbol out altogether. Mackey, who was always so conservative, was quite as radical as this Grand Master, as is witnessed by this statement of his: "It is to be regretted that the letter G as a symbol was ever admitted into the Masonic system."

One writer believes that the G stands for the Greek rendering of "geometry"; another, that it is the initial of the Greek name for "square"; Brother J. T. Lawrence thinks that it may be an old Egyptian snake emblem; others hold that it was originally the square made "gallows shape," and that this gradually became corrupted into a G. The most common theories, however, are that it stands for Geometry; or that it is the initial of our word "God." It will be necessary to examine these last interpretations more at length, for the evidence seems to favour one or the other, or perhaps both together.

One cannot read the old Masonic Constitutions without being struck by the prominence given to Geometry in their descriptions of Masonry. The oldest copy of them makes Masonry to spring from Geometry, as may be seen in the following excerpt:

> "On this manner, through good wit of geometry
> Began first the Craft of Masonry."

Brother Hextall ("A.Q.C.," vol. xxv, p. 97) has pointed out that in every one of the hundred or more copies of these Old Charges, or Old Constitutions, Geometry is placed first among sciences. How can we account for this? The most reasonable explanation would seem to be that Operative Masonry was nothing other than applied Geometry. The builder in that early day had no architectural handbook, no blue prints, no tables of construction; his art was based on Geometry alone, and his skill consisted in knowing by heart many of the processes of Geometry, and his secrets were nothing other than these same processes and the knowledge of applying them. This being the case, it was natural that he should hold his science in high reverence and make its name, represented by its initial letter, to serve as a symbol in his lodge. Such, at any rate, is the reading of the matter as held by a majority of our best modern scholars.

These scholars believe that when Freemasonry became stagnant in the seventeenth century, so that very few lodges remained in existence, Freemasons themselves lost the old explanation of the letter G though they retained the symbol because it was a part of the system which they inherited. This, so it is believed, accounts for the confused explanations made by eighteenth century writers.

II

How did the letter G ever come to stand for Deity? It is almost impossible to answer this question with any degree of certainty, because the available evidence is so slender, but it is thought by some that an explanation may be found in the connection between Freemasonry and Kabbalism (see p. vii), for it is believed that some of the non-operatives "accepted" by the lodges in the seventeenth century brought a certain amount of Kabbalistic lore with them.

The symbolic system of the Kabbala centres mostly about the Divine Name. According to ancient Jewish traditions the real name of God, given to the Jewish people through Moses, was not permitted to be written, except with the consonants only. At the time of the Exile the pronunciation, and consequently the true spelling, of the Holy Name was lost. The consonants, J (or Y), H, W, H, remained, but what the vowels were nobody could discover; to find the Lost Name became one of the great ambitions of Jewish priests and scholars, and this search became one of the principal subjects in the literature of the Kabbala. Not having the Name itself the Kabbalists were wont to inscribe a Hebrew "Y" to the centre of a triangle with equal sides and make this stand for it.

It is supposed that this symbol was brought into Masonry by the non-operatives who were Kabbalists, but that, in the course of time, the common men who made up the lodges substituted for the Hebrew initial of the Divine Name the English initial. Inasmuch as the initial letter of God was the same as the initial letter of Geometry the two symbols became confused, and at last the old Masonic meaning of G was forgotten.

If this history of the matter be correct—I have pieced it together from the opinions expressed by many of our scholars—I do not see that we need to make any choice between G as standing for Geometry and G as standing for Deity; the two conceptions merge naturally together because men have always seen in the Geometry which is everywhere found in Nature the clearest unveiling of the Infinite Mind. The Greek philosopher, Pythagoras, who was the first to raise Geometry to the rank of a science, built his philosophical system on numbers and their relations. "All things are in numbers," he said; "the world is a living arithmetic in its development—a realised geometry in its repose." Of a similar mind was Plato, king of Greek philosophers. When asked how God spends his time, he replied, "God is always geometrising." "Geometry rightly treated is the knowledge of the eternal." "Geometry must ever tend to draw the soul towards the truth."

III

In spite of the enormous increase in knowledge, we who live twenty-five hundred years after those thinkers can still agree with them; science has made more apparent the lucid order, the geometric symmetry, of the universe. The very elements of which matter is composed gather themselves together in regular order; crystals are a solid geometry; the plant, the tree, the construction of an insect's wing, are all symmetrical in their proportion and rhythmical in their motions; the stars move in curves, the wildest comet inscribes a spiral, and the whole universe is one vast realm of order and design.

As science builds itself on the orderliness of Nature so does Masonry seek to build itself upon the equally certain laws of the human mind. Human beings are not exceptions to the universal reign of law. There are laws of brotherhood, laws of the ideal, as certain in their operations and as undeviating in their processes as the law of gravity. When men learn these laws, and when they adjust their actions to them, they will discover that the face of God has been made plain, they will have learned the secret of the letter G.

PART THREE: THE THIRD STEP

CHAPTER XLII

AN INTRODUCTION TO THE THIRD STEP

I

The moment one steps into the Third Degree he finds himself in an atmosphere very different from that of the First and the Second: the opening and closing ceremonies are similar to theirs, but the architectural symbolism which was in them the predominant feature is here crowded into the background by a symbolism of a very different order; for whereas the first two degrees deliver their message in the terms of building, the Third speaks of a living and a dying and a rising again. And so compact is it of profound meanings that it furnishes many of the suggestions, as many scholars have noted, from which the higher grades have developed their magnificent teachings.

By what men the Degree was made, or when, are questions on which our authorities differ so widely that one student—Brother Robert I. Clegg—has collected no fewer than twenty different theories, while another—Brother Hextall—has found fourteen different interpretations. Where so many scholars have failed to discover a satisfactory hypothesis it would require some temerity to offer a theory of one's own, and I must content myself to state, as nearly as I can, such positions as the majority have agreed on.

It is believed that in the beginning of the Grand Lodge period there were at most but two degrees, these being known, as I have already described, as the Apprentice and Fellow Craft or Master Mason parts, the latter being convertible terms. But during this same period so much new material—new, at least, to the ritual of initiation—was introduced that it became necessary to break up the old Apprentice Degree into two parts, leaving the old Second to become the new Third. This was done for the sake of convenience, as the ceremonies had grown too long for only two evenings. This division was made some time between 1723 and 1738.

The new arrangement was a long time in gaining a foothold among the brethren. At first only a few were made Masters and then only in Grand Lodge; in fact, so few knew how to "put on" the degree that for some time special "Masters' Lodges" were organised for the purpose. The progress of the tri-gradal system was even slower in countries other than England; Gould notes that the Third did not become common in Scotch Lodges until after 1770.

Why was the Third so slow in "taking on" if it was the old Second Degree? The explanation of the problem seems to be that so much new material had been added to it that it had become practically a new ceremony. There is even some reason to believe that it was this new material which among many other things gave offence to many old Masons living at a distance from London, who were thereby led to form the rival Grand Lodge of "the Ancients."

By whom was this new material introduced? Some attribute the innovations to Anderson, others to Dr. Desaguliers; others, of whom Pike was one, have held to the theory that at the time of the Revival certain groups of Speculatives seized the opportunity to graft some of their own ideas upon the Ritual. Another theory, more reasonable than these, it seems to me, will be brought out when we seek to answer the next question.

II

What was the new material introduced between 1723–1738? Many of our scholars, perhaps a majority, would answer, "The Hiram Abiff legend." As we are to devote a section to this I cannot go into that matter here except to say that it seems unreasonable, on the face of it, that so elaborate a drama, occupying the greater part of one whole degree, could have been bodily imported into the Ritual as a wholly new thing; the conservative "old Mason," of whom many were remaining in the Revival period, would not have tolerated so huge an innovation. The more reasonable theory is that the substance of the legend, and materials appertaining thereto, had long been a part of the floating tradition of the Craft if indeed, as there is some evidence to show that it was, it was not a part of the old Operative Ritual. This would answer the question, Who imported the new materials? No one man or group of men imported it; "The Third Degree was not made, it grew—like the great cathedrals, no one of which can be ascribed to a single artist, but to an order of men working in unity of enterprise and aspiration." To this it nay be added that the degree has not ceased to grow, in America at least, for it is more elaborate here than in England, even as it is more elaborate there than in other countries—more elaborate, and different.

By whom the degree was made, and when, will furnish material for many debates in years to come, and in the lap of that future must the problem be left; but of one thing we can be very sure—the idea enshrined in the ceremony is so old that we find it serving as the motif of initiatory dramas long before the dawn of history. In a majority of the Ancient Mysteries, to judge by such memorials as we have of them, the action centred in the violent death of some person and his being raised again. In various guises was this idea presented but always did it convey the same truth—that in men there is something that cannot die, that this "something" is akin to the divine, that it can be given the rule of a man during his earth pilgrimage, and that it is the purpose of initiation to discover and to develop this divine element in human life. This is nothing other than Regeneration; it is nothing other than Eternal Life, the life of God in the soul of man lived in the bounds of time and space and under human conditions. Such, I take it, is the secret of our Third Degree.

CHAPTER XLIII

THE VITAL PARTS OF THE BREAST

I

On his entrance to the Third Degree the candidate is received in a manner peculiarly impressive; he is told that as the vital parts of the body are in the breasts so are the vital things of the human world to be found in Friendship, Morality, and Brotherly Love. How vague are these words! We have rolled them around in our mouths so much that they have become smooth as billiard balls; they have been used so often for merely oratorical purposes that they have grown nebulous and abstract; and because they have become smooth and vague we are prone to let them slip through our minds without their depositing their meaning behind them, a thing fatal to an understanding of Masonry, the essence of much of which lies in these three wonderful words.

Man is by nature a social being. It has been proved that he cannot exist as a sane creature except he live among his fellows, for his very personality itself is a social product; the language on his lips implies another to hear and to understand; his emotions and affections seek another in whom to find satisfaction. Not until the individual has found other human individuals who can feel with him, think with him, and act with him can he know the meaning of happiness. But it is a part of the tragedy of our lives that we are so clumsy in uncovering our own souls, and others are so inexpert in understanding our secret feelings, that our fellowship is never complete, so that the music of companionship is continually being disturbed by jangling dissonances of misunderstanding. With a friend, however, it is different; he is one with whom we can live in harmony, as if the two lives could mingle like two streams, his thoughts and our thoughts merging together and the two spirits living as one. Such a union is one of the sweetest experiences in all the world and he who has found his friend may well congratulate himself as being one who has discovered the pearl of great price. Little wonder that our prophets and seers have so often broken into rhapsody on this subject! that our literature may count as its richest treasures such utterances as those of Emerson, Black, Trumbull, Montaigne, Bacon, and Cicero concerning friendship.

II

Morality has been stretched to cover so many meanings, it has been forced into the support of so many conflicting theories, and been made fellow to so many crimes against reason, that we can hardly blame many for not being interested in it. But the word is necessary because the idea of which it is the sign is a real and a necessary idea. If men misuse it there is all the more reason for our learning how to rightly use it.

What is morality? It is derived from a Latin word meaning "custom," and it is probable that the Romans first used it in the sense of living according to the custom. In Christian times a richer meaning was poured into it so that it has come to mean "the life of righteousness." But what is righteousness? It is living the right way, doing the right things, thinking the right thoughts,—a very Masonic behaviour. But what is right? We might answer that question in two ways; we might say that the right is that which gives us the fullest, completest life, for it is the purpose of morality to give us life and give it more abundantly; or, we might say that right is conformity to the law of our being. As the scientist seeks to learn the laws of nature and to conform to them, so does a righteous man seek to discover the laws of his own nature in order to conform to them; he obeys the laws of the body by living healthfully, he obeys the laws of the intellect by thinking facts without prejudice or haste, and he obeys the laws of the heart by loving only that which he finds to be good and true.

Of Brotherly Love much more might be said, though space may not permit, especially the Brotherly Love which Masonry inculcates. How can brotherhood be possible among us men? We are all so unbrotherly, we are so selfish, we are so quick to take or give offence! The solution of this troublesome problem lies in the fact that the one cure for unbrotherliness is brotherliness. We love our enemies that they may cease being enemies. We make friends in order to have friends. Brotherliness is a creative force. Brotherhood is not a thing already made, it is a condition we must create, so that the very presence of unbrotherliness is a challenge to brotherhood to do its best. When our fellows in lodge act thoughtlessly toward us, and bruise and hurt us, it is not for us to retaliate; insofar as we are true Masons we shall love them even though they are not lovable, simply because the only way in which we can make men lovable is by loving them. Brotherly Love, therefore, is a task, a kingly task, one of the greatest and most important inside the whole compass of life. Indeed, we may say that one of the chief purposes of Masonry is to mobilise all men of goodwill in order that they may help to brother the world into a world-wide brotherliness.

CHAPTER XLIV

THE GOLDEN BOWL AND THE SILVER CORD

I

The sacred sentences which fall on the ears of the candidate as he makes his mystic round are so heavy with poignant beauty that one hesitates to intrude the harsh language of prose upon such strains of poetry, so solemnly sweet. We may well believe that the men who introduced the reading here had no other thought than that the words might the better create an atmosphere in which the coming drama of hate and doom might all the more impressively come home to the heart of the participants. If such was their purpose neither Shakespeare nor Dante could have found words or sentiments more appropriate to the hour. There is a music and majesty in the twelfth Chapter of Ecclesiastes that leaves us dumb with awe and wonder and our hearts open to the impressions of a tragedy alongside which the doom of Lear seems insignificant.

For generations the commentators of Holy Writ have seen in the allegory of this Chapter a reference to the decay of the body and the coming of death; to them, the golden bowl was the skull, the silver cord the spinal nerve, "the keepers of the house" were the hands, the "strong men" the limbs; and the whole picture made to symbolise the body's falling into ruin and the approach of death. One hesitates to differ from an interpretation so true in its application and so dignified by its associations. But it must be doubted whether the sad and disillusioned man who penned the lines possessed either the knowledge of human anatomy implied by the old interpretation or the intention to make his poem into a medical description of senility. A more thorough scholarship has come to see in the allegory a picture of the honour of death set forth by metaphors drawn from an Oriental thunderstorm.

It had been a day of wind and cloud and rain; but the clouds did not, as was usual, disperse after the shower. They returned again and covered the heavens with their blackness. Thunderstorms were so uncommon in Palestine that they always inspired fear and dread, as many a paragraph in the Scriptures will testify. As the storm broke the strong men guarding the gates of rich men's houses began to tremble; the hum of the little mills wherewith the women were always grinding at eventime suddenly ceased because the grinders were frightened from their toil; the women, imprisoned in the harems, who had been gazing out of the lattice to watch the activities of the streets, drew back into their dark rooms; even the revellers who had been sitting at their tables through the afternoon, eating dainties and sipping wine, lost their appetites, and many were so nervous that the sudden twitting of a bird would cause them to start with anxious surprise.

II

As the terror of the storm, the poet goes on to say, so is the coming of death, when man "goes to his home of everlasting, and mourners go about the street." Whatever men may have been, good or bad, death brings equal terror to all. A man may have been rich, like the golden lamp hung on a silver chain in the palace of the king; he may have been as poor as the earthen pitcher in which maidens carried water from the public well; or even as crude as the heavy wooden wheel wherewith they drew the water; what his state was matters not, death is as dread a calamity to the one as to the other. When that dark adventure comes the fine possessions in which men had sought security will be vain to stay the awful passing into night. "Vanity of vanities; all is vanity." The one bulwark against the common calamity, the Preacher urges, is to remember the Creator, yea, to remember Him from youth to old age; to believe that one goes to stand before Him is the one and only solace in an hour when everything falls to ruin and the very desire to live has been quenched by the ravages of age and the coming of death.

CHAPTER XLV

THAT WHICH WAS LOST

I

We come now to the crux and the climax of Blue Lodge symbolism, the master symbol by means of which all other symbols have their meaning. Well will it be for us to walk warily, here, not only because the origins of the symbolism of the Lost Word are bound up with an ancient and tangled tradition and, not only because it has been so often prostituted to the level of magic and superstition, even in recent times, but also because it is the embodiment of one of those ideas so high and so deep that they contain whole systems of philosophy and theology within them. It is like the "flower in the crannied wall" of Tennyson's poem; if we could understand it, "root and all, all in all," we would know "what God and man is."

Much has been written about the "Mason's word" as employed in old days, when brethren were sometimes "made Mason" by having that secret term entrusted to them; research has failed to show what this word was though some scholars believe it to have been that sovereign name which stands at the centre of one of the Higher Grades. Some who hold to this last-named theory would have us believe that this transfer of the word from the Blue Lodge to that degree was so disastrous to the symbolic structure of the Blue Lodge that to patch up the damage a substitute word was devised to take its place until the candidate, passed on to the higher grade. But as there is little or no evidence to prove that the great word of the degree is the same as the "Mason's Word" of the old lodges that theory must be left suspended in the mid-air of conjecture.

II

For my own part—and I can speak here for no other—I can not believe that the Blue Lodge system was ever rifled of its chiefest treasure to grace the forehead of a "higher" grade nor can I see why we should think that the Third Degree, just as it is, has lost the one key to its mysteries. The search for a lost word is not the search for a mere vocable of a few letters which one might write down on a piece of paper; it is the seeking for a truth, nay, a set of truths, a secret of life, and that secret truth is so clearly set forth in the Hiram Abiff drama that one is led to wonder why anybody should suppose that it had ever been lost. "The Lost Word" does not refer, so it seems to me, to any term once in possession of the Third Degree and accidentally lost, but rather it denotes the ancient *Tetragrammaton*, or "four-lettered name," for which search has been made these two and a half millenniums.

According to a very old tradition (how much actual history may be in it we cannot know) the Legend of the *Tetragrammaton* goes back to ancient Israel as far as the time of Exile. Like all people of that day the Jews saw in a person's name not a mere handy cognomen whereby a man be addressed but a kind of sign standing for the personality of the one who bore it. Jacob was Jacob because he actually had been a "supplanter," as that name means; and he later became Israel because he grew to be a "prince of God." Jacob's name was a revelation of his character. So was it with all names. Therefore was it that the ancients held proper names in a reverence difficult for us to understand, as is hinted in an old Chaldean oracle:

> "Never change native Names;
> For there are names in every nation, God-given,
> Of unexplained power in the Mysteries."

Bearing this in mind we can understand why the Jews threw about the name of Deity the wrappings of secrecy and sanctity. At first, after the dread secret had been imparted to Moses, the people pronounced the name in whispers or not at all. They were bidden never to use it except on the most solemn occasions as witness the Third Commandment which reads, when literally translated, "Thou shalt not utter the name of thy God idly." As time went on the priests forbade them to do more than hint at it, one of the priestly commands in Leviticus reading, "He that pronounceth the Name of the Lord *distinctly*, shall be put to death." (Ch. 24, v. 16) At last, only the High Priest was permitted to utter the Name at all, and then on some great occasion, such as the day of Atonement. At the same time, it must be remembered, the Jews were using no vowels in their writing; for some strange reason only consonants were ever written or printed; therefore only the four consonants, JHWH, were ever seen.

When the Jews were taken into Exile, all traces of the true pronounciation was lost, either because the High Priest was killed before he could impart it or died in Babylonia before a successor entitled to the secret could be found. Consequently, the Exile was no sooner ended than priests and scribes began their search for the Lost Name. The four consonants only did they have; what the vowels were nobody could learn, nor has anybody since discovered, at least according to the Legend.

III

This *Tetragrammaton* became a storm-centre of theology and around it a great mass of symbolism gradually accumulated. So deeply did it sink into the imagination of Israel that the later theosophists who built up the speculative system we call the Kabbala made it the very core of their teaching; and through the Kabbala, the literature of which was so popular even as late as Reformation times, the legends of the Lost Name made its way into the thought and Literature of Mediæval Europe. But the form of the legend did not always remain the same; "now it is a spoiled sanctuary; now a sacramental mystery; now the abandonment of a great military and religious order; now the age-long frustrations of the greatest building plan which was ever conceived; now the lost word of Kabbalism; now the vacancy of the most holy of all sanctuaries." Whatever the disguise the quest was always the same, a search for something strangely precious which men believed had been lost out of the world but might be found again.

IV

This wonderful symbolic idea still retains its power to cast a spell over us, as witness its use by modern writers. Eugène Sue incorporated it in his haunted tale, "The Wandering Jew." Tennyson wove it into his Arthur epic, where it has assumed the form of the search for the Lost Grail, the cup used by the Lord at His Last Supper. Henry Van Dyke has embodied it in his book of stories, "The Blue Flower," and Maurice Maeterlinck has woven about it a strangely beautiful drama, "The Blue Bird."

Shall we not add to that list the drama of the Third Degree? Surely, "that which was lost" can refer to nothing else, as the evidence, both internal and external, so abundantly seems to show. If that indeed be the case how it does light up with prophetic meaning the whole mystery of the Third Degree: for it shows that the candidate is not on a hunt for a mystic term to be used like a magic spell, still less is it some mysterious individual that he seeks. That for which he really searches is to discover the divine in himself and in the world.

Going out to find God we need not wonder when he finds no one word, or one thing, to reward his labours; nor need we be disappointed if he is "put off with a substitute," for though his search is not fruitless it is not altogether successful, as is fitting when we recall that the complete unveiling of God cannot come to any man in any one lifetime. That hope must ever remain an ideal to us humans in the shadow of our earth life—a flying Ideal, eluding us while it beckons us, leading us over the hills of Time into the tireless searchings of Eternity.

CHAPTER XLVI

THE TROWEL

I

This emblem is like a key; insignificant in itself it opens up matters of such vast import that to pursue its teachings through all their ramifications would itself require a book; consequently I can only hope to set down a few hints of the rich and various applications of it.

There is no need to say that of all working tools it is the most appropriate to the Master Mason Degree; it carries that significance upon its surface. The Entered Apprentice, who can make only a beginning at the task of shaping the ashlar, needs only the gavel and the guage; the Fellow Craft, to bring the stone into completeness of size and form, requires the plumb, square, and level; the Master Mason's task is to set the finished stone in its place, and bind it there, for which purpose the trowel is his most necessary tool. Therefore the Master Mason has been given the Trowel as his working tool because it is most symbolic of his function in the great work of Temple Building; when that tool has done its work there is nothing more to do, because the structure stands complete, a united mass, incapable of falling apart; the stones which were many have now, because of the binding power of the cement, become as one.

II

If the stone represents an individual man, and if the Temple represents the Fraternity as a whole, it is evident that the Trowel is the symbol of that which has power to bind men together. Therefrom arises the question, what is this unifying power? Let us undertake to answer this question from the several points of view of the individual, the Fraternity, and the world at large.

We very frequently meet with men who seem to lack unity in their makeup; a spirit of disorganisation or anarchy is at work in them so that they seem to live at cross-purposes with themselves. What they know they should do they do not, and many things which they do they do against their own will. They may have personal force, but it is scattered and their lives never come to a focus. Of these men we say that they lack character and we say right. Character comes from a word that meant originally a graving tool; after long use the name of the tool came to be applied to the engraving itself, and thus the term has come to stand for a man whose actions give one an impression of definiteness and clear-cuttedness, like an engraving. A man who lacks character is a blur, a confused and self-contradictory mass of impulses and forces. The one salvation for such a man is to find some means of unifying himself, of using himself to some purpose so as to arrive at some goal.

What can he use? We may answer, perhaps, that he can best use an ideal, for an ideal is nothing other than a picture of what one wills to be which he ever keeps before him, as an architect refers to his blue prints. In short, the man needs a plan to live by, a thing we have symbolised in our Ritual by means of the tracing board.

Before the time of the Reformation, builders did not use plans drawn to scale as architects now do, but laid out their building design on the ground, or even on the floor of the workshop or the lodge. In early English lodges this design was often drawn on the floor in chalk by the Master, and the youngest Entered Apprentice would erase it with a mop and water at the end of the ceremony; after a while, to make this labour unnecessary, "the plan of work" was drawn on a permanent board which was set on an easel and exhibited during the degree, as is still done in England. The tracing board of a degree, therefore, is the plan of work for that degree, drawn in symbols and hieroglyphics, and the tracing board itself, as it stands in the lodge, is a constant reminder to the Mason that, as a spiritual builder, he must have a plan or an ideal for his life; and when the Mason does live in loyalty to an ideal he is a man of character; his faculties work in unison, there is no war between his purposes and his behaviour, and he is able to stand among his brethern as a completed temple. Such a man has used a trowel in his own life.

III

It is more difficult to answer the question, What is the force that can unite individual Masons into a unified and harmonious Order, but a practicable answer may be found by asking a further question, What is it that now unites us, even if imperfectly? What is the cement? Perhaps we cannot point to any one thing. When I inquire of my own heart what it is that ties me to my fellow Masons I find myself thinking of many things. There is the sense of a wonderful history which links up to unknown brethren who lived generations ago; there is the symbolism of the Society, in which precious truths and living philosophies have been poured as into golden vases; there is the spirit which pervades the Order, a sense of oneness in purpose and aims, of tolerance, of charity, of patience and forbearing; there is also the remembrance of the obligation which I voluntarily assumed, and which wove into my heart a silken thread, the other end of which is woven into the hearts of my brethren; these and similar influences hold me to the Craft now and ever shall, but how to sum them up in one word I know not, except that word be Brotherhood. Brotherhood has suffered much from over-use, from sentimentalism, and from oratory, but no other word can be found to take its place. Therefore we may say that, so far as the Fraternity itself is concerned, the trowel and the cement spread on by the •trowel, is the kindly, pervasive, irresistible spirit and power of Brotherhood. True it is that

> "Fellowship is heaven;
> The lack of fellowship is hell."

If this be so we have already to hand an answer to our last question, What power can unite the scattered peoples and nations of the earth, especially in a time like this when they are more than ever sundered by passion and hatred? Surely, if the spirit and influence of Brotherhood can call together two million men out of all classes and localities of America and can bind them into the solidarity of a great united Order, that same power can accomplish similar results if applied to the world at large. Diplomats and politicians do not seem to believe it, but it is true nevertheless, trite as it may sound, and Freemasonry's benign genius of fraternity was never more badly needed in the earth than just now. Every device has been used to bind the peoples together; force, money, fear, superstition, and what not; let us hope that sooner or later the race will try the means proved so effective by more than two hundred years of Freemasonry.

CHAPTER XLVII

THE HIRAMIC LEGEND

I

"In all my research and study, in all my close analysis of the masterpieces of Shakespeare, in my earnest determination to make those plays appear real on the mimetic stage, I have never, and nowhere, met tragedy so real, so sublime, so magnificent as the legend of Hiram. It is substance without shadow—the manifest destiny of life which requires no picture and scarcely a word to make a lasting impression upon all who can understand. To be a Worshipful Master and to throw my whole soul into that work, with the candidate for my audience and the lodge for my stage, would be a greater personal distinction than to receive the plaudits of people in the theatre of the world."

When so accomplished a judge and critic as Edwin Booth could speak like this of the Hiram Abiff tragedy we humbler students may be forgiven for approaching such a theme in awe if not in silence; in truth, I may confess that I should not dare to write a line on the subject were it not absolutely necessary to the scope of these studies. The majesty of the drama is not the only deterrent; its origin and its interpretation have engaged our best scholars for many years but they have not yet reached an agreement; many of them remain as wide apart as the poles nor is there any hope for an early uniformity of opinion. Therefore I shall be compelled to lay out for reviews such varying hypotheses as seem most reasonable, leaving to you, reader, the privilege of forming your own conclusions.

II

It is generally agreed, however, whatever may be our theory of the origin of the drama, that it was first introduced into the Ritual, *in its modern form* not more than two hundred years ago. Pike describes it as "a modern invention." Vibert calls it "a comparatively late addition" to the Ritual, and Gould went so far as to fix on 1725 as the most probable date of its introduction into its ceremonies. But while, as I have already said, there is general agreement on this, some scholars, and they not the least considerable, contend that the drama could not have been invented outright in 1725 even if it was amplified or improved, and they believe that the story of the great martyrdom must have existed in *some form* long before the Eighteenth Century. MacBride believes that "there are traces of the Hiramic Legend in connection with the British Craft Lodges prior to 1717." Newton holds that it was in the possession of the French Compagnonage long before that date and that they "almost certainly learned it from the Freemasons." Even Gould, who is so conservative in his opinions, writes that "the traditions which are gathered round Hiram's name" have "come down to us from ancient times."

III

Eighteenth century writers usually accepted the legend as having been based on actual history, even in details; from this position the pendulum swung to the opposite position, one writer going so far as to say that "nowhere in history, sacred or profane, in no document, upon no monument, is there a single shred of authentic historical evidence to support the Masonic Legend;" while another affirms that "in spite of diligent search no reference on the Hiramic Legend has hitherto been found in Jewish writings." We are now in process of reaction from this extreme negative position as is proved by Max Montesole's brilliant article published in the Transactions of the Arthur's Lodge (vol. i, p. 28) in which he shows that the name of Hiram Abiff in Hebrew literally means "Hiram, his father" or "Hiram, his master," and that the term as such is found in II Chronicles 4: 16. This means that the record tells first of Hiram of Tyre, Solomon's architect, and then of a second Hiram, the former's son or pupil which leaves us to infer that the first Hiram may have died or have been killed.

That this latter supposition is not a modern one is proved by a sentence in one of the oldest Jewish writings in which we read that "all workmen were killed that they should not build another Temple devoted to idolatry, Hiram himself being translated to heaven like Enoch." This is doubtless only a Rabbinic legend but it proves that, even to the Jews of ancient times, there had descended a tradition of the Grand Master's death.

Other writers, however, have not agreed with this historical theory but prefer to believe that the drama was devised during Mediæval times. If so it must have come into existence some time before the fourteenth century, for Speth asserts that there are references to it (veiled) in certain of the Old Charges, and Dr. Marks, a learned Hebrew scholar, declares that he found an Arabic manuscript of that date which contains the sentence, "We have found our Lord Hiram."

IV

Some scholars have argued that the drama was brought to Europe by the Knight Templar. Others have seen in it a literary result of popular interest in the Temple which was so frequently the theme of books and speeches in seventeenth century England; but a diligent search among this literature has failed to unearth a single reference to Hiram Abiff. (A.Q.C., vol. xii, p. 142.) Nor has an equally diligent search been able to discover any such references in the Mystery Plays which were once so common in Europe, though some scholars have hoped for light from that quarter. (A.Q.C., vol. xiv, p. 60.) Speth considered that the legend may have originated among early builders as a parabolical story suggested by the old customs of sacrificing a human being under the cornerstone of a building. Pike was of the opinion that it was invented by seventeenth century occultists for the purpose of concealing their teachings. Carr traces it back to a legend still found in Operative Lodges while others hold that it was made out of the whole cloth by Anderson or Desaguliers, while others have seen in it a kind of political allegory devised by Oliver Cromwell (of all men!) or some other republican as a blast against royalty.

To me it seems reasonable to believe that the core of the drama came down from Solomon's day; that it was preserved until mediæval times by Jewish, and especially Kabbalistic, literature; that it found a place among the traditions of the old builders because it was so intimately related to the story of the Temple, around which so much of their symbolism revolved; that it was inherited by seventeenth century Masons, in crude form, and along with the mass of other traditions; that it was elaborated and given its literary form by the early framers of the Ritual; and that it was adopted by them because it embodied so wonderfully the idea at the centre of the Third Degree. As I said above, this theory can not be proved by documentary evidence, but it is the opinion toward which the *drift* of all our data seems to lead one.

V

The confusion which may have been occasioned by this review of the theories of origin will not be lessened, I fear, when we turn to interpretation, for in this also we find a multitude of counsellors, and few agreeing. To make this diversity as plain as possible I shall set down a table of the theories, with their authors' names in parentheses, when known; there are fourteen of them (I borrowed the list from Brother Hextall), but even more could be added by a little search.

1. Real and actual death of Hiram Abiff. (Oliver.)
2. Legend of Isis and Osiris. (Oliver.)
3. Allegory of setting sun. (Oliver.)
4. Death of Abel at hand of Cain.
5. Expulsion of Adam from Paradise. (Oliver.)
6. Entry of Noah into Ark. (*Freemason's Magazine.*)
7. Mourning of Joseph for Jacob. (Oliver.)
8. An astronomical problem. (Yarker.)
9. Death and Resurrection of Jesus. (Oliver; also Pike, in part.)
10. Violent death of King Charles I. (Oliver.)
11. Persecution of the Templars. (De Quincey.)
12. Political invention by Cromwell. (Oliver.)
13. A parable of old age and death. (Oliver.)
14. A drama of regeneration. (Hutchinson.)

It is highly significant that the majority of these theories were born in Bro. Oliver's learned brain; he devoted a life-time almost exclusively to the study of Masonry, and he was a man of unusual intellect. Yet see how bewildered he became in the presence of the drama! how impotent he was to discover any one fact or event to which it might refer! Is not this in itself a solution of the problem? For why should we persist in thinking that the legend as we now have it derives its meaning from any event whatsoever? Why may we not believe that it is simply a dramatic parable of a great experience of the soul in its struggle against adversaries, in its apparent defeat, and its ultimate moral victory? Whatever it may have originally meant, this, surely must be its meaning now.

Hiram Abiff is the type of every Christ-like man who lives as an apostle of light and liberty, and his experiences as set forth in the drama are just those experiences, in one degree or another, which attend every such man who stands true to his principles. Adversaries, whether men or circumstances, seek to undermine his courage and betray his soul; they may even encompass his death and apparent defeat, but he lives while they die, for the man who stands true to his loyalties, whatsoever betide, has that within him which contumacy cannot kill, nor death destroy. Such a man is inconquerable even in mortality, and on his lips we might place, without any incongruity whatsoever, the magnificent exclamation of the heroic Fichte:

"I raise my hand to the threatening rock, the raging flood, and the fiery tempest, and cry, 'I am eternal and defy your might; break all upon me; and thou Earth, and thou Heaven, mingle in the wild tumult; and all ye elements, foam and fret yourselves, and crush in your conflict the last atom of the body I call mine,' my WILL, in its own firm purpose, shall soar unwavering and hold over the wreck of the universe!"

CHAPTER XLVIII

ETERNAL LIFE

I

That which I believe to be the central idea in the whole Hiram Abiff drama, and consequently the profoundest interpretation of it, is that embodied in the term used as the title of this section. I have chosen to consider it in a section apart, not only because its importance is deserving of such emphasis, but also because the truth of Eternal Life is so confused, so mingled with other very different ideas in the minds of men, that we have need of a careful analysis of the matter.

By Eternal Life we do not mean quite the same thing as we meant by a Future Life. Future Life, by virtue of the very words used to describe it, is a life that is supposed to lie in the future, beginning after death; Eternal Life will be lived in the great future, true enough, but is something more than that.

Nor is Eternal Life the same as Immortality, for Immortality means deathlessness that is, an existence of endless duration. It suggests a picture of life lived on a level line, of which line there is no end. Eternal Life includes this conception of infinite duration but it also includes much besides.

Again, Eternal Life is not to be identified with Resurrection. According to this latter hope the man who dies will be raised from the dead and will be the same man that he was before death. This also may be true, in some sense doubtless is true, but the idea is not the same as that meant by Eternal Life.

II

What, then, do we mean by Eternal Life? Briefly it may be put thus—there is something in every man, call it spirit, soul, a divine spark, or what you will, which even now belongs to another order of reality, and is not to be numbered among the things that go "into that utter passing away from which there is nothing to return." It is possible for a man to discover in himself those things that are most akin to God, and to keep these things at the centre of his being: and it is possible for him to do this here and now, and under the very conditions which seem to us so broken and so unfavourable to high living, and not wait until after death. All of God, and all of the Universe, and all of the powers of human life—these are present with us now, and it is not necessary to postpone real life until after death.

III

It is the great tragedy in the life of many men that they so entirely devote themselves to the body's needs that they forget, or neglect, the spirit's needs. Giving themselves up to the search for temporalities, they leave the divinest cravings in them to go unsatisfied; as a result they become materialistic, self-centred, vain, greedy, and animalistic; the soul becomes dissatisfied, God becomes unreal, and the future life uncertain; and they even fall into the fatal habit of making such Goodness, Truth and Beauty as they do find in themselves or others into a mere means to temporal gains. Such a man's whole life revolves about himself; he becomes his own world and his own God, and out of such a state grow the fears, doubts, superstitions, quarrellings, graspings, prejudices, envyings, and hatreds, which so often make life a mere scramble after the things of self. In other words, small things are set at the centre of existence so that all the man's life is made up of temporalities.

The one remedy for this condition is to change the centre of gravity so that the spirit is master, and body is servant, so that search is made for the eternal things instead of wholly for the things that pass away. When this occurs, selfishness, envy, and materialism, vanish; the soul becomes the great reality; God draws very near and becomes very certain; the perspective of life is changed, and its scale of values is reversed. To be honourable and true, to love others, to live in pity, charity, and kindliness, to know eternity as present and the present existence as a brief phase of an endless life, all this becomes for such a man the great ideal toward which all his energies are bent. Loss and disease may be serious but they are not fatal; even death is robbed of its terrors because the man's treasures are out of the reach of destruction.

This is Eternal Life. This is the "life of God in the soul of man," eternity in the midst of time, a divine-human experience possible in the Here and Now. To reach such an existence is in the power of every man; nay, it is the birthright, the God-intended plan, of every child of the race.

Herein, it seems to me, we have the reality of which the Lost Word is the mystic symbol; and he who has found that word within himself is victorious always, whatever betide. If he is betrayed by the friends in whom he has trusted, waylaid by ruffians, put to death in the midst of his creative and benignant work, and thrown into an unmarked grave, he is not defeated or destroyed; the God-like spirit within him, dedicated to the Eternal Values, raises him up from the level of death to the perpendicular of the life that is endless.

IV

If this be the true interpretation of the Raising, we can no longer agree with those who see in it merely a ceremony in witness to the Future Life of the soul. How could it be? The Raising is not accomplished on the other side of the grave but on this; out of the very disaster that overwhelmed him, out of the midst of that dreadful "masterful negation which men call death," the master is lifted up and made victorious. The Spirit is conqueror even Here.

Furthermore, and as I have already hinted, this interpretation makes void the theory which would have us believe that the Lost Word must be sought outside the Blue Lodge Ritual. When is the Master raised? Is it not in the Third Degree? Is not the very Power that raises him itself the thing we mean by the word? It is true that no word of a certain number of letters is given us; it is true that the secret is elaborated and made plain in a higher degree, but the power, the actual upraising energy of which such a word must be a symbol, is present, and does its work, inside the limits of the Degree!

As this understanding came home to me, and opened up within my mind, the whole of the Blue Lodge Ritual, nay, the whole of Masonry itself, became transfigured. Dark places filled with light, and obscure symbols, often so cryptic and dim, became eloquent with endless meanings. I found that every ceremony, from the first simple acts of the preparation room to the climax of the tragedy of the Third Degree, arranged itself in a solemn order that moved easily to its predestined goal. Freemasonry rose in my vision to the most divine heights, and I saw that it has in its heart an Eternal Gospel which gives it a place among the great witnesses to religion, and among the noblest of all the philosophies wherethrough men have sought for light on the brief, broken, bewildering mystery of existence; and strength to live, unconquered and unashamed in the midst of so many enemies and defeats.

CHAPTER XLIX

THE LION'S PAW

I

The Mackey Encyclopædia article on this subject is very brief, as may be seen from the following: "A mode of recognition so called because of the rude resemblance made by the hand and fingers to a lion's paw. It refers to the 'Lion of the tribe of Judah.'" This is true as far as it goes, but it doesn't go far enough, for it leaves unanswered the questions of origin and interpretation. Nor does the companion article on the "Lion of the Tribe of Judah" give us much more information. If Mackey refrained from saying more because he knew no more we can sympathise with him, seeing that at this late day there is still very little known about the matter. But we have learned something since Mackey wrote, enough maybe, to set us on the track toward a satisfactory understanding of the matter.

Owing to its appeal to the imagination, and to the fear and reverence it has ever aroused, the lion has often been a favourite with symbolists, especially religious symbolists. Our modern anthropologists and folk-lore experts have furnished us with numberless examples of this, even among primitive folk now living, who are sometimes found worshipping the animal. Among the early peoples of India the lion was often used, and generally with the same significance, as standing for "the divine spirit in man." Among the early Egyptians it was still more venerated, as may be learned from their monuments, their temples, and especially their sphinxes; if we may trust our authorities in the matter, the Nile dwellers used it as a symbol of the life-giving power of the sun and the sun's ability to bring about the resurrection of vegetation in the spring time. In some of the sculpture left by the Egyptians to illustrate the rites of the Egyptian Mysteries the candidate is shown lying on a couch shaped like a lion from which he is being raised from the dead level to a living perpendicular. The bas-reliefs at Denderah make this very plain, though they represent the god Osiris being raised instead of a human candidate. "Here," writes J. E. Harrison in her very interesting little book on "Ancient Art and Ritual," "the God is represented first as a mummy swathed and lying flat on his bier. Bit by bit he is seen raising himself up in a series of gymnastically impossible positions, till he rises . . . all but erect, between the outstretched wings of Isis, while before him a male figure holds the Crux Ansata, the 'cross with a handle,' the Egyptian symbol of life."

II

The *crux ansata* was, as Miss Harrison truly says, the symbol of life. Originally a stick, with a cross-piece at the top for a handle, it was used to measure the overflow of the Nile: but inasmuch as it was this overflow that carried fertility into Egypt, the idea of a life-giving power gradually became transferred to the instrument itself, in the same manner that we attribute to a writer's "pen" his ability to use words. A few of our Masonic expositors, among whom Albert Pike may be numbered, have seen in the*crux ansata* the first form of that Lion's Paw by which the Masonic Horus is raised. If this be the case, the Lion's Paw is a symbol of life-giving power, an interpretation which fits in very well with our own position as outlined in the two preceding sections.

III

But it is also possible to trace the Lion's Paw symbolism to another source. Among the Jews the lion was sometimes used as the emblem of the Tribe of Judah; as the Messiah was expected to spring from that Tribe the Lion was also made to refer to him, as may be seen in the fifth verse of the fifth chapter of the Book of Revelation, where Jesus Christ is called the "Lion of the Tribe of Judah." It was from this source, doubtless, that the Comacines, the great Cathedral Builders of the Middle Ages, who were always so loyal to the Scriptures, derived their habitual use of the lion in their sculptures. Of this, Leader Scott, the great authority on the Comacines, writes that, "My own observations have led me to the opinion that in Romanesque or Transition architecture, i.e., between A.D. 1000 and 1200, the lion is to be found between the columns and the arch—the arch resting upon it. In Italian Gothic, i.e., from A.D. 1200 to 1500, it is placed beneath the column. In either position its significance is evident. In the first, it points to Christ as the door of the church; in the second, to Christ, the pillar of faith, springing from the tribe of Judah." Since the cathedral builders were in all probability among the ancestors of Freemasons it is possible that the Lion symbolism was inherited from the Comacines.

IV

During the cathedral building period, when symbolism was flowering out on all sides in mediæval life, the lion was one of the most popular figures in the common animal mythology, as may be learned from the Physiologus, the old book in which that mythology has been preserved. According to this record, the people believed that the whelps of the lioness were born dead and that at the end of three days she would howl above them until they were awakened into life. In this the childlike people saw a symbol of Christ's resurrection after He had lain dead three days in the tomb; from this it naturally resulted that the lion came to be used as a symbol of the Resurrection, and such is the significance of the picture of a lion howling above the whelps, so often found in the old churches and cathedrals.

The early Freemasons, so the records show, read both these meanings,—Christ and Resurrection,—into the symbol as they used it. And when we consider that most of Freemasonry was Christian in belief down at least to the Grand Lodge era, it is reasonable to suppose that the Lion symbol may have been one of the vestiges of that early belief carried over into the modern system. If this be the case the Lion's Paw has the same meaning, whether we interpret it, with Pike, as an Egyptian symbol, or with Leader Scott, as a Christian emblem, since it stands for the life-giving power, a meaning that perfectly accords with its use in the Third Degree. This also brings it into harmony with our interpretation of Eternal Life for in both its Egyptian and its Christian usages it refers to a raising up to life in this world, and not to a raising in the world to come.

CHAPTER L

THE EMBLEMS

I

The Weeping Virgin. This monument symbol was unknown to the Ritual in the eighteenth century; it is not now found in European systems, nor even in some American jurisdictions. According to such slender evidence as we possess it seems to have been invented by Jeremy Cross, the famous New Hampshire ritualist and pupil of Thomas Smith Webb, though some deny this. According to one tradition, Cross borrowed the idea from a tombstone; according to another he adapted an old picture of Isis weeping over the dead Osiris. Whatever may be the truth of the matter, the symbol is not of such importance as many others. It is an elaborate construction utterly lacking in that quality of naturalness and inevitableness which is found in all the older emblems, so that its very artificiality and complexity invites every man to fashion his own interpretation. Until new light is thrown on its origin we can make no better use of it than is made by the Lecture itself, where it is transformed into a kind of allegorical picture of Hiram's death.

II

The Temple. The great Temple of Solomon was erected on a table of rock which crowned a Jerusalem hill called Mount Moriah. This hill itself occupies a most conspicuous place in Hebrew tradition, according to which it was variously the spot where Adam was created, where Cain and Abel sacrificed, where Noah built his altar at the subsidence of the Flood, where Abraham offered Isaac, and David erected his altar. The Mohammedans, who inherited so much from the Jews, described it as the "Centre of the World," and "The Gate of Heaven," and Mohammed persuaded his followers that it was from this same hill that he had made his famous "ascent to heaven."

The Temple which Solomon erected there by the assistance of Hiram of Tyre has had an even larger place in the traditions of mankind. Few realise now how high that Temple on Mount Moriah towered in the history of the olden world, and how the story of its building haunted the legends and traditions of times following. Many a church in the Middle Ages was patterned on it, and many a writer, such as Durandus and Bunyan, used it as a symbol of religious truth. In making so much of their symbolism to cluster about this dream-haunted building the early Masons were only following in the footsteps of many others.

Until a half century ago Masonic writers believed that our Craft had been organised during the building of the Temple, even in detail, and that the Order had survived from then until the present. To-day, there is no need to say, we cannot hold that position, at least, many of us cannot. We have a fairly accurate conception of the size and form of the structure, and we know that it was built by Phœnician workmen, even as our legend asserts, for archæologists have uncovered Phœnician Masons' Marks on the original foundation stones. What the actual historical connection between the Temple Building and our own Fraternity was still remains covered by obscurity. But while we wait for future research to establish that connection, or lack of connection, we need not abate our interest in the Temple or minimise its importance to our Ritual, for the Masonry of to-day is interested in it as a symbol rather than as history.

How the Temple found its way into our system is also a debated question. If we accept Vibert's contention that "there is no evidence that we possessed it at all before the eighteenth century" we are still left with the question on our hands, How did it come to be adopted at that time? In 1724 Villalpandus exhibited a large model in London, accompanied by an explanatory handbook, and this created an immense amount of interest in the subject. Some have believed that the Freemasons of that period were so caught by this wave of interest that they worked it into their symbolism; but Brother S. P. Johnston, who went through the records with a fine-toothed comb, announced that he was unable to find one shred of evidence to support this theory. ("A.Q.C.," vol. XII, p. 135.) Brother Rylands, who was second to none as a Masonic scholar, supported this position in the following statement: "No satisfactory reason has so far been offered why the Temple of Solomon and its builders have been selected to play an important part in one division of our legendary history."

Since Brother Rylands wrote the above sentence, Brother A. E. Waite has come forth with a theory that seems reasonable whether it can be accepted as a "satisfactory" reason or not. Holding as he does that many of the Speculatives who were "accepted" during the eighteenth century were Kabbalists in one degree or another he believes that we may have inherited the Temple symbolism from that source. The Kabbalists had made the Temple one of their principal symbols for more than four hundred years and many of their interpretations were strikingly similar to ours. If we accept the theory of Kabbalistic influence—as I, myself, am inclined to do, at least to a certain extent—we may well believe that our use of the Temple was borrowed from that very influential group of teachers. Be that as it may, we shall always retain the Temple symbolism, for nothing could more adequately portray that which is the great ideal of our Craft—the building up of a Divine human brotherhood here among men.

The Temple was built of wood and stone, and metals taken from the earth; but these materials were so prepared, and so adjusted one to another that a miracle of solemn beauty resulted. We also are gathering together materials which seem earthly or common—men with their fleshly nature, their appetites and passion—and we hope so to prepare and to shape them that in the very act of brotherly union a holy structure of heavenly loveliness will come into existence, a House not made with Hands, in which our human nature will be transfigured. The Temple of Solomon was not an ordinary house of worship, for the worshippers remained in the outer courts; nor was it patterned after the earth or the sun as other temples were, for its entrance faced the East instead of the West. By its orientation and its construction it suggested the system of Heaven and it was designed to be God's dwelling place among men. We also would build a House for God; but whereas the Jews would have Him dwell in a Temple of Stone, we would fain prepare for Him a Temple of Flesh; and our hope is that through the regeneration of men, and through their banding together in a fraternity, the All Highest will tabernacle with us, so that God and Man may abide together in a Holy Eternal House.

III

The Pot of Incense. The use of incense in worship is almost as old and as universal as religion itself. In ancient days when the gods were supposed to be merely magnified invisible human beings it was believed that they would enjoy sweet odours as much as men did, so incense was burned on the altar that they might inhale its "unctuous smoke." Where the custom of slaughtering animals on the altar was in use incense was also employed to cover up the odour; this was especially necessary in warm climates where the malodorousness of a dead carcass soon became intolerable. As religious rites became more spiritualised the burning of incense was usually retained, but in a more symbolic way. Thus, in both the Old and the New Testaments, incense is used as an emblem of prayer, as many texts will testify. In the early Christian period when occultism began to take root, the occultists employed incense in their magic rites, believing it to possess some mysterious potency, like a spell. At the time of the Reformation the custom of using incense in Christian churches became almost abandoned, at least by Protestant bodies, but there is a tendency abroad now to renew the custom, not for any occult or theological purpose but simply to add to the pleasures of the church ceremonies.

In Masonry incense is now used only as a symbol "typifying prayer," and such is its significance in the Third Degree lecture. But it must be noted—for it is usually overlooked, in spite of the Ritual's insistence on it—that our symbol is not only the incense itself, but also the pot, or vessel, in which it is kept. If incense means prayer then the pot of incense means the human heart from which prayers arise, and the purport of the symbol is to remind us that only such prayers are acceptable to God as rise from a spirit guileless and pure.

IV

The Beehive. Both the Bee and the Beehive have been used symbolically from a very old time. In some cases, for what reason it is now hard to guess, the Bee was made the emblem of heaven, as may be seen in certain old Hindoo pictures of the god Krishna wherein Bees hover over the deity's head, and also in similar early pictures of Jesus. Both the Persians and the Egyptians sometimes embalmed their dead in honey because they believed it to possess antiseptic properties; out of this custom, we may believe, arose the latter habit of using the Bee as a symbol of immortality. Alexander the Great, so it is said, was embalmed in this manner; and so, also, were certain of the Merovingian kings. The last fact may explain why the Bee has so often been used symbolically by the French, and why Napoleon, to lend the lustre of age to his upstart dynasty, adopted the insect as his royal emblem. The Bee was used as a symbol of immortality by the Mithraic cult, so popular in the time of the Cæsars, and also by the early Christians, as the catacomb pictures still witness.

The Bee was also used in another order of symbolism. Theocritus tells a charming tale in his Idylls of how Cupid complained to Venus of bee stings and how the goddess archly replied: "Thou too art like a bee, for although a tiny child, yet how terrible are the wounds thou dost inflict!" Anacreon includes the same conceit in his Odes as do other Greek poets, as well as a few of their more modern imitators, such as Manuel de Villegas, the Castilian; Felice Zappi, and even the German, Lessing. Sometimes one will see bees flying about the head of Cupid on old Greek pottery; this is to suggest that as bees steal honey from the rose so does love steal honey from the lips of maidens; and as the stings of the bee are very painful so are the sharp darts of love.

Bees were not domesticated in Europe until the age of the monasteries, when the monks considered a hive an essential part of the equipment, owing to which custom the Beehive came to be used frequently in Christian symbolism. In their exhortations to the monks the church fathers would point to the hive as an example of industry. In the old Ely cathedral of England a woman weeping over a broken beehive evidently represents a home when ravaged by indolence or drunkenness.

The Egyptians called the bees "an obedient people" because of their faithfulness to the rules of the hive and to order. They are a far-sighted people, always preparing for the future, and their industriousness has become proverbial. Alas! as many Masters have learned, in the lodge as in the hive, there are often many drones! The brother who could discover a remedy for the drone evil would lay the whole Fraternity under everlasting indebtedness to his genius. The bees, as we know, kill their drones with scant ceremony; that would be a swift, but unhappy manner of disposing of ours! How to destroy the dronishness without killing the drone, that, as Hamlet would say, is the problem!

CHAPTER LI

THE EMBLEMS (CONTINUED)

I

The Book of Constitutions. During the period lying, say, between 1000 and 1400, when Operative Freemasonry was enjoying its plenitude of power, it is probable that no written constitutions were in use. According to such meagre evidence as we possess it seems that the candidate, at the time of his initiation, was given an oral account of the traditional history of the Craft and that the Master gave him the charges of instruction and duty in such language as he might choose to employ at the time. As would inevitably happen under such circumstances these traditions and charges gradually assumed a more or less stereotyped form until at last, to make uniformity more certain, they were committed to writing.

The oldest MS. form of the Old Charges now in existence, as I have already noted, is that which was written by some unknown cleric somewhere near the year 1390; it is known as the Regius, or Halliwell MS., and is written in the form of doggerel verse. Our next oldest copy is the Cooke, which was written early in the following century. Many copies were made of these from time to time, and other versions of the Craft's story were composed; through the labours of Brother W. J. Hughan, the great pioneer in this field, and through the efforts of his colleagues we now possess close on to a hundred copies of these old documents.

Many copies of the Old Charges were in the hands of brethren in the beginning of the eighteenth century.

When the Revival came, and outsiders began to probe into the secrets of the Order certain of these brethren, to guard against their falling into strange hands, burned several of their manuscripts. Not all, however, were destroyed, and it appears that an attempt to collate the Ancient Constitutions was made as early as 1719.

Shortly after the formation of Grand Lodge some members expressed dissatisfaction with the existing Constitutions and Grand Master Montagu ordered Dr. James Anderson to make a digest of all available manuscripts in order to draw up a better set of regulations for the governance of the body. It is thought by some that it was Dr. Anderson himself who first urged this on Montagu. A committee of fourteen "learned brethren" examined Anderson's work and approved of it, except for a few amendments, and it was accordingly published in the latter part of 1723. This Book of Constitutions "is still the groundwork of Masonry" and stands to our jurisdictions very much as the Constitution of the United States does to our nation.

II

Holding such a position it is fitting that the Book of Constitutions serve as a symbol in the Third Degree. Being, as it were, the title deed of our Fraternity it is much more than a mere instrument of law, and links us on to the great past and binds us in an organic unity to the generations of old builders who, in departing this life, left behind them so shining a monument. As a symbol, therefore, the Book of Constitutions reminds us of our debt to the past, of our solidarity with the vanished generations of kindly workmen, and of the necessity of law and of seemly order if the Craft is to hold itself together in a world where everything is always falling to pieces.

III

The Tiler. If the Tiler is set to guard the Book, it is to remind us that secrecy and watchfulness must ever be at hand to guard us against our enemies, for the Tiler is here introduced as a symbol rather than as an officer of the lodge. When the Craft first began to employ such a sentinel we know not, nor can we be sure how the word itself originated. Some believe that the first tiler was literally what the word implies, a brother employed to make roofs, himself a member of one branch of the old guilds of builders. Others think that as the sentinel is to protect the secrecy of the lodge he was called tiler in a figurative sense since it is the roof which conceals the interior of a building. Accepting such views for what they are worth, and acknowledging the practical necessity for such a guardian, we may also see in the Tiler, in the present connection, a reminder that each and every one of us must become a watchman, seeing to it that no influence shall undermine our organic law, and that no enemies shall be permitted admittance to our fellowship. Every loyal Mason must be a Tiler, watchful lest he recommend an unfit candidate, and careful lest, in his own person, he admit such influences into the lodge as make for disunion and disharmony. To keep off cowans and eavesdroppers, figurative and actual, is one great duty of membership.

Cowan is a Scotch term. It was used in early Scotch Masonry in more than one sense but seems originally to have meant "a man who uses round unsquared stones for building purposes, whether walls or huts"; in other words, the cowan was originally an unskilled Mason. Oftentimes a cowan was loosely affiliated with the Craft but never given its secrets, for which reason he was often known as a "Mason without the word." The term was also employed to describe a non-affiliated skilled Mason, one who had unlawfully obtained the secrets of the Craft—as we would say, a scab.

The word was employed by English Masonry in the Grand Lodge period; Brother J. T. Thorp believes it was Dr. Desaguliers who first used it after his visit to Scotland in 1721; Brother Vibert believes it was imported by Dr. Anderson in 1723 or later. Be that as it may the word found a permanent place in our vocabulary albeit with gradual changes of meaning. Literally speaking, as the word is now employed, a Cowan is a man with unlawful Masonic knowledge; an Intruder is one with neither knowledge nor secrets who makes himself otherwise obnoxious; a Clandestine is one who has been initiated by unlawful means; an Irregular is one who has been initiated by a lodge working without authorisation. In all these senses a man is designated who makes use of the Fraternity in an illegal or obnoxious manner, who uses Masonry for un-Masonic purposes. Manifestly such men cannot be kept out by the Tiler alone; every member must assist in this work of the guardianship of the Order.

IV

Sword Pointing to the Naked Heart. Mackey notes that in old initiation ceremonies, still preserved in some places, the candidate found himself "surrounded by swords pointing at his heart, to indicate that punishment would duly follow his violation of his obligation"; he suggests that in this old ceremony we may find the origin of the present symbol which has been undoubtedly introduced into our system by some modern ritualist, Thomas Smith Webb, perhaps. This is a reasonable account of the matter and may be allowed to stand until further light is available.

The Heart is here the symbol of conscience, the seat of man's responsibility for his own acts; the Sword is the symbol of Justice. The device therefore tells us that Justice will at last find its way to our inmost motives, to the most hidden recesses of our being. This may sound trite enough but the triteness must not blind us to the truth of the teaching.

For centuries men believed that God, the Moral Lawgiver, lived above the skies and dealt with his children wholly through external instruments;—agents of the law, calamities, and physical punishments, such things as these were considered the Divine methods of administering Justice. Entertaining such a view of the matter it is of little wonder that men held themselves innocent until punishment would come, or that Justice could be avoided simply by staying clear of the instruments of Justice. In this wise Morality came to be an external mechanical thing, operating like a civil code of law which depends on policemen.

But now we have a better understanding of the matter. The Moral Law, so we have learned, is in our very hearts, and it is self-executing. Sin and punishment, as Emerson says in his great essay on Compensation, a profoundly original and stimulating study of the subject, grow from the same stem. Conscience, like the physical body, is under a universal Reign of Law that swerves not by a hair's breadth. A man may cherish an evil thought in some chamber of his soul almost outside the boundaries of his own self-consciousness, but such secrecy is of no avail; the law is in the secret places as well as in the open and always does the point of the Sword rest against the walls of the Heart. The penalties of Justice are unescapable because Justice and Conscience are of the same root.

CHAPTER LII

THE EMBLEMS (CONTINUED)

I

The Anchor and Ark. Simple as it is, the Ark and Anchor symbol is very, very old, and around it clusters a cloud of associations drawn from many lands and times. The Anchor's significance is self-revealing and needs no interpreter; it is a type of that security which holds a man fast and prevents his drifting with the winds. Nor is it difficult to learn what is this security, for mankind, with an almost unanimous consent, has found it in Deity who, while all else changes, changes not but overarches the drift of the years with His Eternal Purpose, unyielding Will and everlasting Love. Mrs. Jameson, in her "Sacred Art and Legend," says of the Anchor that it was among early Christians "the symbol of immovable firmness, hope and patience" in which sense it is often displayed in the Catacombs and on ancient Christian gems, and Lundy says that among the same Christians it was also used as a symbol of Christ's divinity, for in that, as the first believers held, was man's one stay against sin and human overthrow.

II

Of the Ark it is somewhat more difficult to speak. Laurence Dermott, the erratic but brilliant Grand Secretary of the Ancients, saw in it an allusion to the Ark of the Covenant, but this is most certainly an error. In company with the Hermeticists with whom it was a familiar emblem, our Ritual sees in it a reminder of the Ark, wherein, according to the old legend, Noah found refuge for himself and family when all else was given over to the Deluge. But the story of Noah's Ark itself rests on more ancient traditions, as any reader of such a work as Dr. Ellwood Worcester's "Genesis in the Light of Modern Knowledge" will remember. Long before that story was conceived the Ancient Mysteries were repeating the story of how some hero god, such as Osiris, was slain, and how his mutilated body was placed in a box, and set adrift upon the waters. The Greeks called such a chest an "ark," a word having the meaning of "containing that which was sacred."

III

Among the first Christians the Ark was used as a symbol of the church, not only because it was a place of refuge for bruised and hunted souls, but also because the church was then thought of as a home for all the family of man. In that great household of faith the individual found security and fellowship and protection from enemies, spiritual or otherwise. This faith found expression in an old, old hymn:

"Behold the Ark of God,
  Behold the open door;
Hasten to gain that dear abode,
  And rove, my soul, no more."

Those Christians found their Ark in their brotherhood of believers; is it not the same with us? Is not our Masonic ark the great Brotherhood itself? In that world-embracing fellowship the individual, often so harassed and lonely, finds help, inspiration and companionship, and many a man on whom disaster "followed fast and followed faster" has found the Order an Ark of quiet and protection. Shall we not believe that even in the future life such privileges will be granted? Eternity would grow a solitary place without the "dear love of comrades" and the binding closer "of man to man."

CHAPTER LIII

THE EMBLEMS (CONTINUED)

I

The Forty-seventh Problem of Euclid. Here is a symbol the sovereign importance of which has been recognised by almost every student of our mysteries. Hoffman wrote a book about it; Sydney Klein devoted a magnificent study to it which will be found published in the Transactions of the Lodge Quatuor Coronati under the title of "The Great Symbol"; Dr. Anderson used it on the title page of his Constitutions and therein described it "as the foundation of all Masonry if duly observed"; scholars have vied with each other in attempting to uncover all the riches stowed away among its lines and angles.

Most of these interpreters, it must be said, have shown considerable dissatisfaction with the account of the Problem as given in the Lecture. There it is said that it was discovered by Pythagoras and that he was so overjoyed by it that he sacrificed a hecatomb to celebrate his discovery. This has behind it the authority of Vitruvius but even so it is hardly credible and that for the following reasons: the Problem was known to the Egyptians long before Pythagoras, and it is not possible that Pythagoras, who forbade the killing of animals, should have sacrificed a herd of oxen so needlessly; also, the explanation that this Problem is to teach us to be lovers of the arts and sciences is not very convincing.

Those who would defend the Monitor here urge that while the three, four, five triangle may have been used before Pythagoras he may have been the first to understand the Problem as a whole; that his "hecatomb" may have been made of wax figures of oxen, as was sometimes the practice; and that the Problem is so important to mathematics that it may well stand as an emblem of all arts and sciences. Between these two views one may take his choice.

II

Whatever may be the attitude of our authorities to the Monitorial interpretation they are all agreed that the Symbol is of the greatest importance. Dionysius Lardner, in his edition of "Euclid," writes: "It is by the influence of this proposition and that which establishes the similitude of equilateral triangles (in the sixth book) that geometry has been brought under the dominion of algebra; and it is upon the same principle that the whole science of trigonometry is founded." The Encyclopædia Britannica calls it "one of the most important in the whole of geometry, and one which has been celebrated since the earliest times. . . . On this theorem almost all geometrical measurement depends, which cannot be directly obtained." On its Masonic uses, our interpreters have written with equal enthusiasm; thus one, Brother J. F. Thompson, says that "in it are concealed more ancient symbolism than all other symbols used by, or incident to, our order. . . . In it we find concealed the jewels of the Worshipful Master, the Senior, and Junior Wardens," and also, he might have added, the Apron, the Square, the Tau square, cross, etc.

The brother who wishes to experiment for himself can easily do so by drawing the triangle after the following fashion; lay out a base line four inches in length; at one end erect a vertical three inches high; connect the ends of these two lines and the figure is drawn; this is not the strictly scientific way of going about it but it will serve. The point of this procedure is that whenever the vertical is three and the base is four, the hypotenuse, or long side, will be five; and the angle at the juncture of the base and the vertical will always be a right angle. After this manner a man can always prove a right angle with no mathematical instruments whatever. What this meant to the ancient builders, before such instruments were devised, or had come into common use, is plain to be seen.

III

But our concern here is not with the Problem as a geometric theorem but with it as a Masonic symbol. What is its Masonic meaning? Many answers can be given to this, none exhaustive, but all valuable; of these I can suggest but two or three.

If we experiment with a group of numbers falling into the series corresponding to three, four, five, we will find that they will always bear the same relationship to each other. In other words, the Problem establishes a harmonious relationship among numbers apparently unrelated. Does not this suggest something of the secret of Masonry? We select a large group of men; they seem to have little in common; but through our teachings, and the application of our principle of brotherhood, we are able to unite them into a harmonious fraternity. The Problem is in this view a symbol of Brotherhood.

The Egyptians made the base line to represent Osiris, the male principle; the vertical, Isis, or female principle; the hypotenuse represented Horus, the product of the two. Suppose we follow such a method and let the base represent our earthly nature; the vertical our spiritual nature; by a harmonious adjustment of these two a complete, or perfect man, will result—the same meaning which we found in the Three Lesser Lights.

IV

Along with these two readings of the symbol we might place an historical interpretation. The ancient builders, as has been repeatedly said, did not have algebra and trigonometry, nor were they in possession of architectural tables or instruments such as we have; nevertheless they were obliged to fashion right angles in the erection of their buildings; how could they have done this without the Forty-seventh Problem, a method so simple that any Apprentice could use it? It is not too much to say that there would have been no ancient Masonry without the three, four, five triangle, or the principle embodied in it; therefore it has for us a peculiar value in that it represents the skill of our early brethren in surmounting their obstacles. Since this principle is so essential to the exact sciences we may agree with our Ritual in seeing in it a symbol of all the arts and sciences. Just as a crown may serve as an emblem of all government so may this triangle serve as an emblem of all science. And since Masonry undertakes to make character building into an art or a science we may also find in the triangle, as Dr. Anderson said, "the foundation of all Masonry if duly observed."

CHAPTER LIV

CONCLUSION

I

The Hour Glass. In writing of Masons' Marks, Brother Gould notes that one of the commonest has ever been the figure of an Hour Glass. "The Hour Glass form, very slightly modified, has been used in every age down to the present, and in almost every country. According to some good authorities, it was a custom (at the period immediately preceding the era of Grand Lodges) to inter an Hour Glass with the dead, as an emblem of the sands of life having run out." What could more clearly prove the hold which this simple but eloquent symbol has ever had on the imagination of man? "The sands of life! they are swiftly running away. Be up, mortal, and about your task. Soon the night cometh when no man can work. In the grave man will seek him out no more inventions; what you do you must do while it is still called To-day!" Such is the message of the Hour Glass, too simple to need any interpreter. He who has learned how to transform time into life, and how to make the years leave behind them that which perishes not, who lives the Eternal Life in the midst of time—such a one has learned the lesson of the Glass.

II

The Scythe. If the Hour Glass is the symbol of the fleetingness of a mortal life in which all do fade as Both the leaf, in which the sands are ever running out, the Scythe is the figure of Time which is itself that stream in which the sands are borne along. Time! What a mighty theme! The libraries of the world could not hold the books that might be written about this eternally fascinating, eternally elusive mystery! so infinite are the suggestions of one small symbol in Masonry's House of Doctrine.

III

Time is ever with us, flowing through our minds as the blood courses through our veins, yet does it mystify us; and the more thinking we do about it the more mysterious does it become. We divide it into Past, Present, and Future. But what is the Past? Has it ceased to exist? If so, why does it continue to influence us? If it continues to exist why do we call it the Past? What is the Future? Is it something already made, awaiting us Out There as the land waits for its explorer? What is the Present? We feel that it exists, yet it eludes us. Before I have said "Now" it is still future; the moment I have said it, it belongs to the past. How can one's mind lay hold of that which is always becoming but never is? If one's mind can not apprehend it, how can it be said to exist? It is such puzzles as these that have led our most opulent minds to despair of ever surprising its secret from Time.

Nevertheless, Time is here, a part of the scheme of things, for good or for bale; indeed, it seems to be the very stuff of life itself, as Bergson has argued so brilliantly in his "Creative Evolution." Existence itself is a process of duration and man begins to die the moment he is born.

IV

The stately solemn words of the Lecture, offered in elucidation of the symbol, leave the mind saddened and weighted with a sense of the frailty, or even futility, of life. William Morris, who is in so many ways the poet of architecture, felt in the same way about it. All through his pages one feels its presence like a shadow against which life's little events become etched into brighter relief, so that the little amenities of the day become all the dearer in that they flutter so fragilely over the abysm of eternity, all the more precious because "the sweet days die."

But there is no need that we be shadowed by the sad-sweetness of this melancholy. Time is a part of the scheme of things, it is the very form of life, so that he who accepts life must also accept Time and look upon it as friend and ally rather than enemy. Time helps to solve our problems, assuages our griefs, and always carries us farther into the strange adventure of existence. The most triumphant minds have trusted themselves to it, as a child to its mother, learning how to transform it into ever richer life, not lamenting the past, nor impatient for the future, but living in an Eternal Now which must be such Time as heaven knows. "Man postpones or remembers," complains Emerson; "he does not live in the present, but with reverted eye laments the past, or, heedless of the riches which surround him, stands on tiptoe to foresee the future. He cannot be happy and strong until he too lives with Nature in the present above time!

"Great souls live many an eon in Man's brief years,
To him who dreads no spite of Fate or Chance,
Yet loves the Earth, and Man, and starry spheres,
Life's swiftness is the pulse of life's romance;
And when the footsteps fall of Death's advance
He hears the feet; he quails not, but he hears."

V

It is above all things fitting that the Ritual which began with the candidate's birth into the world of the lodge should end by bringing him to that death which is but a larger birth into the Grand Lodge above; thus does our sublime symbolism, like the sky, gather all things into its embrace and overarch the end as well as the beginning. So also is it fitting that the Ritual should throw about the instruments and trappings of the grave the memories of the slain Master, thus reminding us that death may be transfigured by a great soul into a pæan and a triumph.

To die is as natural as to be born. Death is no interloper in the universe, but at one with its laws and its life; in truth, it is itself the friend and servant of life in that it keeps fresh the stream and removes the outworn and the old "lest one good custom should corrupt the world." The very act of death proves this, for, however much we shrink from its approach, we yield peacefully to it when it comes. Of this all our physicians testify, as witness these words from one of the noblest of them, Dr. Osier

"I have careful notes of about five hundred death beds, studied particularly with reference to the modes of death and the sensations of the dying. Ninety suffered bodily pain or distress of one sort or another; eleven showed mental apprehension; two positive terror; one expressed spiritual exaltation; one bitter remorse. The great majority gave no sign one way or another; like their birth their death was a sleep and a forgetting."

Natural as it is, however, death will ever remain solemn, and even sad, not only because of what comes after, or "because of the body's masterful negation," but because, as the Lecture reminds us, the day of death is a kind of judgment day, for it brings to an end and sets a lasting seal upon the life of a man. The world with its problems, its imperious needs, its grey tragedies, and ancient heartbreaks, is left behind; the man's career is ended, and the influences of his life, the harvest of his deeds—all these are now taken from his control. What he has done he has done, and death places it beyond his changing. Surely, it must be an awful thing for a human being to realise at the last that, so far as he has been concerned, there is less happiness, less love, less kindliness and honour among men than before he entered life. To so live in the midst of this mystery-haunted world, to so work among the winged days that little children may be happier, youth more joyous, manhood more clean, and old age less lonely; to so live that men will hate less and love more, be honourable in public dealings as in private acts, create more than destroy; to so live that the great Kingdom of Brotherhood may be brought near and man be bound closer to man, and woman closer to woman; that it is to be a Mason!

APPENDIX

APPENDIX

QUESTIONS FOR DISCUSSION

The following paragraphs are designed solely for the use of Study Clubs and such other classes or groups as may systematically study the ritual of Freemasonry by means of the present book. The method pursued in arranging these queries will be immediately apparent; they are constellated in the same order as the chapters and numbered accordingly. No attempt has been made to represent every point made, and often questions have been devised for the purpose of leading discussion outside of the limits imposed upon me in discussing "Symbolical Masonry."

CHAPTER I: AN INTRODUCTION TO THE FIRST STEP

I.—When was the first Grand Lodge of Modern Speculative Freemasonry organised? Where? What was the First Degree then called? How were Masons made in Scotland? Where was the most complete Freemasonry then? What do you know about the famous so-called "schism"? What had come to be the condition of the Fraternity prior to 1717? What, do you suppose, brought about this condition? How many degrees were there at the time of the Revival? What was done with the old "First"? with the old "Third"? By what date was the "three degree" system completed?

II.—What was "Operative Masonry"? What were the Old Charges? Give from memory, and in substance, the picture of an old initiation as given by Hawkins. In what essentials does that initiation differ from the one now in use? What, do you suppose, was the Volume of the Sacred Law then used? Was it the Holy Bible or was it the old Book of Constitutions?

What qualifications were required for initiation? What was an "indenture"? how long did it last? why did it have to last so long? Were the conditions of apprenticeship governed merely by the rules of the Craft or were they also controlled by the laws of the state? To whom was the Apprentice bound? What were the Apprentice's duties? What were the moral requirements of an Apprentice? How could he become a Master? where?

What does the word "Apprentice" mean? What is it to be a "learner"? How did you set out to "learn" Masonry? Is Masonry, do you think, worth the time and trouble of study, real study? Why is a learner said to be in "the Porch"? What would be meant by "Solomon's Porch"? What are the rights of an Apprentice to-day? what are his disqualifications? What is meant by the phrase "in a symbolical sense"? What is a symbol? What is symbolical language? Can you furnish an original example? In what sense is it true that an Apprentice is "born into a new world"? What is meant by obedience? Give examples of your own of how obedience must precede mastery and freedom. Which is morally free, the man who obeys the moral laws, or the man who disobeys them?

III.—What is an "art"? In what sense is life an art? What kind of a building is it that a Speculative Mason is set to build? What are his materials? what are his tools? Which is more difficult to build, a man or a building? In how many various ways may the Apprentice be pictured? In what sense is he a babe about to be born into a new world? in what sense is Freemasonry a "new world"? Did you find it such? What was new in it to you? What is the central idea in Dr. Buck's interpretation? What can you find out about Dr. Buck? who was he? when did he live and where? what did he do? Who is Dr. J. F. Newton? have you read his book, "The Builders"? Does your lodge "put on" the First Degree with solemnity an d beauty? How could you improve it?

CHAPTER II: PETITION FOR MEMBERSHIP

I.—What is the first step to be taken by one who desires admittance to Freemasonry? What is contained in a petition? What are the "constitutional questions"? When is the petition read to the lodge? By whom? What is then done with it? What is an investigating committee? Who must recommend a petition? What is done when a petition is rejected? How is a petition rejected? Can a rejected petitioner make another application? How? When? What is a "jurisdiction"?

II.—Can you discover when the present laws governing petitions first came into use? Give the main points covered in a petition. Tell what you can about John Paul Jones as a Mason? Was his petition substantially the same as yours?

III.—What change of conditions made an investigating committee necessary? Have you ever served on such a committee? How did you perform your functions? Do you believe it to be a good system? Among the last dozen petitions presented to your own lodge how many have you known personally? How can a Master of a lodge safeguard membership? How can he hold a committee up to the highest standards? Have you ever known a lodge to fall to a lower plane of usefulness through the poor materials admitted to membership? if so, tell about it. Have you ever seen a questionnaire? what questions were asked? What do you think of the use of questionnaires? What are the objections? Under what conditions is the questionnaire necessary? For what purposes is it necessary to have filed such information as a questionnaire contains?

IV.—What is meant by "solicitation"? In what way does the problem of solicitation lead a student into the inner soul of Masonry? In what way is solicitation a wrong to the man solicited? What is he asked to swear to at the door of the lodge when he comes to be initiated? In what way does that conflict with his having been solicited? How would solicitation be in danger of misleading him as to the real character of the Order? Why is solicitation an evil to the Order? If solicitation were freely permitted, in what way would it cause a deterioration in Masonry? In this regard compare Masonry with other orders that encourage solicitation. Have you had experience in such? what was the difference?

V.—To what extent can you go in acquainting your non-Masonic friends with the history and principles of Freemasonry? How can you tell a non-Mason what Masonry is? Who was Albert Pike? what great Masonic book did he write?

CHAPTER III: THE BALLOT

I.—What is meant by a "ballot"? Describe the machinery of balloting now employed in Masonry as you understand it. What kind of a man would make bad material for the Fraternity? Do many such gain admission? If so, how? Why is the ballot question so "irritating," as one brother is quoted to have remarked? Could you devise improvements in the method? What are the abuses that creep in under the present system? Could you think of an entirely different system for selecting members?

II.—When is a petition put to the ballot? In how many cases is it one month? two weeks? In how many jurisdictions is a re-ballot required for the Second and Third Degrees? When may a rejected petitioner re-apply? When can a member refrain from voting? What is meant by a "unanimous ballot"? What is the universal custom in America? What is the practice in your own lodge? What is the objection to the unanimous ballot? what do you think about it? What system is employed in England? What may be said in favour of the "three blackballs reject" rule? Does the ballot exist in order to get good men in or to keep bad men out? What does Gibson say about it? Are there landmarks to go by? What is to decide what is the wisest system of balloting? What is the usual custom in France? To what extent should the method of balloting be left optional with the subordinate lodge?

III.—What is meant by "secrecy of ballot"? Do you believe in it? Who was Dr. Mackey? Have you ever seen his system of landmarks? What custom of balloting was used before 1720? Why did the methods for balloting change? What is a viva voce vote? What are the objections to it? Why is the present system "as good a method as can be devised"? Why is the present system of balloting difficult to manage in a large lodge? How can its difficulties be overcome? Has your Grand Lodge dealt with balloting methods recently? What is meant by "Masonic jurisprudence"?

IV.—What is the difference between a Masonic ballot and any other? What determines your choice of political candidates? Have you exactly the same things in mind when you cast your ballot on a petition? In what way does the ballot pass upon a petitioner's character? What are the qualifications for membership in the Order? When should you vote against a man? Should you vote for or against a petitioner who is a stranger to you?

CHAPTER IV: "WORTHY AND WELL-QUALIFIED"

I.—What is meant by "qualifications"? Are they now too rigorous, do you think? What is the "certain purpose" for which Freemasonry is organised? What is the criterion by which the fitness of a candidate is judged? Who was Tolstoy? what is the point of the quotation made from his book? How would you defend the high demands made on candidates as against those who criticise Freemasonry for being "aristocratic or exclusive"?

II.—What were the Old Charges? what are they otherwise called? Name the oldest of them: what is its date? How does it describe the qualifications of membership? Who was James Anderson? When was his version of the constitution made? What qualifications are described in it? What qualifications are demanded by your own Grand Lodge?

III.—Give your own reason why "no bondmen" could be admitted into operative lodges.

Were women admitted to the old guilds? were they admitted to the Masonic guilds? If not, why not? Who was Gould? what did he write? What is he quoted to have said? What does MacBride say?

Give your own reasons at length why an immoral man cannot be admitted. What is "an immoral man"?

IV.—Why does not Masonry accept bad men in order to make them better? What are the reformative agencies in society?

Why cannot we admit women to membership? Under what conditions did Freemasonry evolve into its present form? What would have to be done in order to admit them? Are you in favour of it? To what would you object? From what book are the verses quoted? Have you ever read a History of Masonry? Can you name three such histories?

What is meant by "free born"? What does your own Grand Lodge require on this point? What is Gibson quoted to have said?

What is meant by "mature" age? How old were Apprentices in operative days? What have been the regulations in force in England with regard to age? What are the rules in your own Grand Lodge? What is the point of MacBride's comment? do you agree with him? Have you ever visited lodges in a foreign country? How could a Grand Lodge maintain its requirement for legal age in such wise as to enable a member to visit a jurisdiction in which eighteen years is permitted?

V.—Why has the question of "physical qualifications" so long been a storm-centre? Have you ever debated it? What does the Regius Manuscript say about it? Why was physical soundness necessary in operative lodges? What is the position maintained by the Grand Lodge of England? Why have Grand Lodges in this land maintained the doctrine of physical perfection? What is your own opinion about the matter? Give substance of statement issued by the Board of General Purposes of England. Who was Dr. Oliver? can you name any of his books? What was his position? Who was T. S. Parvin? what position did he take?

VI.—What is meant by a "right motive"? Are you taking Masonry "seriously"? Were you serious when you came in? What is said by Hughan? Who was Hughan? What is a cowan? What is a "watch-fob Mason"?

CHAPTER V: THE HOODWINK

I.—Why is the question "Where were you prepared?" so important? In what way does its answer reveal many of the secrets of Freemasonry. Why, do you suppose, did the Ancient Mysteries demand a long process of preparation? What can you tell about the Mysteries? How much of the Ritual did you understand after you had completed your Third Degree? What is meant by "prepared in the heart"? When is a candidate duly and truly prepared? What kind of preparation room have you in your lodge? How is it protected against jest and derisive remarks?

II.—How did Mackey describe the hoodwink? How would you yourself describe it? What is the symbolical meaning of it? How long has the hoodwink been used in initiations? Who were the Cathari? who was Innocent III? In what sense is it true that the purpose of the hoodwink is NOT to hide things from the eyes of the candidate? What effect did wearing the hoodwink have on you?

III.—What is meant by the word "revelation"? Give examples of your own that explain its meaning. In what sense did Jesus, according to the V.S.L., bring "life and immortality to light"? In what sense has love ever been "the law of the world"? What did Newton discover? Watt? Copernicus? Give other examples that would illustrate the same point. What is the difference between "reveal" and "discover"? In what manner may it be said that Freemasonry "confers the power of vision"?

IV.—What does Freemasonry reveal to us? How? In what sense has brotherhood always been a reality, a "law of the world"? Does Freemasonry create brotherhood? Define the kingdom of heaven. Can you think of a better definition? In what sense was brotherhood "true" during savage times? Does brotherhood seem like a frail tender thing to you? In what sense is this an erroneous thought? What are the enemies of brotherhood? What is the hoodwink that prevents men from discovering it in their own lives? What is the real hoodwink? Give examples of this same idea from religion, politics, and science.

CHAPTER VI: THE CABLE TOW

I.—Why was the noose whereby early man learned to control wild animals of such great importance to him? What part did animals play in the life of primitive man? (See "The Dawn of History," by J. L. Myres.) What led primitive peoples to make symbolical use of tools and implements? Is the symbolising process still going on? If so, give examples. Repeat the examples of the early use of the noose as a symbol given in the text. What is meant by "A.Q.C."? How did Operative Lodges use the cable tow? What is meant by "Operative Lodges"? How is the cable tow used in English lodges? How used among us?

II.—How does Mackey define "cable tow"? The Standard Dictionary? What is said by the author of this last definition? How is the term defined by Pike? by Lawrence?

III.—What did the cable tow mean to you during your initiation? How would you now interpret it? How does Pike interpret it? Do you agree with him? If not, why not? What is Waite's opinion? Paton's? Churchward's? Give the "obedience theory" of the cable tow. Give examples of "bad" obediences; of "good." Why does a symbol always have many meanings? In what sense is this an advantage? Give a list of symbols, emblems, and symbolical acts in every day use about you.

IV.—Repeat the author's interpretation. Do you agree with it? Could you write out your own interpretation? Give substance of Dr. Buck's interpretation. In what sense are you bound by law as a candidate is bound by the cable tow? Is law a thing that gives us liberty? or does it take away liberty? Give examples of other "cable tows" that bind us in every day life? How about the ties of friendship? marriage? business contracts? Does the principle made clear by the interpretation of the cable tow enable you the better to understand the meaning and use of all human ties?

V.—In actual Masonic practice how do you interpret "the length in your cable tow"? What does Castello say? Give Mackey's interpretation. What was the Baltimore Convention? Would "the length of my cable tow" mean the scope of your ability toASSOCIATE with a brother as much as to ASSIST a brother? should it be given that larger interpretation?

CHAPTER VII: THE LODGE

I.—What is Pierson's theory of the meaning of the word "lodge"? Give the various definitions of the word. What is its meaning among Masons? What did it mean to Operative Masons? How did the Fraternity as a whole come to be called "lodge"?

II.—What is the symbolical meaning of "lodge"? What did ancient people believe about the earth? What does Professor Breasted say about Egyptian homes? What does Albert Pike say about ancient temples? Of what is the lodge a symbol? Give a description of the symbolical lodge. What are the Three Pillars on which it is supported?

III.—What does the lodge do for men? How does co-operation increase the power of men? In what way is the lodge a symbol of brotherhood? In what way does lodge life prepare for brotherhood?

CHAPTER VIII: THE ENTRANCE

I.—What is the first step taken toward introducing a candidate into a lodge? What worthy motive might a man have for entering a Masonic lodge? On what must a candidate depend when he enters a lodge? Why must a candidate knock for entrance? Give examples of the way in which one must knock for entrance to the arts and sciences.

II.—How is Freemasonry defined to the candidate? How did MacBride define Masonry? How does he define Speculative Masonry? Give Thomas Green's definition. What is the Royal Arch definition? Give Dr. Buck's definition. Give Brother Waite's definition. What is the author's definition?

III.—How is Masonry defined from the point of view of architectural symbolicism? What is it "which was lost"? What is Brother MacBride's illustration of this idea? What is meant by a "drama of regeneration"? In what way can Masonry be thus described?

IV.—What is meant by "a merely natural man"? How can one live the eternal life now? Give Albert Pike's definition of Freemasonry.

CHAPTER IX: THE SHARP INSTRUMENT

I.—What is the meaning of "sharp instrument?" What is the only real penalty? Why have penalties led to attacks on Freemasonry? What is MacBride's theory concerning them? What are the actual penalties of wrongdoing? What are the penalties for transgressing the laws of any art.

I.—What is the place of prayer in human life? What is Thorp's theory of the Apprentice's prayer? Why is prayer found in the Masonic ceremonies? In what way is prayer a force? How may prayer be described as "spiritual work"?

II.—Why should man pray if God is all-knowing and all-powerful? Give examples of the way in which God and man must work together. Why do men pray? What are the effects of prayer? Do any other living beings on this earth ever pray? Who was the author of the stanzas quoted? What do these stanzas mean?

CHAPTER XI: CIRCUMAMBULATION

I.—What is the meaning of the word Circumambulation? From whom have we inherited this rite? What do primitive people believe about the sun? Among what people was the rite of Circumambulation practised? What is said about the Greeks, Romans, Hindoos, Druids and early Christians? In what way does Mackey compare Masonic Circumambulation with the Greek?

II.—How did the old Legends explain Circumambulation? What was Pike's explanation? In what way is Circumambulation "a drama of the development of the individual life"? What is Pierson's theory? What did Circumambulation mean to you at the time of your initiation? What is the last explanation given?

III.—What does the sun represent? In what way does Circumambulation suggest "the secret of human accomplishment"? Give some examples of this.

CHAPTER XII: APPROACHING THE EAST

I.—Into how many parts may the ceremony of approaching the East be divided? Why did early peoples come to look upon the North as a place of darkness? What does Fort say about the North in the Middle Ages? What does Evans say about the symbolism of the North? Milton? Shakespeare? Why is the North in the Masonic lodge the place of darkness? What is the symbolism of the South? How did the church builders make use of this symbolism? What part does the South play in a Masonic lodge? What is the symbolical meaning of the West? Who was Sophocles? How does Tennyson use the symbolism of the West? What does the East mean in a Masonic lodge?

II.—What is meant by Orientation? How were ancient temples situated and dedicated? How was the city of Rome oriented? How were early Christian churches situated? How did the Jews orient their temples? Why is the Master's station in the East? How is the Masonic lodge oriented?

III.—What is the meaning of the approach to the East? What is the Masonic ceremony of approaching the East? What is the meaning of that ceremony? How do you approach the East in your daily life?

CHAPTER XIII: THE ALTAR

I.—Where does the Altar stand? How should the Altar be made? With what should it be furnished? Where is the Masonic life lived? Of what is the Altar a symbol? In what way is it the symbol of gratitude? What is the theory of human stewardship?
II.—How was the Altar used as a sanctuary in early centuries? In what way is the lodge a sanctuary? In what way is the Altar a station of sacrifice? What is meant by sacrifice? How do you yourself make use of sacrifice?

III.—Give in your own words the substance of the paragraph quoted from Dr. Newton. Why is man a "seeker after God"?

CHAPTER XIV: THE OBLIGATION

I.—Define the word "obligation." Have oaths and obligations been in universal practice? Why? Can you name oaths administered outside the Fraternity with which the Masonic obligation may be compared? Are the marriage oath, the President's oath, etc., such forms? Why is a religious sanction thrown about an oath? Does the taking of an obligation imply that the candidate cannot be trusted? Does it make his obligation or does it define it? What does Tyler say about the universality of oaths? How do Philo and Cicero define an oath? Can you give a better definition of an obligation than any herewith offered? If so, will you send it in to the Society?

What does Gould believe to have been the original of the Masonic oath? Why was the oath taken by the freemen adopted into the forms of the Masonic lodge? Do we see to-day any institutions copying the forms of oaths employed by some other institution? Name them. Were the earliest Masonic obligations short or long? How did the obligation evolve into such length? Is this legitimate? Have any other parts of the ceremony evolved similarly? Are Masonic ceremonies still changing and growing? If so, why? If not, why not? What was the substance of the earliest obligations? Why were the building secrets so jealously guarded? How did these secrets come to be public property? What effect did such publicity have upon the Freemasons?

What is the whole point of the present obligation? Have we any trade secrets? If you believe that a simpler, more effective obligation might be written, will you offer one? Why should Masonic secrets be still so jealously guarded? What is the function of secrecy in Masonry? Does friendship have its secrets? Business? Diplomacy? What would happen to the Fraternity if it should abandon its policy of secrecy? Does secrecy attract men to it? Why?

What is the meaning of "due form"? Whence came the term? What is the difference between form and formality? When two friends meet do they shake hands in "due form"? Does the form in which the obligation is given add to its dignity and impressiveness? Do you permit any flippancy in your own lodge's ceremony of initiation? Why not?

Why are the penalties kept so secret? How much can you talk about Masonry without violating your obligation to secrecy? Did the earliest obligations have any penalties attached? If not, why not? What is the "Harleian Manuscript"? What is meant by "Old Charges"?

What do Old Testament writers seem to feel concerning the sea? When the sailors cast Jonah overboard did they suppose they were putting him out of reach of the God he had offended? Would you as soon be buried in the sea as on the land? What is meant by "consecrated ground"? What churches still bury their dead in consecrated ground? Why? Does the custom of setting apart a special tract of ground for burial add dignity to the thought of death? Would you as soon think yourself dead lying in the sea as lying in a grave?! Who added the present penalties to our obligations? When? What hint do you get from Brother Clegg's suggestions?

II.—Why have anti-Masons so rabidly attacked the obligation? Is a man scared by penalties which he knows will never be inflicted? Who was John Quincy Adams? Why did he fight the Fraternity? Do you agree with what Brother MacBride says about the obligation? If not, why not? If you do, why? Is there any way in which the obligation could be recast? Who would have the authority to do so? Would it be of any advantage to have a General Grand Lodge of America to take care of such matters?

Why is the cable tow removed when it is? What does it signify? Is the obligation an appeal to a man's sense of honour? Or is it a slam against his sense of honour? Does the wedding oath add to or detract from the stability and dignity of marriage?

If marriages were left to private wills could the law have any control over them? How could Masonic law be brought to bear upon a man who had never taken an obligation? What is the real "Masonic Tie"? Does that tie draw you to other Masons? Does it ever restrain you from doing a wrong to a brother Mason? Why?

CHAPTER XV: THE THREE GREAT LIGHTS

I.—Why is the Holy Bible called the V. S. L.? To what extent are the materials in our ritual drawn from it? In what sense is the Bible true? What constitutes its "unity"? How many books in it? Can you tell how these books came to be gathered together? Can you tell the difference between the canon (or "collection") of books used as the Bible by the Greek Catholics, the Roman Catholics, and the Protestants? What is inspiration? In what way is the Bible inspired?

What does "infallible" mean? Is the Bible infallible as history? As a book of science? In what way is it infallible? If it is infallible in any manner at all how can we prove it? How can its teachings be verified? How are scientific teachings verified?

Of what is the Bible a symbol? What are the sacred books of other races? When, and for what reason, can those books be substituted for the Bible on a Masonic altar? In what manner can other sacred books serve as a symbol of that of which the V. S. L. is the symbol?

II.—In how many ways is the Square used in our ritual? Describe the Square as it is used Masonically. Why did early peoples think that the earth was cubical or square-shape? How did the Square come to have its present significance? What is the Great Light of which it is a symbol? Why do we say of an honest man that he is "square"? What do we mean by "the square deal"? Why do we say that a dishonest man is "crooked"? Is dishonesty ever justifiable? Is a dishonest man like one who walks in the dark? Why?

III.—Why did ancient peoples believe the heavens to be circular? What did the Compasses signify to them? What do they signify to us? Do you believe that there is a divine element in you? Is there a divine element in a murder? How can we discover the divine in others? and in ourselves? How can we learn to let it rule us? Explain the various positions of the Compasses with relationship to the Square and explain the reason for this.

CHAPTER XVI: THE LESSER LIGHTS

I.—What are the Lesser Lights? What is meant by Hermetic? What was the Hermetic symbolical explanation of the sun? of the moon? Give illustrations of the way in which nature is divided between male and female, active and passive. Who was John Woolman? What kind of a nature did he have? Who was Friedrich Nietzsche? What did he stand for? Who were Isis, Osiris, Horus? What does the Worshipful Master represent in Masonic symbolism?

II.—What is Steinbrenner's theory of the Lesser Lights? How could this symbol have been suggested by lodge windows? What do you think about Steinbrenner's theory? What did the Lesser Lights mean to you?

CHAPTER XVII: "LUX E TENEBRIS"

I.—Repeat in your own words Brother Newton's paragraph about light. What was the nature of the first religions of the world? Repeat quotation from Norman Lockyer. Who is Norman Lockyer? What does he say about the Egyptians and their beliefs concerning the Sun? Why did ancient peoples worship light?

II.—What does the Bible say about light and darkness? Who was Jamblichus? Zoroaster? What is the meaning of "Lux e Tenebris"? Why are Masons called the sons of light? In what way does initiation bring a candidate to light? What is meant by light in Masonry? What is the difference between truth and knowledge?

III.—What meaning does the author give to the symbolism of light? In the world at large? In the individual? What is the word that Masonry utters to man? What is the lost word?

CHAPTER XVIII: WORDS, GRIPS AND TOKENS

I.—Give examples of the use of secret modes of recognition in past times. What does Gould say about the use of signs, grips, etc.? Why, do you suppose, are these "common features" of all secret societies? In what way do they protect secrecy? Why should secrecy be protected? Can you name any political, social, religious, or literary clubs which employ secret modes of recognition? If so, why do they use them? Chemists and druggists employ arbitrary signs to stand for various formulæ, and these are understood only by themselves. Are such signs analogous to our own?

II.—What evidence is there to show that Freemasons used signs in old times? Why is the evidence so slender? Why were not these signs published and explained? What is the point of the quotation from Fergusson? Even if the early Operative Masons had been able to read and write, could they have dispensed with their signs and grips? We can all read and write: why have we not dispensed with them?

Can you guess what the Scotch "Mason Word" may have been? What was the significance of "words" among Masons in other countries at that time? How, and for what purpose, do we use words? Can you define a "password"? What are its usages and advantages? Does the army employ passwords? Why? What other organisations do so? In what way is "Word" used in the Third Degree? What is the meaning of "The Lost Word"?

III.—What is the "Due Guard"? Why was it invented and taken up by American lodges? What is the meaning of "an Americanism" as Mackey employs the term?
In what way are grips and tokens different from passwords? Can you give any examples of your own use of these outside the lodge room? When we say we have given a friend "a token of our esteem" do we use the word in its Masonic sense? Why are Masons entitled to use secret modes of recognition? Can you give reasons not given in this paper?

CHAPTER XIX: THE RITE OF SALUTATION

I.—What is the meaning of "salutation"? How is it used in general society? Is tipping your hat to a lady a salutation? Why does a private salute an officer in the army? Give all the reasons you can think of to explain why the candidate should salute the Wardens. In what way do they represent the law and authority of the lodge?

What is there in the principles of Masonry that has ever caused it to be the champion of liberty? Can you offer examples not given in the paper? Can you tell the story of Masonry's part in the Revolutionary War? What great leaders in that day were Masons? Was Lafayette a Mason? Washington? Franklin? Where was the Bible obtained on which Washington took his oath of office?

II.—Can liberty exist in a monarchy as well as in a democracy? What is the difference between "freedom" and "liberty"? Between "liberty" and "independence"? Can a nation be independent without enjoying liberty? Did Italy secure liberty when she gained independence from Austria and France? What is a "free thinker"? Are Masons "free thinkers"? Why is law necessary to liberty? What would become of liberty if laws were destroyed?

What does law do for us in our daily life? Why should a man desire to be free? What are the advantages of freedom? What are the relations between liberty and authority? Are they opposed to each other? Why are Masons bound to uphold the dignity of law and order? What is meant by "civil scepticism"? Does the habit of speaking sarcastically of law and of courts help to uphold man's respect for social order? What should be a Mason's attitude toward the laws of his own community? Suppose, as was the case in Italy, that Masonry itself were declared unlawful, should a Mason under such circumstances oppose the law? If so, why? In what way should such opposition be different from lawlessness?

Is the desire to substitute a good law for a bad law, lawlessness? How were the laws of Masonry instituted? How are they enforced? In what way do they protect the liberty of each member? Would you say that the Masonic organisation is a constitutionalism or a democracy? What is the difference?

CHAPTER XX: THE APRON

I.—Why has the apron been interpreted so variously? Give,; a list of the interpretations you have heard. Why is it dangerous to seek for symbolisms in the present shape and size of the apron? How long has it had its present shape and size? If the shape and size has changed from time to time is it safe to build any symbolism thereon?

II.—Can you give any examples of non-Masonic use of the apron not mentioned in the text? Why, do you suppose, has the apron been so widely used? Why did the Operative Mason wear an apron? What do you imagine its material and size to have been? If it was once of leather, why? Why was it changed to its present material? Why is the apron we usually wear in lodge different from that given to us during initiation? What led Speculative Masons to change its material and shape? Give usual dimensions of aprons as worn in American lodges. Why are they sometimes varied for different degrees and offices?

III.—What is a badge? What is the badge of a Mason? What is the difference between a badge and an emblem? A symbol? Has the Masonic use of the apron done anything to wear down the old prejudice against manual labour? Why were men ever so prejudiced? How long has it been since the prejudice began to break down? What were the causes? What are the labours of a Mason? Are they of any great value to society?

IV.—In what way is the apron as now used the symbol of sacrifice and innocence? Why have men so frequently thought of white as a symbol of innocence? Give examples of the early use of the colour as such symbol. What is the meaning of innocence? How can a grown man be innocent? What is the Masonic meaning of innocence?

What do you think of Brother Crowe's argument as given in the text? Why is the lamb the symbol of sacrifice? Can you give examples from the Bible of such a meaning? What is sacrifice? Why is sacrifice necessary? What is a Mason's sacrifice?

What was the Golden Fleece? The Roman Eagle? Star and Garter? Why is the apron more ancient and honourable than these? How would it affect human society if all men accepted the Masonic meaning of toil, innocence and sacrifice?

CHAPTER XXI: DESTITUTION

I.—What is the significance of the way in which the candidate is prepared? What is the difference between humility and humiliation? Why should the symbols in a Masonic lodge cause a man to feel humility? What is meant by discalceation? What is Mackey's interpretation of discalceation? What is the meaning of this ceremony in the terms of every-day life?

II.—What is the meaning of the word holy? What does the Holy Bible teach concerning holiness? What is meant by sacredness? What is astrology? alchemy? What was the astrological theory about the influence of planets? What does A. E. Waite say about destitution? What is your theory of destitution?

CHAPTER XXII: THE NORTHEAST CORNER

I.—Why is the candidate "reinvested with that of which he had been divested"? Why not wait until the end of the degree? What means "Northeast"? Is a boy halfway through school standing in education's "Northeast"? What is the Masonic meaning of "profane"? Why is the North a place of darkness and the East a place of light? Why is an Entered Apprentice said to be midway between the two? Do you know of any members of your lodge who are still in the Northeast? Has your study club helped you to find the East?

Describe the posture of the candidate as he stands in the Northeast Corner. Why is he made to stand thus? When is a man morally upright?

What is the function of a cornerstone in a building? Have you ever attended a ceremony of cornerstone laying? If so, describe what happened. Why a ceremony? What would you describe as a cornerstone of government? Of education? Of religion? In what way is the Entered Apprentice the cornerstone of Masonry?

Describe the cornerstone ceremonies in early times. Why was a living man sacrificed? What is the real meaning of sacrifice? Have you ever made sacrifices for Masonry? In what way has the Fraternity a right to expect sacrifices from its members? Would you agree with this definition of Masonic sacrifice: "Masonic sacrifice is the surrendering of all that conflicts with the principles of Masonry"? Name some things which men commonly do that would so conflict. What sacrifice has Masonry as a whole been making during the war—not subordinate lodges, but the Craft as a whole?

II.—What is your opinion of human nature? Do you believe that man is by nature depraved? Is our hope for the race built on what man is now, or on his capacities? What can be meant by the divinity of man?

Has man a capacity for the god-like? If so, how does Masonry appeal to that? How does Masonry help to develop it? What is the point of Brother Markham's poem? Do you agree with him? Is it mere sentimentalism to deal with men in such a way as to call out the best that is in them? In what way does Masonry make its appeal to the best that is in us?

CHAPTER XXIII: WORKING TOOLS OF AN ENTERED APPRENTICE

I.—What can you add to the quotation from Carlyle? What particular accomplishment of man is cited by Bergson to distinguish man from brute? In what manner do the tools of the brute differ from those of man? How has man's superiority over the brute developed? Where does man's superiority lie?

What is the key to Masonry's use of the "working tools"? What is their use? How are they symbolised? What is the ultimate design to be accomplished by the use of the working tools of Masonry? Can a Mason shape his own destiny or be instrumental in shaping the destiny of others without the aid of his Masonic working tools?

Why is not the newly initiated candidate at once intrusted with all the working tools or implements of Masonry? With what tools is he intrusted and instructed in the Masonic application of, in the Entered Apprentice degree? in the Fellow Craft degree? in the Master Mason degree?

II.—What is a "twenty-four inch guage"? Of what is it the symbol, in our Monitors? Give the Monitorial exposition of the twenty-four inch guage in the language of the standard "work" of your Grand Jurisdiction. What reference to it was made by the old writers in connection with Saints Ambrose and Augustine and King Alfred? Do you agree with what the author says regarding the right use and division of time? If not, why not?

What is your definition of "Time"? What definition of it does the author give? Does Time symbolise to you opportunities to be grasped and improved upon? Who wastes time, the laggard or the successful man? Do you consider it a waste of time to attend the Study Club meetings of your lodge or Study Club? Are you wasting time by not attending these meetings? Are you applying the twenty-four inch guage to your time as did Abraham Lincoln and Albert Pike and other busy men?

What is the fundamental reason for so many men developing into "human failures"? How may we protect ourselves against becoming failures in life? How has man heretofore divided his actions? What test should we apply to our actions? What foundation are Masons laying for the morality of the future? What great secret have we to learn from the twenty-four inch guage?

III.—What was the symbolism of the gavel in the Middle 'Ages? Whence was this symbolism derived? Of what was the gavel a symbol in Scandinavian mythology? What other peoples attribute to it the same symbolism? What is the Masonic derivation of the gavel? Give the Monitorial reference o the gavel as used in the standard "work" of your Grand Jurisdiction. Is the common gavel a symbol of authority? How is it distinguished from the implement of authority wielded by the Master of a lodge? What functions are combined in the common gavel? What is Mackey's explanation of its probable derivation? What use did the Operative Masons make of the common gavel? What is a "knob" on a stone? an "excrescence"? What do these suggest to the author? Do you agree with him in his deductions? If not, why not?

Does Masonry demand more from its members in the foregoing respect than do other organizations of their members or employés? What is the first lesson to be learned by a soldier, or an employé of a corporation? Why must they learn this lesson? Is "team work" and "co-operation" necessary to the success of a lodge? of a Grand Lodge? of Masonry as a whole? Could Masonry successfully cope with the questions which are arising each day in connection with the great work of reconstruction which the world is now facing, without some such united organisation as the recently launched "Masonic Service Association of the United States"? Did the necessity of "team work" and "co-operation" demand the organisation of such a Body?

CHAPTER XXIV: AN INTRODUCTION TO THE SECOND STEP

I.—What is the meaning of the term Fellow Craft? What were the Schaw Statutes? What do they say about Fellow Craft? What was a Mason's mark? What was the ceremony of passing in Operative lodges? When was the term introduced into England? What was the old-time meaning of Fellow Craft? How did the term come to have its present meaning?

II.—What was a masterpiece? What is the key word of the Second Degree? Who was William Preston? What did he set out to do? Who was Hemming? When were his lectures adopted? Who was Philip Webb? What was the dominating idea in Preston's time? What did Preston do with the Second Degree?

III.—What does Pound say about Preston's theory? What is your own theory concerning the matter? What did the Second Degree mean to you when you were initiated?

CHAPTER XXV: PASSING

I.—What is the meaning of indentured? What space of time do American Jurisdictions require between the First and Second Steps? What does Gould say about marks in Solomon's Temple? How did Operative Masons use the mark? What is meant by essay? How could present-day lodges make use of the old custom of the essay or masterpiece?

II.—What do you think about the memory test? What was an intender? What is the function of custodians of the work? How could the Fraternity carry on schools of Masonry? What should be demanded of a candidate who wishes to pass from the First to the Second Degree?

CHAPTER XXVI: SQUARE ON THE BREAST

I.—What is meant by the phrase "arts, parts and points," etc., familiar to every Mason? What teaching do they convey? Is a Mason expected to be square and upright only in his dealings with members of the Fraternity? What has always been expected of him in his relations to the Craft? Is a Fellow Craft under any stronger tie to the Fraternity than he was as an Apprentice? Why?

What was the original meaning of virtue? What is its present-day definition? What is your definition of "rectitude"? Should Masons be content with merely observing the conventions of society, or should they strive to be active at all times in things that tend toward a higher plane of morality?

II.—Of what is the breast a symbol in Masonry? What are we to realise from the Fellow Craft application of the square? Has the man who has two codes of ethics, one of which he practises for effect in his own community and the other when away from home and among strangers, fully learned the truth designed to be conveyed by the application of the square? What kind of a moral code does Masonry demand that its votaries follow?

CHAPTER XXVII: THE SCRIPTURE READING FROM AMOS

I.—What custom was observed by the Greeks during their ceremony of Circumambulation? Why did this custom obtain? What similar custom is practised in Masonic lodges of the present day? Why?

What did Amos seek to do in his day? What is the end to which the Fellow Craft should apply the knowledge gained in his Masonic studies? What was the state of society during the time of Amos? What penalty was inflicted upon Amos because of his teachings? What was Amos' method of teaching?
II.—What picture does Amos portray to us in the Scripture reading? What is the author's interpretation of the reading? Have you a better interpretation?

What was the lesson learned by Job? Can we expect to escape from punishment for our wrongdoings?

CHAPTER XXVIII: THE OBLONG SQUARE

I.—In what particular does the Fellow Craft's approach to the East differ from that of the Entered Apprentice? What is the significance of this variation? Prior to the time of reading this chapter, did you ever try to discover the origin and meaning of the term "oblong square"? If so, what did you learn concerning it?

What is Mackey's definition? What reference does he find in it? Whence does he seek to trace this reference? What inference does the author take from Mackey's deductions?

II.—What other interpretations are cited by the author? What objections are advanced to these interpretations? How are squares classed by Brother Hunt? Do you agree with him in his deductions? If not, why not? How is Brother Hunt's theory supported by Irwin?

What theory does the author advance as to the possible manner in which the "oblong square" was handed down to us? What lesson does he think the framers of our present-day ritual intended to convey when they retained the phrase?

CHAPTER XXIX: DUE FORM

I.—Describe the "due form" assumed by the candidate in the Fellow Craft degree. In certain jurisdictions whenever the signs are given the brethren must also be on the step of that particular degree at the same time. It is held that the signs cannot be properly given unless this is done. The brethren thus place themselves in due form to give the signs. Try this, and see if the body is not thus brought into the proper position to facilitate giving the signs properly. Then try giving them without first being "on the step." Possibly you will thereby discover the reason for practising such "forms."

Define the words "form" and "formality." What is a "formalist"? What is "formality"? Is "form" necessary in our every-day business and social life? Is it necessary in Masonry? If so, for what purpose? Why do we use the term "due form"? Is a candidate expected to comply with these "due forms"? What does his compliance signify?

CHAPTER XXX: WORKING TOOLS OF A FELLOW CRAFT

I.—What are the working tools of a Fellow Craft? How have you explained them to yourself? What is their meaning in your understanding now? Why do you always think of goodness, holiness, heaven, God, as being above you? What is the difference, in your judgment, between morality and righteousness? Do you think of your ideal of your own life as being above and beyond you? If so, what efforts are you making to attain to that ideal? May this not be one of the suggestions in this working tool of the plumb?

What do you mean by "a hero"? How can a man erect himself above himself? What influence has the memory of Washington, Pike, Jefferson and Lincoln had for you? In what way may a true Mason be a hero to his friends? his family? his race?

II.—What do you understand yourself when you use the word "level"? Do you really believe that you are equal in all ways to every other individual? Is every other individual equal to you in all ways? If there are fundamental differences between you and other individuals, just what is the nature of these differences? What do you understand by "pride"? "superciliousness"? In what way are all Masons on a level with each other? What becomes of your pride when you sincerely stand in a lodge room on a level with your brother countryman?

III.—How would you explain the meaning of the square when that symbol is used as one of the working tools of a Fellow Craft? How can the sense of manly pride and the feeling of equality be joined together in your own experience? Do you really use your gifts to help your brethren and to help others in this world? How can a healthy man use his own strength to help those that are ill? How can a learned man use his learning to help those that are ignorant? How can a man who has money really help those that have little or no money? Should not we try to help others in such a way that they do not even know that we are helping them? How should parents help their children? How should teachers help their pupils?

How may the Master and officers of a lodge help the members of that lodge without their knowing it? What is meant by not letting your right hand know what your left hand is doing?

CHAPTER XXXI: THE ASHLARS

I.—What is your understanding of the Ashlar symbolism? hat is meant by saying that a profane man, using the word in a Masonic sense, is but like a rough block of stone? Is not an ignorant, unclean, profane, dishonest, unbrotherly man like an unshaped piece of rough rock from the quarry? If you know of such a man, how can you help him to become a man more square, cultured and brotherly? What is the Masonic Fraternity as a whole now doing, in your own honest estimation, to help this old world to cease to be a wreck of a world?

II.—Is not this present world but a great crude piece of rock in your eyes? What can our Fraternity do to help make this living human race more square with the everlasting laws of life, righteousness, health, happiness and God? Which are you in your own lodge—a rough ashlar or a perfect ashlar? What do you do with the members of your lodge who make trouble? Do you grow impatient with them, or do you help them? You see that all these questions are designed to lead Masonic students to understand that Freemasonry tries to help us in our daily lives.

CHAPTER XXXII: THE MIDDLE CHAMBER

I.—In what light have you heretofore interpreted the existence of the "Middle Chamber" of Solomon's Temple—as a literal fact or simply as a symbol? What is Sir Charles Warren's opinion? What is Mackey's opinion regarding it? Do you agree with them? If not, what reasons have you for disagreeing with them?

What is the modern Biblical interpretation of the term "chamber" as used in the present connection? How many such chambers were there in the Temple, and what were their uses? Were they used as "paymaster's offices," or as chambers of instruction?

What is a "myth"? Were our ceremonies contrived as vehicles for the conveyances of historical facts to candidates? What thought should we continually bear in mind while pursuing our Masonic studies?

Of what is the Middle Chamber a symbol? What does it represent in the Second Degree ritualism? How are we benefited by "learning" or education?

What part does the Second Degree occupy in Ancient Craft Masonry? Would the system have been complete without it? Have you gained a new conception of the Second Degree from this section of the author's present study paper from that which you formerly held of it?

CHAPTER XXXIII: OPERATIVE AND SPECULATIVE

I.—Describe Operative Masonry. Why did Operative Masonry decline? Give substance of MacBride's theory? What specific elements existed in Operative Masonry? What is Mac-Bride's theory about this? Give substance of A. E. Waite's theory. What elements in modern Masonry could not have come from Operative Masonry? What did Speculative Masonry inherit from Operative Masonry? What is Masonry's general idea concerning the world? What is the point of the Browning poem?

How were builders organised in mediæval times, and for what purpose? Why were they intrusted with signs, words and grips? why were they called "Operative" Masons?

Why were persons who had no connection with the building trades admitted into the Order prior to 1717? What attracted them to it? What was the result of their admittance?

How does Brother MacBride describe the transition from Operative to Speculative Masonry?

What influence has the speculative element on the operative organisation?

What did the non-operative element undertake to do after their acceptance into the organisation, according to Brother Waite? How were Kabbalistic and Rosicrucian ideas and symbols introduced into the Order?

What did Speculative Masonry inherit from the Operatives? Was all of our philosophy and mysticism handed down from the Operatives?

What was the work of the Operative Mason, and what were his wages? What is the work of the Speculative Mason, and what are his wages?

Do you believe with those who claim that the race cannot be improved; that because evils of one kind and another have always existed, that they are always to remain with us? What is the mission of Masonry?

CHAPTER XXXIV: THE TWO GREAT PILLARS

I.—Why did early peoples set up pillars before their places of abode, about their villages and over the graves of their dead? What did they believe such pillars to symbolise? What did pillars portray to the Mayas and Incas? How were they looked upon in Bible times? By whom were monoliths most widely used? In what manner, and for what purposes? In the course of religious development what did they come to symbolise? What did the obelisk symbolise?

Whence did the custom of placing pillars before temple entrances proceed from Egypt? What did Hiram probably use as his models for the pillars placed before Solomon's Temple?

What do the pillars used in the lodge room represent? What is the height of the pillars as given in the Book of Kings? In the Book of Chronicles? What is the author's theory concerning these variations? How does Mackey describe the original pillars?

II.—What was the shape and composition of the pillars? What was their combined weight? What were they respectively called and what were their positions? How are these names interpreted Masonically? What part did they occupy during celebrations? Where were the pillars supposedly cast?

What should be the height of the pillars used in our lodge rooms? What are the heights as adopted by American Grand Lodges? What was the height of the pillars as now accepted by present-day authorities? Is it imperative that we know the actual height of the pillars to pursue our Masonic studies? In what light should we consider them?

What did the pillars symbolise to Preston? To Caldecott? To Covey-Crump? To Mackey? To the old Jewish Rabbis? What is the author's interpretation?

Where do you keep the pillars in your lodge room during the time they are not in actual use? Has such position any particular significance? In some jurisdictions we find them at either side of the entrance from the preparation room; in others they stand in front of the Senior Warden's station. Can you give a reason for either or both of these locations other than "for convenience"? How did the pillars impress you when you first saw them? What do they mean to you now?

CHAPTER XXXV: THE GLOBES

What are the two globes called? Why are they so-called? Describe the Egyptian symbol of the Winged Globe. What is the objection to the theory that our globes came from Egypt? What is the author's theory of the origin of the globes? Why did Preston give the globes a place in the Second Degree? What do the two globes represent? What sciences deal with the earth? What sciences deal with the heavens? In what way can a Mason gain enlightenment from this science?

What two theories have been offered by Masonic scholars concerning the origin of the globes? How was the first theory suggested? What is the symbol of the winged globe? What did its oval shape suggest or symbolise? Do you accept this Egyptian theory? If so, why? If not, why not?

Why does it appear that Preston modified the chapiters of the pillars into globes? How is Preston's theory verified? Do you agree with the author that we of to-day have the same right to interpret the symbols in our own way as did the ancients? If not, why not?

CHAPTER XXXVI: THE ASCENT

I.—To what extent is the origin of the symbolism of the Winding Stairs generally known? Is it essential that we discover the exact facts in order to intelligently pursue our present study?

Have there ever been advanced satisfactory answers concerning the source of the symbolism? To what extent should discussion of the origin be considered of value?

Do you agree with the contention of early scholars that there was actually a winding stair of three, five or seven steps in Solomon's Temple? What can you offer in support of such contention? Could the semicircular stairway at the Gate Nicanor where the Levites chanted the "Psalms of Degrees" have been taken as the prototype of our winding stairs? What is your opinion concerning this theory? What does Sir Charles Warren say concerning the staircase?

What is the "Theological Ladder"? When and by whom was it introduced into the ritual? What was the symbolism of the "Theological Ladder"? Have we anything similar to it in our ritual of the present day? What does the author say about this interpretation?

What is the theory of the Operative origin of the symbolism? Can this theory be depended upon? If not, why not?

Since the origin of the Winding Stair symbolism cannot be accurately traced, how should we view the use of the stairs in our work?

II.—What does the use of the mystical numbers suggest to you? Of what is the Winding Stair as a whole a symbol?

What is Pike's theory concerning the number "15"? What would happen should our present symbolic arrangement of the Winding Stairs be changed? Would a change be of any material advantage?

Is the use of numbers in symbolism of modern origin? Can you give a reason for even numbers being used to denote earthly or human things and odd numbers to suggest divine or heavenly truths? Has this always been the case?

What was "the number of the beast" and its interpretation? How were ancient temples usually approached? Why should we feel gratified that the symbolism of odd numbers is retained in Masonry?

What is the "triad" or "ternary"? How was it considered by philosophers?
III.—How does the author explain the number "5"?

Of what is the number "7" the symbol? How was knowledge divided in mediæval times? What does Gould say about the seven sciences?

How can our ritual be made to be of assistance to us in our every-day life?

What is our most familiar explanation of the "three steps"? How does Masonry help the individual? Should a Mason feel that he is being left apart and alone in his endeavours to improve his physical and spiritual condition?

What great lesson is revealed to us in the five steps?

How is the group of seven steps interpreted? Is this teaching a necessity? Does Masonry approve ignorance? Is the expression "I have no time to read or study" one of yours? How did Burritt, Franklin, Livingstone and others secure their education? What grows out of ignorance?

Do you believe that the human race is still progressing? What must we avoid in measuring progress? In what manner alone can the human race progress? What are your answers to the author's closing questions?

CHAPTER XXXVII: THE BUILDERS

I.—Why, do you suppose, were so many allusions to the art of Architecture incorporated in our Ritual and monitorial lectures? What was Preston's idea in the formation of the Second Degree Lecture? What advantage has the boy or man of our day over the Masons of Preston's time?

What is Morris' definition of Architecture? Is a structure erected with a view of catering to physical needs only worthy of being designated as "architecture"?

Is Morris' definition borne out by facts?

What do the Parthenon and the colonnades at Thebes tell us? What part did art play in the Middle Ages?

To what have the buildings of men always had a reference? What is the story of the Tower of Babel?

II.—What is the secret of Masonry's use of architecture? How are Masons at present interested in building? Is the use of builder's tools as symbols of modern origin? Is such symbolism to be found in the Bible? Can you quote illustrations? Are similes in use at the present day? Name some of them. In what sense do we usually speak of a "builder"? a destroyer? Is there a connection between the present-day mission of Masonry and the language of architecture? From what source do we derive our Masonic institution of the present day?

Is a Mason an "architect"? Why? What manner of a structure is each individual Mason engaged in the building?

Do you agree with the author's assertion that Masonry is a "world-builder"? If so, why? If not, why not? When will Masonry's work be completed?

CHAPTER XXXVIII: THE FIVE SENSES

I.—What part of the ceremonies or lectures most impressed you on the night you took your Second Degree? How were you impressed by the lecture on the "Five Senses"? How have you expressed or carried out your impressions? Have you ever given the matter any further thought? Have you "Masonized" your Five Senses?

What thought have you gained from the author's short discourse on the part played by the senses in a man's life? What is the underlying idea of the series of paintings in the Congressional Library at Washington mentioned by the author?

In what direction should our senses be trained?

II.—How does the author interpret the sense of feeling? the sense of tasting? the sense of smelling? the sense of hearing? the sense of seeing?

III.—Can you give a different interpretation of any or all of these senses?

What important lesson has the author endeavoured to emphasise in the present chapter? What new understandings have you gained from the foregoing pages?

CHAPTER XXXIX: THE LIBERAL ARTS AND SCIENCES

I.—How many branches of learning were taught in the schools of the Middle Ages? What were these two groups called? What is the meaning of "trivium"? "quadrivium"? What branches comprise these two groups? What does Conder say about the London Society of Masons? What was the Ahiman Rezon? When was our oldest MS. written? What was Preston's purpose for the Second Degree? What have the Liberal Arts and Sciences to do with Masonic light? What did scholars of the Dark Ages study? Who were the Humanists?

II.—How do the Liberal Arts and Sciences "improve us in social intercourse?" How does education help a man to he a better lodge member? How does enlightenment make for brotherhood?

CHAPTER XL: THE EPHRAIMITISH WAR, AND CORN, WINE AND OIL

Have you ever heard a satisfactory explanation for the connection of the use of a sheaf of grain with the war between Jephthah and the Ephraimites? If so, what is it?

What was the cause of the Ammonitish war? Who was Jephthah? How did he intercept his enemies?

How did the custom originate of placing gifts on altars to appease the gods in early times? How was the nature of the gifts determined?

Whence originated the present-day custom of depositing records and valuables in the cornerstones of buildings?

What is the author's interpretation of the symbolism of corn, wine and oil? Can you give a different interpretation?

CHAPTER XLI: THE LETTER G

I.—Before reading the article on the letter G by the author what was your conception of its symbolic meaning? Did you accept the ritualistic explanation as authentic and final? Or had you at any time subsequent to receiving your Second Degree investigated the subject from other sources? If so, what conclusions did you reach? Did the Masons of the eighteenth century know why the letter G was adopted as a Masonic symbol? Are Masonic students of the present day agreed upon the subject? What is said about it in the article in Mackey's Encyclopædia?

Name several interpretations of the symbol as quoted by the author. What are two of the most common theories?

What branch of the sciences was given the greatest prominence in the old Constitutions of Masonry? What is a reasonable explanation for this?

How are the confused explanations of the symbol by eighteenth century writers accounted for?

II.—How did the letter G ever come to stand for Deity? What was the Kabbala? Around what did the symbolic system of the Kabbala centre? What restrictions were placed upon the real name of God by the ancient Jewish people? What was the result of these restrictions? What symbol did the Kabbalists adopt for the lost name of Deity? In what manner is the letter G supposed to have been substituted for the Hebrew *Yod?*

III.—When will men have learned the secret of the letter G?

CHAPTER XLII: AN INTRODUCTION TO THE THIRD STEP

I.—In a study of the Third Step shall we expect to find architectural symbolism as in our preceding studies? In what terms were the teachings in First and Second Steps given to us? Of what will our new studies treat?

Who originated our Third Degree? and when? Have these questions ever been satisfactorily answered?

How many degrees were there at the beginning of the Grand Lodge period? What were they? Why was the old Apprentice Degree divided into two parts? When was this division made?

Did this change meet with unanimous approval? Was the new degree universally worked immediately after the division? Why was the new degree so slow to meet with universal approval? Was it welcomed by Masons outside of London?

Who is believed to have been responsible for the introduction of this new material?

II.—What was the new material introduced between 1723 and 1738? Why does the author not believe that it was the Hiram Abiff legend? What is the author's theory concerning the substance of this legend? Give his answer to the question, Who imported the new material? Was the Third Degree as elaborate from the first as it is now? Is it worked uniformly in all countries? In all Grand Jurisdictions in the United States?

If you received the degree in another State than the one in which you now reside, state for the benefit of the other members of your Study Club some of the details in which the work as you received it differs from that of the Jurisdiction where you now live.

What is the possibility of our learning the full details concerning the origin and early working of the degree in the very near future? Do we have record of similar legends in existence before our present Masonic system was established? Can you cite some of them?

What is the purpose of this degree? What is its secret?

CHAPTER XLIII: THE VITAL PARTS OF THE BREAST

I.—At the time you received your Third degree what particular impression did the method of reception make upon you? Did you look upon this particular part of the ceremony as simply a matter of routine, or did you endeavour to think out for yourself the true meanings of the words "friendship, morality and brotherly love"?

Can a man who lives a secluded life apart from his fellows be said to know the true meaning of happiness? Has the friendship of fellow-members of your own lodge and those of other lodges with whom you have come into close contact been a help to you since you became a member of the Fraternity? Has this friendship caused you to change your opinion of any of the fellow-members of your own lodge with whom you had but a speaking acquaintance prior to your becoming a Mason? Has your own mind been broadened by such friendships?

II.—What is your conception of the word "morality"? Has this word been misused? Is a system of morality necessary to the advancement of the human race? Why?

What is the derivation of the word "morality"? What was probably the sense in which it was first used? What has it become to mean in Christian times? What is "righteousness"?

Give a few concrete examples of which you may have knowledge. What is "right"?

"How can brotherhood be possible among us men?" asks the author. What is his solution? What is your idea as to how it may be accomplished?

CHAPTER XLIV. THE GOLDEN BOWL AND THE SILVER CORD

I.—Read the chapter from the Book of Ecclesiastes on "The Golden Bowl and Silver Cord." What is the old-time interpretation of this chapter? Give in your own words the author's interpretation.

II.—What does death mean to you? In what way does trust in T. S. G. A. O. T. U. destroy in us the fear of death?

CHAPTER XLV: THAT WHICH WAS LOST

1.—What is the master symbol of Blue Lodge symbolism? Why should we be cautious in our endeavours to ascertain the origins of the symbolism of the "Lost Word"?

How were brethren in the early days of Masonry sometimes "made Masons"? Have our researchers yet been able to discover what the "Lost Word" was? What would those who hold to the theory that the Royal Arch Word is the "Lost Word" lead us to believe? Is there any evidence to prove beyond a doubt that this word was really the "Lost Word"?

II.—Do you agree with the author that the "Lost Word" was never a component part of the Blue Lodge work which was later taken away from the Blue Lodge and transplanted into the Royal Arch Degree? If so, what are your grounds for so agreeing? If not, what are your reasons for disagreeing with him?

What is the Legend of the Tetragrammaton? What was the custom among the Jewish people relative to pronouncing the name of Deity? How was the use of the name restricted? What finally became the penalty inflicted upon one who spoke the name aloud? What further restrictions were placed upon the use of the name? How was the name spelled?

When and in what manner did the true pronunciation of the name become wholly lost? What did this result in after the Exile was ended? What did the priests and scribes have left upon which to base their search? What were the vowels of the word?

III.—Of what did the Tetragrammaton become the centre, and how did the search for the word spread?

Did the form of the legend always remain the same? What various forms did it take?

IV.—Has the symbolic idea centred in the search for the "Lost Word" been confined to Masonry alone? Do we find it in modern literature?

CHAPTER XLVI: THE TROWEL

I.—Have some brother recite the monitorial lecture on the Trowel as the working tool of the Master Mason. Why is the Trowel most appropriate to the Master Mason Degree? What are the working tools of an Entered Apprentice, and their uses? What are the working tools of a Fellow Craft, and their uses? What is the function of a Trowel in the hands of a Master Mason? Why is the Trowel most symbolic in the work of temple building?

II.—Of what power may we consider the Trowel to be a symbol?

What do we say of men who lack unity in their makeup? Whence came the word "character"? What is its present-day meaning? What may a man who lacks character do to better himself?

What can he use to accomplish this end?

How did the builders of ancient times lay out their building designs? How and by whom was the degree work laid out in early English lodges? What was the duty of the youngest Entered Apprentice after the conclusion of the ceremony? How was the "plan of work" later displayed? What is the tracing board of a degree? Are the tracing boards of the several degrees represented in your lodge? How? Of what is the tracing board a symbol?

III.—How would you answer the author's question, "What is the force that can unite individual Masons into a unified and harmonious order"? What is it that ties you to your fellow Masons? What is your conception of the "Brotherhood of Man"?

CHAPTER XLVII: THE HIRAMIC LEGEND

I.—Who was Edwin Booth? What is his opinion of the Hiramic Legend?
Give your own opinion on the Legend in your own words. Are Masonic authorities agreed as to its origin and interpretation?

II.—What have Pike and Vibert to say of its introduction into our ritual? When does Gould believe it to have been made a part of our ceremonies? Are other Masonic scholars in agreement with these brethren? What do MacBride and Newton have to say on the subject?

III.—How was the Legend accepted by eighteenth century writers? Was their position held to by later writers? What are we to infer from findings of more recent times?

Had the Jews a tradition of the Grand Master's death? Can we deny positively that the Legend is not historically true? What is the belief of other writers, who do not agree with the historical theory? When do they believe the drama to have had its inception? What are the assertions of Speth and Marks?

IV.—Is there any good evidence to support the Templar theory? What were the theories advanced by Speth, Carr, Pike and others?

What is the author's theory? Does this theory seem logical to you?

V.—Do all writers agree as to the interpretation of the Legend? How many theories were offered by Oliver? What were they? What were some other theories advanced?

What is the author's present-day interpretation?

After receiving the Third Degree how did you interpret the drama?

CHAPTER XLVIII: ETERNAL LIFE

I.—What does the author consider to be the central idea of the Legend of the Third Degree?

In what respect does the term "Eternal Life" differ from Future Life? Immortality? Resurrection?

II.—What is the author's definition of "Eternal Life"? How would you define it?

What are the two component parts of human nature?

III.—What group of our activities has reference to the body? What is man's "spirit"? Why is this "spirit" eternal?

What is the principal fault of many of us? What is the result of this fault?

What is the remedy for this condition?

Why is the "Lost Word" the symbol of "Eternal Life"?

IV.—Do you agree with the author's conception of the "Raising"? If not, wherein do you differ from him? (A general question.)

Is it necessary for us to seek outside of our Blue Lodge ritual for the "Lost Word"? If so, why?

Has the present Study Club lesson given you a new conception of the Legend of the Third Degree, and opened up any new thoughts on the subject? If so, what are they? (A general question.)

CHAPTER XLIX: THE LION'S PAW

I.—What does the article in Mackey's Encyclopædia have to say concerning the Lion's Paw? What is the substance of Mackey's article on "The Lion of the Tribe of Judah"?

Why has the lion always been a favourite subject with symbolists? What was the symbolism of the lion among early peoples in India? Of what was it a symbol to the Nile dwellers? Give an example of the use of the lion symbolism in Egyptian sculpture. How does Harrison describe the raising of Osiris?

II.—What was the crux ansata, or "ansated cross" originally? In what manner did it develop into the "symbol of life"? What did Albert Pike see in the crux ansata?

III.—How was the lion as a symbol used by the Jews? Whence is it supposed that the Comacine Masters derived their habitual use of the lion in their cathedral building? What has Leader Scott to say concerning the lion in architecture? What is the author's theory as to how the symbolism of the Lion's Paw came into Masonry?

IV.—What power did the people of the cathedral building period believe the lioness to possess? Of what was this a symbol to them?

Of what did the early Freemasons consider the lion a symbol?

Is there any difference between the real meaning of the symbolism of the Lion's Paw as interpreted by Albert Pike and as interpreted by Leader Scott?

Does the symbol refer to a raising in this life or in a future life?

CHAPTER L: THE EMBLEMS

I.—Recite the monitorial lecture on the Weeping Virgin monument.

Was the Weeping Virgin monument known to the Ritual of the eighteenth century? Is it now generally found in European systems and in all American jurisdictions? Is there a brother present from a jurisdiction where this emblem does not appear in the monitor of his mother jurisdiction? By whom is the emblem supposed to have been invented? Who was Jeremy Cross? What is the tradition as to where Cross borrowed the emblem? What is another theory? How should we view this emblem in the light of such meagre information concerning its origin as we now possess?

II.—Recite the monitorial lecture describing the Temple of Solomon.

Where was the Temple erected? For what other things was the hill on which the Temple was erected noted in Hebrew tradition? How was the hill described by the Mohammedans? What great event in the life of Mohammed is claimed by him to have occurred there?

What influence did the temple have on the legends, history and traditions of the people of early times?

Until how long ago was it the general belief that our present-day Masonic organisation was formed at the time of the building of the Temple? After receiving your degrees did you believe this to be a fact? (A general question.) What sort of marks have been discovered on the original foundation stones of the Temple? Are we certain of an actual historical connection between the Phœnicians and our present organisation? How is the Masonry of to-day interested in the Temple legend?

How did the Temple find its way into our Masonic system? What is Vibert's contention? What was the theory of it having been adopted in 1724? What is the position of Johnston and Rylands on the subject?

What is Brother Waite's theory?

How does the author compare our "work" with the building of the Temple?

In what manner did the Temple differ from our present-day houses of worship? In what manner did it differ from other temples? What is our object in building a "spiritual" temple?

III.—Recite the monitorial lecture on the Pot of Incense. Why was incense burned in ancient days? What is the reason for using it to-day? Of what is incense an emblem, in both the Old and New Testament?

How is incense used in Masonry of to-day? What should we bear in mind regarding the symbol?

IV.—Recite the monitorial lecture on the beehive.

Of what was the bee an emblem to the Hindoos? What may be believed to be the origin of the custom of using the bee as a symbol of immortality? Why did Napoleon adopt the bee as his royal emblem?

How was the bee symbolism used by the Greeks and some of their modern imitators?

How did the beehive come to be used in Christian symbolism?

Why did the Egyptians call the bees "an obedient people"? How does the beehive symbolise a lodge of Masons? Are there any "drones" in the "hive" of Masonry? Can you suggest how these "drones" might be transformed into "workers"?

CHAPTER LI: THE EMBLEMS (Continued)

I.—Recite the monitorial lecture on "The Book of Constitutions guarded by the Tiler's Sword."

Were written constitutions known to Operative Freemasons in the eleventh to fifteenth centuries? How were the traditions and charges communicated to the candidate in those times? What is supposed to have been the gradual evolution of these traditions and charges?

What is the oldest manuscript of the Old Charges? In what form was it written? What is the next oldest copy? To whom are we indebted for our present collection of these old documents? How many copies of these have been collected and preserved?

What happened to a number of the Old Charges that were in the hands of Masons at the beginning of the eighteenth century? When was one of the first attempts made to collate them?

Who made the first digest of these old manuscript constitutions shortly after the formation of the Grand Lodge of England? In what light is Dr. Anderson's work looked upon at the present day?

II.—What symbolical interpretation may be placed upon the Book of Constitutions?

III.—What is the symbolical significance of "The Book of Constitutions guarded by the Tiler's Sword"? What is the origination of the word "Tiler," and when was that office first created? What is one theory of the derivation of the word? What is another theory? Of what should the Tiler be a reminder?

Whence was the word "cowan" derived? What is supposed to have been the original meaning of the word? In what other sense was the word used?

When was the term introduced into English Masonry? By whom was it supposed to have been introduced? What is its present-day literal meaning? Is it the Tiler's duty alone to "keep off cowans"?

IV.—Recite the monitorial lecture on "The Sword Pointing to a Naked Heart."

What is Mackey's theory of the origin of the symbol of the "Sword Pointing to a Naked Heart"? How is it presumed to have come into our Ritual?

Of what is the heart a symbol in this instance? the sword? What was one of the early beliefs concerning God? What did the term "morality" mean in those days?

How is the "moral law" interpreted by Masons of the present day?

CHAPTER LII: THE EMBLEMS (Continued)

I.—Recite the monitorial lecture on "The Anchor and Ark." Is the Anchor and Ark symbol a modern or an old one? What does the Anchor typify? Of what was it a symbol among early Christians? How was it displayed in those early times? What does Lundy say of it?

II.—Is the symbolism of the Ark as well known as that of the Anchor? What symbolic significance did Laurence Dermott attach to it? What did it symbolise to the Hermeticists? Was the symbol used in the Ancient Mysteries? In what manner?

III.—Of what was the Ark a symbol to the early Christians? Why? What does the Ark mean to us, as Masons?

CHAPTER LIII: THE EMBLEMS (Continued)

I.—Recite the monitorial lecture on this emblem. Why should the emblem be one of particular importance to Masons? What prominence did Dr. Anderson attach to it?

Is our monitorial lecture on the emblem generally accepted as accurate in all details? Why is its alleged discovery by Pythagoras doubtful? What is the argument of those who defend the monitorial interpretation? Which of the two views given in the chapter do you believe the most convincing? What is a "hecatomb"?

II.—What does Dionysius Lardner say on the subject? The Encyclopædia Britannica? Brother J. F. Thompson? What might be added to Brother Thompson's statement?

III.—In what manner is the Proposition a symbol of Brotherhood?

How did the Egyptians use the Problem to portray the principle of the "perfect"? How is this symbolism displayed in "The Three Lesser Lights"?

IV.—Was a knowledge of the principle of the Forty-seventh Proposition vital to the existence of early operative Masonry? Why? Why is the triangle of symbolism of importance to present-day Masonry?

CHAPTER LIV: CONCLUSION

I.—Recite the monitorial lecture on "The Hour Glass."

In what manner was the Hour Glass symbol commonly used by operative Masons? Is the emblem a modern one? How was it used in funeral ceremonies in early days? What is the lesson we should learn from this emblem?

II.—Recite the monitorial lecture on the "Scythe."

III.—Have you any answers to the questions asked by the author in this section of his chapter?

IV.—Recite the ritualistic lecture on these emblems.

V.—What does the First Degree symbolise? The Second? What does the drama of the Third Degree symbolise? Did you realise the symbol of the Hiramic Legend the night you were raised? Was its meaning entirely clear to you at that time, or did you have to study it out later?

CPSIA information can be obtained at www.ICGtesting.com
Printed in the USA
LVOW11s0242290115

424826LV00003B/143/P

9 781505 686777